Jobs and community action

This volume has been edited by Gary Craig, Marjorie Mayo and
Nick Sharman in co-operation with the Editorial Board
appointed by the Association of Community Workers:

Gary Craig
Paul Curno
David Jones
Martin Loney
Marjorie Mayo
Nick Sharman
Leo Smith
John Ward

It is no. 5 in the Community Work Series.

Jobs and community action

edited by
Gary Craig, Marjorie Mayo and Nick Sharman

Routledge & Kegan Paul

London, Boston and Henley

First published in 1979
by Routledge & Kegan Paul Ltd,
39 Store Street,
London WC1E 7DD,
Broadway House,
Newtown Road,
Henley-on-Thames,
Oxon RG9 1EN and
9 Park Street,
Boston, Mass. 02108, USA
Set by Hope Services, Abingdon
and printed in Great Britain by
Lowe & Brydone Ltd
Thetford, Norfolk

British Library Cataloguing in Publication Data

Jobs and community action. — (Community work series;
no. 5).
1. Labor supply — Great Britain — Case studies
2. Social action — Case studies
I. Craig, Gary   II. Mayo, Marjorie   III. Sharman,
Nick   IV. Series
331.1'377   HD5765.A6   78-41240

ISBN 0 7100 0241 6

Contents

Part IV   Recent State Initiatives

Part V   Production for Community Needs

Contributors

Linda Clarke is a research student at University College, London. She is currently investigating the building industry.

Tom Clarke is a lecturer in Industrial Sociology at the Trent Polytechnic, Nottingham.

Ken Coates is an ex-miner and is now senior lecturer in sociology at the Adult Education Department, Nottingham University. He has been a city councillor and is an active member of the Institute of Workers Control.

Bob Colenutt is a planner working for the North Southwark Community Development Group in London. He is joint author (with Peter Ambrose) of *The Property Machine.*

John Connolly was a shop steward in the West India and Millwall Docks, London. He is now a district officer in the Transport and General Workers Union.

Mike Cooley has been chairman of the Lucas Aerospace Combine Shop Stewards Committee, and Chairman of AUEW-TASS.

Gary Craig was a community worker in Chesterfield and Stoke-on-Trent for three years, and worked for Benwell Community Development Project (CDP) for five years. He is a NUPE shop steward and organizer for Newcastle-upon-Tyne Trades Council.

Tom Davies is a lecturer in the School for Advanced Urban Studies, University of Bristol. He was formerly a planner with the London Borough of Wandsworth.

Bert Edwards was a founder member of the National Unemployed Workers Movement. He later played a key role in the development of national shop steward committees in the car industry. He was also active in the tenants' movement.

Mark Hill is a member of the Aberdeen People's Press and was the author of their book, *Oil Over Troubled Waters*.

Keith Hodgson worked for Liverpool CDP for two years and is now a research worker for the Trade Union Studies Information Unit, Newcastle-upon-Tyne.

Jane Leighton was formerly Merseyside organizer for the British Pregnancy Advisory Service and is now secretary of the Liverpool Central and Southern Community Health Council.

Martin Loney is Senior Lecturer in Community Work, Polytechnic of the South Bank. He was formerly general secretary of the National Council for Civil Liberties and taught in the School of Social Work at Carleton University, Ottawa.

Marjorie Mayo works at the Joint Docklands Action Group Resource Centre. She previously worked for the Community Development Project and lectured at Surrey University in Community Work.

Richard Minns is a research worker at the Centre for Environmental Studies, London.

Peter Morris is currently studying at Warwick University. He previously worked for the Canning Town CDP in London.

Joe Noble works as a community worker in Hackney, London. He has lectured at the North-East London Polytechnic and was one of the founders of the Homeworkers Campaign.

Nick Sharman works at the Joint Docklands Action Group Resource Centre. He has worked for a number of community projects, including the Benwell CDP.

Pete Smith was formerly TGWU convener at Shell Chemicals,

Carrington, before establishing Sunderlandia, a building co-operative and working with it for four years.

Jenny Thornley is a research worker at the Centre for Environmental Studies, London.

Kevin Ward worked for Batley CDP before becoming a lecturer in Adult Education at Leeds University. He has helped to establish a Trade Union and Community Resource Centre in Leeds.

Roland Watkins was a planner and community worker before working for Birmingham CDP for four years. He is currently unemployed.

Introduction

Gary Craig, Marjorie Mayo and Nick Sharman

There are over five million people without jobs in the Common Market countries alone, nearly 6 per cent of the working population. In Britain there are one and a half million unemployed, three times the figure of the early 1960s. Although unemployment has been rising generally, particularly in the 1970s, certain areas in the country are bearing the sharpest impact. Here unemployment is up to five times the national average. Vast areas of industrial land have become derelict as firms have closed or moved out. The process of decline has affected the whole community, not just the local work force. Unemployment, declining incomes, deteriorating social fabric and community services, have reduced opportunities, especially for young people. All these problems have led inevitably to mounting social bitterness and racial conflict, symptoms already all too well known to social and community workers.

It is important not to take this area-based analysis too far: low incomes, unemployment, restricted job opportunities and poor services are not, of course, confined to particular areas, nor are their causes. None the less, an *area-based* analysis can be a helpful starting-point for analysing economic changes — and certainly, as our contributors show, it has some importance as a base for political organisation.

Jobs — and the local economy generally — are increasingly of central concern to a wide range of professionals, from community and social workers, planners and lawyers to trade union organisers and researchers. Although this collection of essays is directed at this broad group, it is primarily aimed at the workers and residents directly affected. If they are able to organise against the systematic rundown of their areas, they will have taken the first step towards democratic control of the economy. In the longer term this would mean socially useful work for all, production for people rather than profit, instead of the demoralisation caused by widespread unemployment. Achieving this will ultimately involve fundamental political and economic change. The discussion of these broader issues, however, is beyond the scope of these essays.

Scope

This introductory chapter has three aims. First, it discusses the reasons for the economic changes which have wreaked such havoc particularly in working-class communities. Can the problems caused by economic growth and decline be isolated, and solved within these communities or can they only be tackled as part of a wider national — and even international — strategy for creating jobs and reviving these communities?

Second, the chapter examines the state's policies, at both local and national level. How much have they improved conditions? How much have they merely supported the reorganisation of the economy and thus made the local crisis worse by placing the burden of this reorganisation onto working-class communities?

Third, the introduction looks at the response from the people and organisations within these communities, residents and workers. How have they organised themselves to fight back? What links have been built up, especially between local trade union organisations and resident-based community groups? In many cases the focus on jobs in a particular area is relatively new. The most immediate problem then is to devise strategies for action, based on an analysis of the needs and circumstances of the area, which effectively combine trade union and community groups. One of the major intentions of this book is to help promote strategies for action and to bring together organisations which have developed around the separate bases of home and work yet which increasingly share a common concern with the future job prospects of their area.

The nature of the jobs crisis

The decline of one phase of industrial technology and the development of the next in another area is not new to the 1970s.

Manufacturing industry in Britain, as in other advanced capitalist countries, is facing one of these recurrent crises in its profitability. In an effort to increase productivity and thus to restore profits as competition becomes sharper, British industry has been concentrated into larger and larger enterprises. This process is designed to maximise the economies of scale in order to compete more effectively at national and especially international level. Concentration of ownership has occurred by merger and take-over — smaller competitors are taken over (and their plant often closed, especially in sectors where demand is static or falling). Within the firm, production is reorganised and rationalised to achieve speed-up. This will typically involve investment in new, capital-intensive plant, often automated or semi-automated, employing a smaller and less skilled workforce. Planned capital investment in five Welsh industries (including the British Steel Corporation) for example, in 1977–8 totalled £1,445m but was expected to bring only 2,900 new jobs. At the same time, the closure of British Steel's East Moors Works in Cardiff resulted in the loss of over 3,000 jobs.

Britain has seen a dramatic decline in industrial employment, losing over 10 per cent of its workforce since the early 1960s. Output from particular sectors of the economy, like steel and ship-building, has been cut back with enormous losses in jobs: new orders secured by British shipbuilders for 1975 were at their lowest level for thirty years. Other sectors like electrical supply industries have been reorganised so that one or two firms now dominate the industry, with a vastly reduced workforce. In the space of ten years, GEC, the country's largest manufacturer of electrical supply equipment has cut its workforce by 64,000. And these processes are continuing: in the Northern Region, for example, the Northern Economic Development Council warned in 1977 that between 66,000 and 93,000 further jobs were at risk in shipbuilding, coal-mining, chemicals and mechanical and electrical engineering.

While mergers, rationalisations and the consequent loss of jobs are seen as the solution to capital's drive for higher profits, the impact of economic change on labour, especially in older industrial areas, has been shattering. These areas typically contain the firms and plant most vulnerable to take-over and closure, that is firms with older, more labour-intensive plant, in older buildings on small sites. These are all obstacles to the process of rationalisation and concentration outlined above. Firms in these areas thus tend to be more vulnerable to closure. Consequently job losses in these areas have been up to three times the national average; in the period 1961–74, for example, there was a fall in manufacturing employment of 30 per cent in London, compared with a national figure of 10 per cent. It is important to point out that these losses were very largely the result of large firms either closing down their branch or taking over a smaller competitor in these areas. In either case the remaining production or new investment has been moved to a new site, or increasingly out of the country altogether. Multinational firms like Vickers, for instance, have run down the workforces in their traditional sectors and expanded both into other countries (where wage and transport costs are lower) and also into new, more profitable forms of activity. Since 1971, while the workforce has remained roughly constant, the proportion of Vickers workers employed outside the UK has risen from 17 to 25 per cent.

This pattern is repeated in every city and hundreds of thousands of jobs are lost in the process. These moves serve two functions; first, they make it easier to reorganise production methods and reduce the size of the workforce. Second, they enable firms to take advantage of lower costs (wages and land especially) elsewhere. In some cases they have enabled firms to sell off valuable inner-city sites or redevelop them for more profitable purposes, for example commercial or light industrial building. However it is done, the overall aim is the same — rationalising investment to maximise profits.

The impact on communities

Often the local plant will be making quite considerable profits — but not as much as in alternative forms of investment open to the company. So the plant is closed, irrespective of the devastating social and economic consequences for the local community which may still be heavily dependent on this one particular employer. Several chapters in this book illustrate how these processes work in practice.

But these policies and economic pressures are not confined to the private sector: nationalised industries, many of which were taken into public ownership because they provided essential products or services, have shown the same disregard for the social consequences of their investment programmes, as chapter 7 demonstrates. The Coal Board's proposal to relocate its activities from Ashfield was not discussed with councillors let alone the communities involved. And in Hartlepool, for example, a small town heavily dependent on steelmaking, 1,500 steel jobs were lost in early 1978 as part of the British Steel Corporation's plan to axe nearly 40,000 jobs in five years. As a result the town's unemployment rate reached 14 per cent. This kind of social irresponsibility on the part of nationalised industries is inevitable, given successive Governments' directives to them to make profits. It has meant that with reinvestment in even larger plant these industries have contributed very largely to the loss of industrial jobs. This again especially affects the 'declining' communities where much of the utilities' older plant was located. As a result the Gas and Electricity Boards and the Water Authorities are among the major holders of derelict land in inner cities. A typical example is in South-East Birmingham, where the British Gas Corporation owns almost 100 acres of land: once employing over 4,000 workers, the land has been virtually empty and derelict for years.

The pressures to rationalise, concentrate and substitute capital-intensive plant for labour are not confined to manufacturing industry and the utilities. The decline of dock and transport labour with containerisation, the spread of supermarket (and now hyper-market) retailing, the growth of computerised warehousing are examples of technological developments in other sectors which require a smaller and less skilled workforce. Even in sectors still experiencing an overall increase in jobs, such as offices, these pressures are becoming evident. Office machinery is now being substituted for clerical labour on a massive scale in Central London. Despite a growth of 16m sq ft of office building in the late 1960s and early 1970s, there was a *fall* of 30,000 clerical jobs. There are now very high rates of clerical unemployment throughout inner London. It is clear then that there is no growth sector in the economy which can readily absorb those thrown out of work by the processes we have described above. The so-called 'growth services', where employment has grown significantly over the past decade, and continues to grow cover a restricted number of services — notably tourism, some areas of public administration and public service, banking and finance.

Frequently, then, sufficient alternative jobs will simply not be available in declining working-class areas. And those jobs which are available present other problems — the skills and experience of those thrown out of work aren't suitable for the 'new' jobs, which typically have a low 'manual' content. Retraining programmes are completely inadequate in scope and number. Moreover — as we have already argued — these 'growth' sectors are themselves becoming increasingly liable to rationalisation and labour-shedding. There can be no reliance on the service sector to 'mop up' unemployment as industry declines. This has become particularly clear in the light of the series of public expenditure cuts made by the Labour Government since taking office in 1974. The package of cuts announced in July 1976 were estimated to have cost at least 110,000 jobs in the public services.

New growth in certain sectors of the economy, for example in property development, is financed from the less profitable sectors, particularly manufacturing, whose operations are then restricted or halted altogether. Where the latter have traditionally been concentrated in the older urban areas, as is the case with manufacturing industry, the consequent impact is enormous. The older areas are therefore the victims of our particular form of economic development. The fundamental solution to their problems of economic decline cannot be found through programmes which concentrate on these areas alone. Only far-reaching changes affecting the control of the form and location of investment can ultimately make any impact on their economic fortunes.

Such an analysis, however, does not mean that there is nothing that can usefully be done within the declining areas to affect these problems in the short term. The final section of this introduction, and the contributions themselves, demonstrate that successful resistance to economic run-down and to closures is possible. More importantly such organisation makes an essential contribution to the building of democratic control of the economy. We outline the first steps in such a strategy in the next section.

State policy

Over the last forty years the state has increasingly intervened in the economy. Broadly the aim of state policy has been to support directly and indirectly, the efforts of British industry to restructure itself to cope with declining profits and growing international competition. This has been done in two main ways. First, a succession of incomes policies have attempted to keep down labour costs. Second, an elaborate and comprehensive system of subsidies to capital investment have encouraged British industry to re-equip its ageing plant and technology. As part of this policy firms have also been encouraged to merge, to create larger and stronger units, by organisations like the IRC[1] and latterly the NEB.[2] There have of course been a plethora of other measures (from state support of essential but non-profit making services, railways, electrical supply and so on, to subsidies to support training), but these key themes stand out.

There has, however, been another aspect of state policy which has run alongside these mainstream economic policies, a policy of subsidising jobs in areas of high unemployment. The motives for this are for the most part political and social, a reaction to the organised labour movement's demands for work, and a fear of social instability. The central example is regional policy, pursued by all Governments since the depression of the early 1930s. At that time Government policy attempted to encourage unemployed workers to move to other areas for jobs. Since World War Two, however, an array of bribes and directives has attempted to steer new and expanding firms to the regions where unemployment has remained persistently above the national average.

Other government programmes have also attempted to cushion the effects of economic decline, particularly in the older urban areas. The Urban Programme, started in the late 1960s, mainly as a way of improving social conditions, has now taken on the explicit aim of regenerating employment. More generally the Manpower Services Commission has directed resources to create jobs and to subsidise training, especially in areas of high unemployment. There are also subsidies available to firms taking on more workers, the temporary employment, youth employment subsidies, and now the small business employment subsidy. This range of programmes, described in chapter 14, has had only a modest overall impact on unemployment levels. In November 1977, when total unemployment in the UK was over 1½ millions, the Department of Employment estimated that 320,000 people were covered by its special employment and training schemes: 189,000 of these were covered by temporary employment subsidy, 45,000 by 'Job Creation' and 30,000 by the Work Experience programme.

Local authorities are now increasingly encouraged to take an active economic development role, mainly by supporting the expansion of small firms in their areas. In the inner city, this is an important change of direction: up to the early 1970s local authorities were mainly interested in housing development and were often actively encouraging the departure of local industry, through the operation of their land-use planning policies.

State policy then is increasingly schizophrenic — on the one hand it supports the rationalisation and concentration of British industry, with the inevitable loss of jobs particularly in the declining areas. On the other hand, policies have been directed at creating jobs especially in these areas. The contradiction, however, is more apparent than real. The major state effort (and expenditure) is aimed at improving industrial investment and competitiveness. The other measures are little more than political concessions involving relatively small amounts of Government spending. Moreover, even the 'concessions' to declining areas are double-edged and in fact do much to support the mainstream economic trends we have outlined. Regional policy for example now concentrates mainly on subsidies to capital, both plant and building. Considerable sums are involved – over £400m in 1975-6. As the 1972 Industry Act explains, these grants are 'intended to help in the modernisation of existing operations as well as incoming firms *it is not necessary for the new investment to provide additional employment*' (our emphasis). In other words, regional policy is increasingly seen as part of the state's overall economic strategy to promote rationalisation and re-equipment and thus increase productivity and profitability. This in effect means cutting down the use of labour. Regional policy, especially now that a direct subsidy for jobs (the regional employment premium) has been eliminated, does little more than help industry to do what it would do anyway – that is, to move its plant to new sites, re-equip and take advantage of an inexperienced and typically unorganised unskilled or semi-skilled labour force. As such it is another arm of the increasing state support for reinvestment, the so-called Industrial Strategy, embracing the National Economic Development Office sector working parties and the National Enterprise Board.

There is a similar contradiction in both the Government's other major policies aimed at local areas of high unemployment. The *inner city* initiative, an expanded version of the Urban Programme which was announced by Peter Shore in 1977, gives added resources and extra powers to a restricted number of local authorities to help them regenerate their economies. The extra powers described in chapter 12 enable local authorities to subsidise the improvement of industrial property either themselves, or by loans and grants to firms. The extra resources are designed to provide the funds to do this and to modernise infrastructure (roads, housing, public transport, etc.). However, the powers and money are so restricted that they will make little impression, either on a decaying environment or on the economic forces causing the closures. More importantly these extra powers are not linked to mainstream policies for direct investment into these areas (for example neither the Industrial Strategy nor the nationalised industry investment programmes have been altered). At best this programme will merely bribe a few small businesses to come into or remain in the area.

Many of these, moreover, are dubious assets in areas of high unemployment. Local authorities, meanwhile, are forced into the position of bidding against each other to secure a few, often badly-paid, jobs. It is significant that the Department of Industry (the main force behind the Industrial Strategy) has failed to back the Inner City policy of economic revival, except as a location where small businesses can be encouraged. The small firms sector in Britain is smaller than in any other Western country and there is some evidence that large firms are finding this a problem. Small firms can be extremely useful to them, for example, as highly flexible sub-contractors or as 'test-beds' for high-risk innovative projects. Some help to this sector thus satisfies a vocal political lobby and provides support for some of the larger firms, central to the Government's strategy. For these reasons Government recently stressed the importance of small firms in reviving the economies of the inner cities. The Government has also commissioned a special study of the problems facing small firms. The Government sponsorship of the small firms sector will pose real problems for the trade union movement; compared to large firms, this type of company is more often non-unionised, pays lower wages and offers poorer working conditions. At the same time, the Government's refusal to deal with the problems posed by the larger and multinational companies moving out of the inner city must drastically reduce the possibility of real economic regeneration in these areas.

The Manpower Services Commission — the executive arm of the Department of the Employment's manpower strategy — has promoted a range of job creation and training programmes aimed particularly at areas of high unemployment, and at young people. They too can do little to regenerate local economies since the 'jobs' created are of very limited duration and must not be competitive with existing firms. Again, policies like the Youth Opportunities Programme (YOP) serve to quell vocal political forces, in this case by creating subsidised 'make-work', and by trying to reduce young people's alienation from the economy and to instil the 'discipline' of work. Moreover, the emphasis of the training aspect of the YOP is on semi-skilled training, clearly fitting into the demands of modern, automated industry and incidentally removing some of the costs of this training from firms, as Martin Loney's contribution (chapter 14) indicates.

Another aspect of state policy where the same contradictory threads are evident is in the public services, especially those provided by local authorities and by the health authorities. These both underpin the local economy (housing, social facilities, roads, environmental services and so on) and are an important source of jobs in themselves. This type of public investment however tends to follow, and thus support, the economic growth and decline of areas. For services are built up to support new communities with new roads, schools, housing, health facilities, and so on. In contrast, the declining areas, with their falling populations, usually merit little more than patch-and-repair of old buildings (such as the succession of housing 'improvement' programmes which delay demolition by a few years). Resources tend to be concentrated on social services support for a community, made vulnerable by economic decline and depopulation. This high spending on social services, particularly for the old and the unemployed, serves only to cushion the more traumatic effects of industrial decline. It does little to underpin and revive the local economy.

Part of the Government's economic strategy has actually been to cut back the level of public expenditure, arguing that a high level of public spending uses financial resources which could otherwise be used to revive manufacturing industry. Thus, since 1974, there have been a series of budgets which have cut expenditure on public services, notably in 1976 when three separate rounds of cuts totalling £8,100m took place. The attempt to increase investment in manufacturing industry has had limited success: investment in that sector fell by 13 per cent in 1975 and a further 7 per cent in 1976.

These cuts in public spending have reduced even further the level of already inadequate services. For example, the health authorities' decision to switch resources to the 'underprovided' regions within a stationary budget, has meant severe reductions in hospital provision, especially in London and Liverpool. Both cities have large areas which are declining and therefore have high needs, both for acute and primary care.

Despite campaigns attempting to prevent hospital closures (see chapter 10), there has been a steady cut-back. The story of hospital closures is repeated throughout the country: in 1977, up to 100 hospitals were estimated to be threatened with closure in London alone. This run-down or even withdrawal of services has also affected a broad range of local authority provision, including housing, education, social services and public transport (chapter 11). Thus the cut-back in public investment has begun to parallel the withdrawal of private investment from declining areas. This has three effects — first it exposes an already vulnerable community to cuts in services, second it hastens the departure of people and firms from these areas and removes the infrastructural base for economic revival and third it adds to unemployment (the public sector typically provides around 20 per cent of jobs in inner city areas — this figure is even higher in some cities such as Newcastle, which houses three local authority headquarters and a regional DHSS office, itself the largest single employer in the city).

There are, nevertheless, important contradictions in central government's allocation of resources to local services. For alongside a policy of spending cuts, there has been an effort to bias the Government grant to local authorities (the Rate Support Grant or RSG) towards some declining areas in the large cities. The extra Urban Programme resources to the Partnership areas have the same bias and, unlike the RSG, are not supposed simply to buttress the existing pattern of services but to lay the basis for economic revival.

In both cases, however, there are important flaws. In particular the amounts involved are comparatively small; urban aid, for example, will allow an extra 5 to 10 per cent expenditure on capital projects, and the areas involved are extremely limited. (There are only seven such 'partnership' areas in England and fifteen further local authorities which have been asked to prepare even more limited 'inner city programmes'.) Once again the roots of this policy are political (preventing the alienation of voters in Labour strongholds, racial conflict in some inner cities and so on) rather than economic. However, the 1978–9 RSG settlement suggests that several of the partnership areas, notably Liverpool, Newcastle/Gateshead and Birmingham, will be receiving a smaller needs grant than hitherto, thus offsetting to a large extent any extra finance available under the Urban Programme. Although such extra resources as may be made available are designed to restore the confidence of the private sector and induce it to reinvest in the decaying areas, as we argued above, the private sector has in fact very limited interest in these areas. Only if it can replace the working-class community with offices and luxury housing (as Bob Colenutt argues in chapter 15), exploit the most vulnerable sections of the workforce with low wage activities (see chapter 5), or replace old manufacturing plant with more profitable but less labour-intensive activities like warehousing, has it shown any substantial spontaneous interest. So without public direction of private investment to declining areas to provide jobs, any extra resources for local public services can do little except cushion the community against the effects of further decline.

State policy is thus increasingly contradictory. On the one hand it is attempting to carry out its economic strategy and on the other, it has to cope with the social and political consequences of this strategy, particularly where they are manifested as gross disparities between regions or between the older declining areas and the newer centres of growth. This is the central conflict, and not the often expressed *spatial* conflict between new town and the inner city, or between the 'affluent' south-east region and 'declining' northern and western regions. As we have seen, state policies at national, regional and local level all contain this conflict. The Government's strategy has at the moment, then, been broadly settled in favour of 'strengthening' British industry by rationalisation, re-equipment and thus by increasing unemployment.

At national level, the National Enterprise Board, for example, has in the main pursued two aims, 'the promotion of industrial efficiency and international competitiveness' and assisting 'the reorganisation or development of an industry'. Yet the NEB was also set up in response to pressure for an alternative approach. When the NEB was set up under the 1975 Industry Act, it was also seen as a method of creating industrial jobs through public sector intervention. So a third aim was 'the provision, maintenance or safeguarding of productive employment in any part of the UK'. If sufficient political pressure were mounted to bring this aim back to the fore, the NEB could become an agent for promoting more socially responsible economic development rather than a method for technocratic rationalisation.

Planning agreements between private industry and the Government (enshrined in the 1975 Industry Act) is another example of a socially useful policy instrument which has been pushed into the background. Their aim was to make private firms more accountable to the public — thus a regional grant to a firm could, for example, have been made conditional on specific guarantees about the provision and maintenance of jobs suited to the needs of the local workforce. In fact, since the system is voluntary, only one planning agreement has been signed (with Chrysler). Yet if the system were compulsory, planning agreements could be a useful first step in controlling private firms' investment decisions, using the Government's financial subsidies to the private sector (now over £4,000m a year) as a weapon. In turn, investment could then be guided to the 'declining' areas and sectors most in need of jobs. Similarly, the nationalised industries' investment programmes could be made more socially responsible. As we have pointed out, the emphasis on maximising profits means that they behave in many ways like private firms, rationalising their plant with little or no regard for the local effects of their policies.

All these national policy initiatives are essential if a start is to be made in providing jobs as well as rebuilding the industrial base of the country. Yet these policies must have a local dimension to make them sensitive to the needs of particular areas. This must involve strong representation from the local labour movement in any implementing body. One key agency which could do much to initiate and to implement a democratic jobs strategy at this level is the local authority. However, just as with national policy, the tendency of Councils, whether Labour or Tory controlled, has so far been to concentrate on meeting private employers' interests. Competition amongst them for the few allegedly 'footloose' firms wishing to take advantage of 'inner city' incentives could easily take this process one step further.

Such competition tends to lead to a 'jobs-at-any-price' attitude among local authorities, so that grants, loans and premises are offered to any employer regardless of the quantity, let alone the quality, of the resulting jobs. Mark Hill's contribution on Aberdeen (chapter 2) shows a local authority evading this issue. Yet local authorities could avoid this problem by themselves becoming an important generator of local jobs and at the same time enforcing social accountability over wages and conditions in local industries. Thus Tom Davies's review of Wandsworth's policies (chapter 13) shows how the Council took significant steps itself to create jobs (for example by building up municipal enterprises). It also attempted to make employers more socially responsible by insisting on the firm's compliance with a Good Employer Code in return for any public support. Wandsworth Council also floated the idea of local planning agreements with big employers to ensure that their investment programmes are sensitive to local needs. Here central government support is essential if such agreements are to be effective.

In another field, Linda Clarke's contribution demonstrates how local authorities' direct labour organisations can expand local jobs in construction and at the same time increase the social responsibility of the industry.

In general, Councils' powers over employment are restricted. However, as Richard Minns and Jenny Thornley show in their review of local authority initiatives (chapter 12), there are useful opportunities which can be pressed locally. Councils can also take an active co-ordinating role in ensuring that public resources coming through bodies like the MSC are constructively used, instead of merely serving to create an isolated and subsidised 'make-work' economy or to offer inadequate cover for the deficiencies in local services caused by public spending cuts.

There are, then, elements within local and national state policies which could be used as a basis for demands to combat the pattern of unplanned economic growth and decline. These stand in sharp contrast with the present situation, in which, despite internal contradictions, state policies are fundamentally shaped around the interests of private industry and its profitability. Only by political organisation at national and local level can this change be won. Essential to winning these policies and widening democratic control at all levels of the economy are strong locally-based campaigns which embrace both workplace and resident-based groups. We look at these in the next section.

The local response

The first sections have shown how the national economy has developed, by the rundown of the older industrial areas, as both public and private investment is withdrawn, and redevelopment or re-investment of private capital takes place elsewhere, and/or in other sectors of the economy. In this section we look at the groups, organisations and campaigns which have challenged the local manifestations of these processes, and attempted to extend public accountability of investment decisions to achieve greater democratic control over the local economy.

In practice, the starting point has frequently been less ambitious. Often it has been a trade union campaign organised by shop stewards within a factory to resist closure, redundancy or the imposition of a new production process that means a loss of jobs. In some cases this has led to factory occupations, often with the involvement of the local community as described in chapter 4. Sometimes it is a community campaign involving community groups and tenants' associations to fight a cut-back in public services in their area.

Increasingly, links are being made between workplace and residents. The closure of a large firm can bankrupt a community. The cutback in public transport means fewer jobs, not just worse services. These are not just theoretical connections. The workers whose jobs are threatened are also faced with rising rents and fares, and declining school and health services. Moreover, these connections are being reflected at the organisational level. There are, as our contributions show, a growing number of cases where workplace and community campaigns have united. This has not only added strength to particular campaigns but also laid the basis for wider perspectives on both sides. This is crucial if the campaigns are to go beyond resistance to change, an endless repetition of defensive struggles, and develop alternative strategies to show how production can be controlled and related to people's needs. Politically it is vitally important to link the unionised working population with the non-unionised and wageless sections of the population, both to prevent attempts to divide the working class and to involve the widest possible constituency in developing campaigns and policies. In this context the development of unemployed members' branches of trade unions such as the Transport and General Workers Union, or the establishment of links between claimants' unions and trade unions or trades councils represent significant initiatives.

A central theme of this book, then, is the importance of these links, both in action and in developing alternative perspectives and demands. These cannot of course be developed in isolation. Many of the key decisions affecting working-class areas are taken at national and even international level and appropriate organisations and strategies have to be developed at that level. The workforces in a number of prominent multinational companies such as Lucas, Vickers, Dunlop and Ford have responded by establishing national or even multinational combine committees of shop stewards. But a locally organised base is an essential part of any wider strategy to build up strength and fully to democratise measures to control economic change. This in turn means that local labour organisations must break out of the rigid demarcation lines that have tended to separate home-based and work-based organisations.

Such jointly organised campaigns, linking the issues of unemployment and bad living conditions, are not of course a new phenomenon of the 1970s. In chapter 1, Bert Edwards, a leading member of the National Unemployed Workers' Movement, shows that these issues were as inextricably bound together in the depression of the 1920s and 1930s as they are today. Low wages, casual work and unemployment went hand-in-hand with poor housing and harassment from landlords and police. Moreover, locally-based organisation effectively spanned both kinds of issues. Then, as now, the strength of such campaigns lay in their flexibility and immediacy. Organisation was informal and action sporadic, shaping itself around the particular issue of the day.

These strengths, as well as some of the weaknesses of the past, have reappeared in the campaigns and organisations of the 1970s. These have varied widely, as our contributions demonstrate, though it is possible to pick out four important strands — each of which illustrate different lessons for joint community and worker organisation.

The nature of campaigns

First there are campaigns which have attempted to make the investment decision of *employers* more accountable to the workforce and to the community. As we have already pointed out, the investment programmes, particularly of large employers, have a critical impact on the fortunes of both the workforce and the surrounding area, especially where there is little alternative work available or where the firm is of major economic importance to the area. The threat of plant closure can thus become a critical *community* issue. Three of our chapters deal with this issue and show how campaigns were organised to oppose these decisions. The threatened closure of the Tate & Lyle refinery in Vauxhall, Liverpool, led to a campaign based on the shop stewards within the plant. It was significant that this campaign developed links with workers in the London plant which was also threatened. This is a crucial step when confronting multi-plant firms, to avoid one plant being played off against the other, though it is difficult to sustain in practice especially if only one plant is threatened. The local shop-steward base made it possible to develop the campaign in another direction — into the local community in Vauxhall. In this case the fact that some shop stewards were members both of community and of trade union organisations was helpful, for in practice there are likely to be problems in linking the two kinds of organisation with their differing working methods. The research support and community links, provided by a local community resource centre were also important factors.

Both these features, the shop steward base and community resource centre support, were also important in another, similar campaign to prevent the closure of the West India and Millwall Docks in East London, again a key local employer in an area of high unemployment. In this case the links between workers and residents were slightly more formal. An action committee on jobs, linked through the local resource centre, brought together representatives from the dock shop stewards, the local trades council and community groups. This action committee acted as the campaigning arm in the surrounding area. A vigorous local campaign run by the stewards and the committee involved public meetings, a march, lobbying, preparation of alternative plans and so on, and brought in support from the local MPs and the Council. Although the closure was averted, the problem has been to sustain the campaign in the longer term, and in particular to gather wide support for an alternative plan for developing the docks. Without this, the inevitable further attempt to close the docks may be successful.

Our third example of threatened closure deals with a public corporation, the National Coal Board, and its threat to the economy of a whole sub-region. The proposal to close down mining operations in the Ashfield area and move them to the Leicestershire/Nottinghamshire border would involve the upheaval of several communities. Ken Coates demonstrates that this enormous social issue was never divulged even to the local councillors, let alone to the workers and residents involved. This lack of social responsibility for the local effects of investment decisions, characterises most of the nationalised industries as much as the private sector. It clearly indicates the need to work out guidelines so that the social costs of relocation can be estimated and allowed for, and mechanisms for local participation can be built into decision-making.

A second group of joint community and workforce campaigns has been trying to make *small employers* more socially responsible in terms of wages and conditions of employment. As we have seen, areas of high unemployment are especially vulnerable to exploitation by a variety of enterprises. A typical example of this problem is the small non-unionised firm paying below-minimum wages, operating in a run-down old factory. Particular groups within these areas, women and blacks, for example, who face discrimination generally, are especially vulnerable. Two of the chapters describe attempts to combat these conditions. The first (chapter 5) describes a campaign to unionise a small factory exploiting a predominantly immigrant (and non-English-speaking) workforce. It is important to note that many techniques standard to community work were found to be extremely useful in winning trust and organising an inexperienced workforce. Moreover, the community can be an important base from which to organise, for the employer can make organisation impossible within (or even outside) the factory itself. However, it was of course also essential to bring in trade union organisers, right from the start, to give weight and continuity to the campaign. The second account (chapter 6) describes a homeworking campaign. Homeworking, which is on the increase, is especially prevalent in declining, low-income areas (though by no means confined to them). Again this campaign started from a community work base and has subsequently brought in official trade union backing. Homeworkers are a notoriously difficult workforce to reach, let alone organise, despite the fact that local authorities are obliged to maintain a register of homeworkers. However, there have been a number of local initiatives which have successfully contacted homeworkers, and in some cases, won improvements in pay and conditions. The campaign has also successfully won wider commitment from the TUC and from local Councils. The involvement of Councils should be an important aspect of a wider policy to improve conditions in firms of this type. We have already referred to Wandsworth Council's attempt to get firms taking space in Council-built factories to sign a Good Employer Code. This is aimed particularly to persuade firms to comply with Health and Safety regulations, to allow trade unions into the factory and to pay Wages Council rates.

A third group of joint campaigns are based on the issue of *public services*, where again the interests of the workforce and community group are likely to coincide. As we have pointed out, cuts in public spending have reduced the already inadequate level of services, especially in the declining areas, as well as reducing jobs directly. The last few years have seen a mushrooming of organisations, linking 'producers' and 'consumers', aimed at reversing cuts, particularly in local authority and hospital services. Two of our chapters illustrate the problems and possibilities. The campaign to resist proposed bus fare increases in Leeds highlights the difficulty of developing and sustaining an organisation spanning trade unions and community groups. In both cases, perspectives had to be extended. The trade unions for example became more aware of the impact of their service, while the community groups, realising their mutual interest, organised on a city-wide basis. The focus for action was a public inquiry into the fare increases. This tactic of using an official or quasi-judicial mechanism as a peg for a campaign is familiar to many community groups (many, for example have used Compulsory Purchase Order Inquiries in the same way). Although useful, this tactic has drawbacks, as Kevin Ward points out. Inquiries are likely to be weighted to accepting the official, expert line and they rarely allow broadly-based participation or even discussion. Usually, too, they are one-off affairs, making over-reliance on them dangerous. None the less, as the Leeds example, and chapter 10 on the opposition to the closure of Liverpool hospitals show, 'inquiries' and 'consultation periods' can be a useful focus for community and trade union groups to gain joint working experience, to win useful, if limited, concessions.

Another public service, particularly important to many community groups, is the Council's own building and repair service. These direct works departments are important both to extend socially responsible local employment (especially in the building industry where employment is still largely casual) and to ensure an adequate, locally accountable service. As chapter 9 points out, links between tenants' groups and direct labour employers are important both to defend them against the attacks of the private contractors and to improve their responsiveness to tenants' needs. In practice these links have been difficult to make and sustain: most tenants' groups have concerned themselves with *how* and *whether* repair work is done, rather than *who* does it. Direct labour organisations for their part have rarely involved themselves with their consumers, though there are now an increasing number of initiatives from both sides to make good these deficiencies.

The fourth area where community and local workforce have come together is more general and varied, and concerns a number of initiatives to relate the work process itself to the local community. These span the Lucas Corporate Plan's proposals to modify the company's product range, to the co-operative movement. The method of organisation varies widely, in some cases springing from community demands, as in the case of the Green Ban Action Committee (chapter 17) which are subsequently extended into trade union organisations. In others, like Lucas Aerospace, the reverse process has occurred.

Perhaps the most far-reaching of these initiatives is the Lucas Aerospace Shop Stewards Committee's alternative corporate plan (described in chapter 18), which suggests radical reassessment of both the *kind* of product industry chooses to make and the *way* that it is manufactured. If the groups are to go beyond a largely defensive strategy towards local jobs it is essential that these wider issues are raised. In particular the increasing bias towards capital intensity can be resisted in the long term only by extending workers' control over the productive process. As Mike Cooley points out, machines must be the servants, not the masters. He also highlights the essential role of the wider 'community' — for example, in defining the socially necessary products. The mechanisms for doing this have only been tentatively explored. The Corporate Plan has been widely discussed by community-based groups in some areas and the North East London Polytechnic centre referred to in his account provides one starting-point for relating community needs to production. Another important area where community control can be extended with the workers involved is the building industry. This touches on an area more familiar to community groups: the redevelopment of buildings and areas for high profit-yielding activities, often at the expense of more socially-needed projects. Again, only tentative experiments have been undertaken. Roland Watkins demonstrates however how Birmingham's Green Ban campaign to prevent the redevelopment of a Post Office building for offices (suggesting instead its use as a leisure centre) gained widespread support from both building workers and community groups. He highlights some of the political problems both in reaching a consensus about alternative uses for the building and in developing the campaign's tactics with a wide range of groups. As he shows, community-based groups are often limited by their area-based perspective.

Another kind of initiative aimed at redefining the aims and methods of production is the co-operative. Many co-operatives have sprung from a 'community' base, either to meet specific local needs (e.g. Sunderlandia's attempt to modernise working-class housing in Wearside) or, more generally, to reduce local unemployment. Given that the underlying aim is also to redefine the relationships between workers and owners, support has been gained from community groups and some local councils.

Despite these advantages, co-operatives have grave drawbacks: they are small-scale and thus provide few jobs. Most important, they are isolated within the wider market economy and vulnerable to the same pressure to be 'economically viable', an aim which, as the Sunderlandia example shows (chapter 16), conflicts with the goal of socially useful production. For example, the original intention to employ a high proportion of trainees and to concentrate work in working-class areas, had to be modified.

The community worker's role

Many of these attempts to link community-based and workplace organisations have used a local community resource centre, both as an organisational base for joint action and as an important source of research expertise. This in turn suggests that community workers can take an important role in developing a local strategy for employment. This role is an essential extension of community work itself, since, as we have argued, the local economy is crucial to the fortunes of the people and the organisations with whom the community worker operates.

This will mean that the community worker must become familiar with workplace organisations, trade union structures and methods of work. Particularly crucial are the local organisations such as shop stewards' committees and the trades council, and the relationship between shopfloor workers and the full-time paid officials of their trade unions. Most community workers have themselves realised the value of joining a trade union themselves: through becoming involved in inter-union organisation (such as works committees or trades councils) an appreciation of the concerns of other unions can be obtained. Community workers will also need to familiarise themselves with the local economy itself. This should first be done by learning about the issues directly from the workers themselves in each of the key sectors. It is important also to get a feeling for what is happening over the whole area, and this is best done by looking at official data for small areas.[3]

In addition, most local authorities which have become involved in analysing local employment trends have published or hold considerable information about the local economy: this information is generally located in the Council's Planning Department. Further analyses of the local economy are also published by public agencies concerned with local or regional planning or by specially commissioned teams of researchers: in the Northern Region, for example, the Northern Economic Development Council and the Northern Region Strategy Team have published accounts of various aspects of the local employment situation. Valuable information can also be obtained from unofficial bodies such as the trade union research units now established in Southampton, Birmingham and Newcastle (as well as the long-established unit at Ruskin College) and a number of larger trade unions (such as NUPE, TGWU, ASTMS) which have their own local and national research facilities. Many of these bodies have proved to be invaluable support for local campaigns in defence of jobs and services.

Information on the activities of individual local companies, their investment plans, performance, range of products etc., as well as key personnel, especially directors, is another important component in building up a picture of the local economy.[4] Through acquiring such information the community worker will be better equipped to offer resources to local trade union organisations over and above the regular resources of facilities for meetings, hardware such as typing and duplicating and so on.

Conclusions

A major theme of this book is the need to unite organisations at the workplace and in the community in defence of jobs and for the preservation of decent living conditions. Each chapter, in addition, highlights the demands which need to be formulated as part of these broader campaigns. These include the need for strengthening public control over the form and location of the investment decisions of private and public companies, the need to protect the fundamental right of trade unions to organise, to safeguard the quality as well as the quantity of jobs and the need to relate production and technological change to social needs rather than to the requirements of profit.

Each of these represents a significant demand to be fought for and involves, we have argued, strengthening the relationship between trade union organisations and local community groups. However even this will not, by itself, be sufficient to bring about lasting and significant improvements. Ultimately democratic control of production and services needs to be secured and will only come about by change at every level of social, economic and political organisation. These changes have to be fought for in parallel with the more limited demands described above. Until they are achieved, any gains, however useful in the short term, will continue to be partial and transitory.

Notes

1   The IRC was the Industrial Reorganisation Corporation, set up with £150m capital in 1966 to 'help British Industry to adapt its structure and organisation so that it can meet international competition more effectively'.
2   The National Enterprise Board, established in 1975, and which has now developed on similar lines to the IRC.
3   There are several important sources:
     Employment Record data from the annual Census of Employment.
     Population Census, 10% workplace data, for 1961, 1966, 1971.
     Unemployment/Vacancies for men and women from the Department of Employment every month. (The Codot Occupation data break this data down into many hundreds of occupations.)
4   Much of this information is available at local public libraries. The following are the most useful sources:
     The Times 1,000 Top Companies.
     Who Owns Whom.
     Extel Service (providing regular business information on thousands of companies).
     Directory of Directors.
     Kompass Directories (for European firms).
     A detailed guide to investigating companies has been published by *Community Action* Magazine and is available from them (PO Box 665, London SW1X 8DZ). The annual reports of companies, which often give a review of their activities, can generally be obtained from the Company Secretary at the company's headquarters, and both private and publicly quoted companies are obliged to register annual accounts and supplementary information with the Department of Trade and Industry at Companies House (55 City Road, London, E1), records which are available for public consultation. Various journals are also helpful sources of information, notably *Labour Research*, published by the Labour Research Department (78 Blackfriars Road, London, SE1), *Trade and Industry*, published by the DTI, and the *Employment Gazette* from the Department of Employment. Finally, a number of books are now in print which provide helpful information on understanding Company accounts. The most useful is probably *Your Employer's Profits* by Christopher Hird, published by Pluto Press, London.

Further general background reading

Community Development Project, *The Costs of Industrial Change*, and *Gilding the Ghetto*, CDP Interproject Editorial Team, London, 1977 (both available from Publications, 87 Adelaide Terrace, Newcastle upon Tyne NE4 8BB).

Joint Docklands Action Group, *Jobs Now*, London, 1976, and *The Fight for a Future*, London, 1977 (both available from JDAG, 58 Watney Street, London E1).

D. Massey, *Industrial Restructuring versus the Cities*, Centre for Environment Studies, London, 1977.

Policy for the Inner Cities, Cmnd 6845, HMSO, June 1977.

K. Coates (ed.), *Planning by the People: the Right to Useful Work*, Spokesman Books, Nottingham, 1978.

Part I **Historical Connections**

1 Organizing the unemployed in the 1920s

Bert Edwards

Bert Edwards has been a key figure in both the trade union movement and community organisation. He was one of the founders of the Joint Shop Stewards Committees in the motor industry, from the first meeting in 1921, to the formation of a regular Shop Stewards Conference in London and eventually to the National Motor Shop Stewards Committee.

Because of his union activities, he was frequently out of work and thus became involved in organising the unemployed in their local communities. He was a founder member of the National Unemployed Workers' Movement Committee and Organising Chairman of the Southwark Committee. The interview which follows deals with this inter-war period and with the links between the Unemployed Workers' Movement and the growth of trade union organisation on the shop floor.

Subsequently, Bert Edwards played a leading role in another aspect of community organising: tenants' associations. The growth of tenants' associations on the new GLC estate where he lived in Burnt Oak provided a model for similar developments elsewhere. The history of the Burnt Oak association has been described in Ruth Glass's study of *Watling Street.*

The interview, relating as it does to an earlier period, has to be seen in this historical context when tenants' associations were relatively undeveloped and the experience of the rent strike novel.

Bert Edwards is currently completing his autobiography, covering his experiences both in the trade union movement and community action (up to his present age of eighty-three).

What were the economic and social problems which gave rise to the National Unemployed Workers' Movement? The 1920s and 1930s are remembered now as a period of high unemployment and widespread poverty — what were conditions like in Southwark at this time?

First, the percentage of unemployed workers was particularly high. This was because the people there were casual or ordinary rather than skilled labourers. The unemployment rate for Southwark must have averaged over 12 per cent. There were few factories in Southwark, but the docks were close. Being casual workers, a lot of local labourers found work in the docks. The only reasonably big factories were Dewrance Engineering in Old Kent Road, an engineering factory making printing machinery in St George's Circus and a firm making lifts. Apart from these, there was little manufacturing industry in Southwark: the majority of workers were hired on a casual basis. The workers were so badly paid when they were in work that when they were out of work they had no reserves to fall back on.

A lecturer at the Socialist Church spoke of women living, working and sleeping in a small room, sewing for a shilling a day, making childrens' overalls for 2d each, making matchboxes for 22d a gross, and paper bags for 6d a thousand. A man and his wife together earned 20s per week for making artificial flowers. A mother and daughter made 5s a week for twelve hours' work a day making sunshades. One Camberwell Green girl for instance was keeping her mother and herself on earnings of 8s per week, while paying 1s 6d rent.

The social consequences of these low wages were documented for example by Lady Warwick visiting a Lambeth school. In Standard 1, she found that twelve boys had been told not to come home to dinner as there was no food. Sixteen had breakfasted on charity and two had eaten no breakfast at all. In Standard 2, six had eaten no breakfast, forty-five were habitually underfed and thirty-five had no dinner to go home to. At the bottom of Tabard Street the ground floors were empty because they were infested with rats. The houses had been condemned for many years. Southwark was a slum. It was these conditions which created the solidarity between the unemployed, the low-paid workers and also the general public in Southwark. This is what made it possible to organise them, as we did, in the Unemployed Workers' Movement.

How far were these problems solved by the welfare provisions of the time — the Poor Law Relief?

The conditions of getting Poor Law Relief were different from today. You had to go to the Board of Guardians and wait, sitting on benches. You were called before the Board and they asked you all sorts of questions. Then you would leave. Afterwards they would send a Relieving Officer to your house to talk to you about your conditions. He would say, 'You don't want that piece of furniture, you can sell this and that, and that'll give you money.' When you did get Relief you didn't get money, but tickets. You had tea and meal — not oats — and you had a ticket for *cagmag* meat, scrap ends from the butcher. This background still exists in people's minds today; when you talk about going to the social services, they say 'that's charity' — and they don't want it.

How did you become involved in organising the unemployed?

After the First World War I became a founder member of the National Unemployed Workers' Movement with Wal Hannington and Sid Hayes. I became the organising chairman of the Southwark branch of the NUWM. At that time I found it hard to find a job. I had been active in the development of the shop floor movement and as soon as you were found to be an active trade unionist, you were unemployed. So I became active in the Unemployed Workers' Movement.

During this period I was in and out of work. I had a number of short jobs that would last possibly a week or a number of months, then I would be unemployed again. Each time I was in work, I came back into the organised workers movement and carried on my work there. Otherwise, I was active in the NUWM.

How did you contact the unemployed to organise them?

We organised them at the Labour Exchange, then in Newington Causeway in a big empty store, fronting onto the Causeway. We used to hold meetings at the apex of Southwark Bridge Road where it joins the Causeway, right opposite the Exchange. Our members had membership cards and contributed a halfpenny a week so that we had finance. Our offices were in a cellar in Penton Place. We had regular monthly meetings outside the Exchange. When we had a demonstration it would start and finish there. The organisation was so strong that I could go to the manager of the Exchange, tell him I was taking a demonstration and he would arrange for all the men going on the demonstration to sign on because it would disrupt his organisation so much otherwise. I even used to leave my pushbike in his office; after the demonstration I would just walk over and pick it up again.

What form did your organisation actually take?

The organisation of the local branches was fairly loose and

flexible. There was no constitution or standing orders. In addition to the regular mass meetings there was a committee consisting of three elected officers who selected the other five committee members. Each borough had its own committee. When one borough was organising a demonstration to the Boards of Guardians, other boroughs who had their own organisation operating well would bring a company or a group of all their unemployed. They would march into the area and so a very large demonstration of the unemployed workers would develop in the borough in question.

How did the NUWM relate to the trade union movement generally?

We worked on the principle that since a member of a trade union could become unemployed, and if he became unemployed he could become a member of the NUWM, there needed to be a close association between the trade union and NUWM, and that kept it together.

How did the local movement relate to the national campaign?

There was a tremendous organisation developing in the rest of London and in the whole of the country. At this time we held a national conference of the Unemployed Workers' Movement in Manchester. (I was a delegate and there were delegates from all over the country and from Scotland.) We elected an executive committee and launched the nationally organised movement with the slogan 'Work or full maintenance at Trade Union rates'. At this period (1922 and 1923) we organised the first unemployed march, and fifty of us marched from London to Brighton to the Labour Party Conference. We aimed at getting a number of important Labour leaders to speak to us, on the sea-front. But the only member who came out was George Lansbury, the Poplar MP, who was later arrested with twelve of his councillors because they refused to repay the money they had overspent, giving benefit to unemployed workers.

Could you explain the tactics your organisation developed?

For instance, we developed the method of raiding factories that were working overtime. We would cut the telephone wires, march in and take over the office; then we would call the workers to a mass meeting in the factory, get up on one of the benches and talk to them about the problem of them working overtime and getting extra money when there were anything up to 2 million workers unemployed. We were requesting that they should work the normal 52-hour week and force the factory to take on some of the unemployed workers — this was in order to assist the general position of the working class. Generally they were very sympathetic. They would stop work and come to the bench where I was standing and listen reasonably.

Another tactic was to take over the workhouses. One time for example I took over the workhouse at Offord Street. I did it, by understanding what I'd read about the German method of organisation, by the 'tens' method. I had five groups of ten men standing very close to the Offord Street workhouse. Another member of the committee and myself knocked on the door. When the porter came, we just pushed him aside, went into the office and got hold of the workhouse manager. We gave the word to an organiser who sent to a meeting-point where there were five men with bicycles, each of these then called their groups, so that fifty men entered the workhouse before the police knew anything about it. We held this workhouse for a week and we flew the Red Flag from the roof. There was some amusement in it too, you know. I never laughed so much as when I went into the food section and found one of the organisers with a big 5lb pot of jam under his arm, eating the jam with his hands, with the jam all over his face. So you can see that even in adversity we had a certain amount of amusement and fun.

On one occasion we went into another workhouse. We went into the Master's office, another member and myself. The Master was a little chap and it was funny to see him. We banged on the door and he stood on one side while I argued with the Manager. We wanted blankets, coal and more food, for the unemployed people. After all, in the winter you can't live while you're freezing with cold, and the children had to be protected from bronchitis. It was a long argument; afterwards, when we started to leave this little fellow stood with his arms out and said, 'Only over my dead body.'

Did NUWM become involved in housing and other local community issues?

Evictions were a particular problem — there were a lot of men out of work and a lot of men out on strike, so working-class families were often unable to pay the rent and consequently they were evicted under the instructions of the local magistrate. The bailiff would come and haul them out of their houses. So we decided that we should assist these unemployed and low-wage workers. If they were threatened with eviction we would put into the house a defence committee of ten to twenty members, according to the size of the house. We would supply them with a bucket and a rope that could reach from the first floor window down to the pavement. We would send them up food and drink in this bucket and also keep in constant communication. When we had barricaded the front door and the ground-floor windows, back and front, we would fill the street with unemployed workers or sympathetic neighbours so that the bailiffs or the police could not penetrate near the house to do the eviction. Then I would go to the landlord's agent with my friends. We would argue that if they wanted to throw us out of the house there would be more damage done and that would cost a hell of a lot of money. We would repay some of the back rent and some of the regular payments and then we would leave. This tactic became the order of the day. On many occasions the local bailiff would come to me and say, 'Are you going to take up this case, Mr Edwards?', and if I said 'Yes', he would say, 'All right, I won't take it.'

Another tactic was to organise a rent strike. We said that the rents were too high, so the tenants decided to withhold paying it. They would pay it to me and I'd put it in the bank. I appreciated the fact that, if a workman's wife had money she'd spend it — she wouldn't put it away — and consequently, at the end of the dispute she would most likely be in such arrears that she'd run the risk of being removed from the house. The strike didn't last long. What I did was to contact some of the MPs from the Clyde who had been running rent strikes during the war, to get information. Kirkwood, the MP, was very helpful and very friendly over it. Consequently, we won our demands and that was that.

Did any of these tactics bring you into conflict with the police?

We did have difficulties with the police. I went with the Battersea Unemployed Workers Movement on a demonstration for increased Poor Relief, and seeing that it was November, we were asking for blankets and coal for the workers. As I was about to take the demonstration away, the local inspector came down and said, 'The Superintendent would like to have a word with you.' The Superintendent asked me to tell him which factories the committee were going to raid, in return for £5 per week. I refused of course. The Superintendent said, 'O.K. I'll have you inside within a month.' I said, 'Fine, I'm unemployed now. I'll be fed in prison and I will have time to read. I'll come out a bigger rebel.'

Part II Private Capital: Social Accountability and the Community

2 Community responses to the oil industry

Mark Hill

Introduction

In 1970 Aberdeen was a small and relatively self-contained city of about 200,000, regional capital for the much larger area of North East and North Scotland. Its economy was resource-based — fishing with fish processing, farming and food processing, paper-making, whisky distilling, construction and some shipbuilding and marine engineering — and bolstered by a comprehensive array of professional and other services. Because of its unique situation the city had in fact a higher proportion of professional people than any other city in Britian of a comparable size, many of them employed in one of the large public services — the Health Service, the University, the College of Commerce, the College of Education and the two technical colleges. About half of its population could be described as working class and most of them lived on estates seldom beautiful, often badly designed and inadequately serviced, but in general of a higher standard than similar estates in other large Scottish cities.

Despite this relatively large working-class population the city's political tradition was liberal rather than democratic socialist. Between the wars Aberdeen had been noted for its radicalism, and post-war labourism and bureaucracy was, as it were, grafted on to this dominant tradition. The city's unemployment rate in 1970 was already approaching seven per cent. This disguised a steady trickle of emigration but was lower than other coastal towns such as Dundee and Peterhead. It was generally agreed that the city needed more industrial development, and the North East Scotland Development Authority was set up in 1970 to promote this. Until oil was discovered there was not much hope that such development would be forthcoming.

The oil industry, being resource-based, in theory fitted in well with the pattern of the region's economy, but in practice the speed with which the industry developed — a speed forced on it by the 1973 oil 'crisis' and normal market pressures — put enormous strains on the existing administrative, land use and labour market patterns of the region. During the early phases the primary needs of the industry were for offshore service bases, office space, housing, improved transport, labour and engineering services. It is the strains and repercussions of these demands which particularly concern us. During the subsequent phases of refining and petrochemical processing, the really controversial decisions about the siting of such facilities have to be made but since there are no plans to site any such facilities in or around Aberdeen they do not immediately concern us. We have chosen to confine ourselves to Aberdeen simply for reasons of space.

Readers should however bear in mind that the repercussions of the oil industry have been relatively greater in places outside Aberdeen (such as Peterhead and the Cromarty Firth) where populations were smaller and infrastructure was less adequate. While Aberdeen was big enough and well enough developed to accommodate the industry without actually changing its *nature*, the same could not be said of many smaller towns and villages.

Before 1970, oil companies engaged in exploration kept a low profile. The vigilant would have noticed an ever-increasing number of seismic survey vessels putting in to harbours, but for most people there was only the rumour of oil discoveries. The announcement of the discovery of BP's huge Forties Field in the summer of 1970, and the subsequent announcement that BP were planning to set up a major administrative HQ at Farburn, Dyce changed everything almost overnight. Enquiries from other oil companies began to flood in, closely followed by a huge number of planning applications. The boom had started.

Although the arrival of the industry signalled a huge increase in general public aggravation, it was also exciting for a city which had been on the edge of the doldrums for most of the post-war period — so nearly everyone was at least resigned to the industry's presence. The problem, as people saw it then, was to make the most of the opportunity offered and to avoid, if possible, too great a disruption of one's normal way of life.

The impact of oil developments

Before proceeding to an account of the reactions of the community to the industry we will sketch in the statistical background. In terms of employment and industrial development the oil industry has meant over the past six years:

(a) over 400 firms directly involved in the oil industry (oil companies, rig operators, shipping companies, diving and underwater specialists, mud/cement companies, catering and engineering supply firms) have set up offices or supply bases or manufacturing premises in the city. This number continues to expand at the rate of about one per week, and there is still a queue of firms looking for development space. This represents something like 14,000 new jobs created in the Grampian region since 1970, the great majority of them in Aberdeen itself. This is compared with a total of 26,000 oil-related jobs for the whole of Scotland (figures as at June 1977).

(b) at least another 400 firms are indirectly involved in providing miscellaneous services to the industry. This represents a further expansion of some 6,000 jobs in Aberdeen.

(c) expansion of the region's population by 40–50,000 by 1982, most accounted for by the immigration of professional and skilled oil workers and their families. Most of this influx is, or will be, accommodated in a ring of expanding towns within 20 miles of Aberdeen, though a fair proportion live in Aberdeen itself or its immediate suburbs.

(d) a sharp drop in the numbers of unemployed. Since 1970 when unemployment in the region was about 8 per cent and in the city about 7 per cent, the rate of unemployment in the region has fluctuated around 5 per cent and in the city has seldom risen above 3.5 per cent. By comparison, the unemployment rate in Strathclyde in December 1977 was 10.1 per cent.

(e) the building of major administrative HQs by eight major oil companies.

(f) the development of at least 450 acres of industrial land within the city boundaries; the development of a further 400 acres by local authority and private developers on land around the airport; and the development of a further unspecified acreage by private interests elsewhere in the city.

(g) the setting up of three large, and a larger number of small oil field equipment manufacturers in the city, representing long term employment well in excess of 1,000.

(h) an investment of more than £20m in the following facilities in the harbour area: conversion of harbour from tidal to non-tidal; six integrated oil field supply bases; reconstruction of the fish market (£2m); a new graving dock; a new plant for manufacturing drilling and associated chemicals; and a new roll-on/roll-off ferry terminal.

(i) an investment by the British Airports Authority of over £6m in providing a new terminal building, apron space and runway extension at Dyce Airport; an investment of over £20m by the main helicopter companies in their local fleet, by far the largest in Europe; an annual increase in passenger traffic of about 35 per cent since 1971 with passenger movements now totalling over one million per annum.

(j) the setting up of a training school with courses in oil-related geology and engineering, and general training facilities for offshore workers.

The effects on existing services

The scale and pace of developments outlined above represents a massive expansion of industrial and other activity in the city. This has had inevitable repercussions on existing services in the city, beginning with the Town Council and sending its shock waves through every department of local administration and public service and amenity.

1 *Aberdeen Town (later District) Council*

For the past 30 years the city has been administered by a Labour Party majority, though in the last local elections the Labour Party lost its overall majority while still remaining the largest single party. In a city as remote and provincial as Aberdeen the quality of the local Council and local government administration can be a crucial factor in the success or failure of large-scale developments of the kind represented by the oil industry. Provincial administrations tend to be paternalistic rather than participatory; if *they* do not take the initiative then the community is unlikely to do so on its own account. If Aberdeen folk related to the local power structure at all they tended to do so through their local councillor rather than through any grass roots organisation; and they also tended to accept as inevitable whatever their councillor told them. This was certainly the case in Aberdeen in 1970.

Faced with large-scale economic development, any local government administration is immediately faced with an important question — do we try to obtain extra-ordinary powers to plan, co-ordinate and control developments; or do we simply use existing legislation to administer developments while allowing ordinary market forces of supply and demand to dictate their scale, speed and direction? This question is especially crucial for any Labour administration because the Labour Party purports to be the party of the working class.

It has to be said that in 1970, after twenty-five years in office in a city with a paternalistic liberal tradition, the Labour Council and local administration was predisposed to play a purely administrative role. This is no place for an excursion into the history of the Labour Party in local government, but in passing it is worth noting that it is, par excellence, the party of the negotiated compromise and will in general go to almost any lengths to avoid exacerbating class conflicts. Had Aberdeen's Labour Council chosen a more positive planning role they would undoubtedly have received the support of working class organisations in the city, but they would also have offended deeply entrenched traditions.

There were other powerful reasons to explain the Council's 'do nothing' attitude. There was a Tory Government in office which they did not wish to offend; their own local organisation had decayed over the years and they had lost contact with the aspirations of their electorate. Quite simply the quality of ideas and initiatives produced by the local Council had gradually degenerated since the war, and their electorate had lost interest. Active participation was very small, and lines of communication with local trade unions had fallen into disuse. The local Trades Council was kept alive by a handful of activists and a larger number of old worthies who came for the beer and the conversation, but since so few people and unions actively supported its work, its pronouncements were largely ignored, not least by the local Council. This was to heavily influence subsequent events, at least up until the election of the new District Council in 1974–5.

2 Local government planning

The attitude of the Labour Council to the oil industry was at first defensive. Under constant pressure to grant planning permission quickly, they were undoubtedly reduced to a degree of panic planning. In a year from mid 1971, the two qualified planning officers had to deal with an increase in planning applications from the normal 1,200 to 2,200. The arrival of the oil industry triggered off a wave of speculation in land and property, starting at the harbour and working its way through the city centre during 1971–4. In a six-week period in 1972, fourteen separate applications were made for hotel developments and office sites changed hands up to four times without a brick being laid. The Council came under heavy public pressure to control speculation but did not act until the late summer of 1974, by which time most of the damage had been done. Empty office blocks and gap sites proliferated up to 1974, land and property values in the city shot up astronomically, and the Council eventually decided to refuse to grant planning permission unless the developer could show he had a client interested, and began to refuse to give detailed planning permission if plans were not submitted within six months of the original application.

In this orgy of city centre development, the unique character of the old city centre was trivialised and commercialised. The granite facades and austere beauty built up over the centuries from local materials gave way to cheaply designed and built office and tower blocks. Many listed buildings simply disappeared. Luckily the city had at its disposal fairly large areas already zoned for industrial use, mainly on the edge of the city; these were rapidly taken up. A 33-acre extension to the East Tullos Estate attracted applications from thirty-five companies requiring a total of 175 acres; and in response to this demand the Council was forced to zone further land for industry, including a huge 180 acre estate at Altens. After some minor skirmishes, the farmers involved secured a reasonable price from the Council.

3 The harbour

The Council were not so lucky in the harbour area, because space there was strictly limited. This came to a head in 1971 when Shell Expro applied to build an oil storage and marine base on the site of Old Torry, a traditional bungalow-type community of fishermen's houses on a prime site overlooking the harbour. The threat of development had been hanging over this area for years, with the Council adopting a strategy of attrition, neglect, threat and persuasion to demoralise the residents. Some owners had left and their houses stood empty, but others continued to resist steadfastly.

Then in the late 1960s the residents seemed to have won when the Council gave them a 15–20-year 'no development' guarantee; but this proved to be shortlived.

Shell made its application after consultation with the Council, and in the knowledge that the Council had itself been gradually wearing down the resistance of the residents with constant threats of development during the 1960s; the final demise of Old Torry has to be seen in this light. When Shell submitted their application it quickly became obvious to the Torry residents that they were not going to get any support from their Labour councillors and that, in effect, further resistance was hopeless.

After meetings of the Council's Select Committee on Industrial Development, which recommended that the Council acquire the land and rezone it for industrial use, and of the full Council, whose Labour majority duly ratified this decision, the Torry residents managed, without much difficulty, to raise a storm in the local Press. But once the Council had made its decision there was little the residents or the Press could do to reverse the momentum towards development. A futile public enquiry was subsequently held and the question was more or less settled when Shell threatened to leave the area unless their demands were met. Old Torry was duly razed to the ground in February 1974 within days of the last residents leaving, though one old lady established a firm place in local legend by refusing to leave, even as the bulldozers arrived, until she had received what she regarded as suitable alternative accommodation from the Council's Housing Department.

The persuasive force of Shell's threat to leave the area has to be seen in the context of intense inter-city rivalries and competition for development, which are themselves the logical result of relying for development on the unplanned and uneven distribution of capital investment. In a market economy, where capital migrates in search of the highest profit, different cities are forced to compete in a way which can only be destructive to the long-term interests of their inhabitants.

4 *The airport*

The other major area of development was at the airport at Dyce. There the problem was not the shortage of development space but the loss of amenity caused by the gradual rise in the noise level, especially after the introduction of jet flights in 1972. At that time planning for the area was controlled by the Conservative Aberdeen County Council, who were under constant pressure from the British Airports Authority (BAA), the Civil Aviation Authority (CAA) and commercial airline and helicopter companies to expand facilities and open the airport to 24-hour use. In October 1974 the BAA was granted outline planning permission by Aberdeen County Council to proceed with a £6m development involving a runway extension, more apron space and a new terminal building. This outline planning permission was granted with the provisos that:

There should be no flights between 10.30 pm and 6 pm and
all take-offs and landings should be routed to and from the North, away from residential areas.

These provisos did not satisfy the commercial interests involved and early in 1975 the BAA submitted more flexible plans including:

(a) an extension of flights up till 11 pm
(b) discretion to the BAA to allow night flights they considered of importance to industry or the community and
(c) discretion to the BAA to decide flight direction, weather and traffic conditions permitting.

These new proposals were accepted by Aberdeen County Council at a meeting in May 1975.

The stage was then set for a head-on collision between residents in the affected area and the BAA; but at this point, with the re-organisation of local government, the new Aberdeen District Council assumed responsibility for planning decisions affecting the airport and, under intense public pressure, upheld the original planning conditions. The BAA and others objected, and on the strength of their objections the Secretary of State ordered a public enquiry to be held, which duly took place on 14 June 1976, and which upheld most of the planning provisos insisted on by the new District Council. More importantly it supported the District Council's submission that it was the District Council, not the BAA, who had the legal right to control planning conditions at the airport. The BAA is at present appealing against this decision.

5 Roads and transport

Plans for an inner ring road were first mooted in Aberdeen in the early 1950s, but they had never really received the wholehearted support of the Labour Council because prior to 1970 there was not a sufficient volume of traffic coming into the city centre to justify the expense and disturbance this would entail. The oil industry of course brought with it a huge increase in traffic, both private and commercial, and added a new urgency to the search for a solution. This in turn brought residents on the proposed routes under renewed pressure, especially on certain sections on the route from the airport to the harbour.

In other areas of the city, for which no plans existed, traffic congestion built up and there was increasing pressure on parking space. Congestion was particularly bad on the bridge over the River Dee in Torry, which carried the main access road for harbour-bound traffic coming from the South, and this gave rise to a community campaign described in the next section. Pressure on city centre parking was however somewhat alleviated by the siting of most major industrial developments on the edge of the city.

The inner ring road has meantime only been developed in small sections. This is partly the result of lack of finance following from the cuts, partly the result of localised opposition, but more probably the result of the lack of suitable alternative accommodation for those threatened with being displaced to make way for the road.

6 Housing

In 1970 the Council administered a housing stock of about 26,000 houses, of which at least a quarter were sub-standard. In 1972 the chief sanitary officer for the city claimed that 7,000 houses in the city were actually slums and a total of 15,485 officially sub-standard. In 1970 the Council received 4,312 applications for housing and re-housing and completed 1,169 new houses. The cost of building a 2–3-room flat was then (disregarding loan repayments) between £3,000 and £3,600, and a steady labour force of about 1,000 men were employed on Council building projects.

Because the housing programme was 'going well' the Housing Committee considered cutting back on the number of new houses being built, and decided to transfer some of the labour force (and about one-third of the £4m housing budget) to modernising old pre-war sub-standard housing. The following year the waiting list was down to 4,119; 836 new houses were completed and 594 were modernised.

During 1972 the situation changed drastically. When the nine-week national building strike finished in October, many skilled men did not return to Council building projects having been lured away by the high bonuses offered by commercial and industrial developers. During the year the waiting list rose to 4,686 and the Council's building programme ground to a halt. Between 1972 and 1975 a huge backlog of partially completed houses built up, and only 730 houses were completed in the years 1972–4. Since well over half the population depend for housing on the Council the effect of this slowdown was drastic. Between 1973 and 1975 the waiting list was effectively frozen at about 4,500. It would have been much higher, but many families knowing the situation simply didn't apply for housing or re-housing. At the same time the cost of building a 2–3 apartment flat rose to between £9,000 and £10,000.

This meant that by 1975 the number of families living in over-crowded conditions (mainly in Council houses where young couples were forced to share with in-laws) had increased six-fold from 1967; that the number of families living in sub-standard conditions had also multiplied enormously; and that a huge boost was given to speculation in the private sector.

In 1971 there was already a move in the privately rented sector away from unfurnished to furnished lets. Landlords who would normally have let furnished accommodation on the open market sought lucrative company lets instead, thus immediately reducing the number of private lets available. Speculative landlords began to buy up old tenement property and divide and sub-divide already tiny rooms. As far as space allowed, caravan sites proliferated on the edge of town, and rents of £30–£35 a week were not uncommon. Rents for lodging and bed and breakfast accommodation soared, and many single men working on oil-related projects found themselves sharing four to a room and paying £20 a week for the privilege.

'To obtain a Council house in 1974,' wrote Judy Payne,[1]

> a young couple would have to either share a house for 11 years, or live in unsuitable housing for 11 years and both suffer ill-health. Under the present system of points alloca-tion, the quickest way to obtain access to Council housing is to have more children or to share a house to such an extent that there is a bedroom deficiency. One young couple with one child living in a small two-roomed tenement flat with no bathroom and an outside toilet were told that unless they

had another child they would have to wait eight years before getting a Council house.

The housing situation now, four years later, has only improved marginally.

In 1976, as the pace of development elsewhere in the city slackened and as more money was made available by the Government, building workers returned to work on public housing projects and the Council set itself the target of 1,000 new housing units a year for the next five years. In two years, 1976-7, they managed to keep to that target, but because of the enormous backlog built up during the crisis years 1972-5, this only eased the housing problem. The waiting list is still over 4,000 and it will be some years yet before that total will drop substantially. In time those workers employed offshore will probably move off the list as they become owner-occupiers; but they are really very few and will not radically alter a dismal situation.

Those who have suffered most from the housing crisis are the most vulnerable groups in the community — young couples, pregnant women, couples with young children, the young children themselves, and the elderly. People remain badly overcrowded and single people find it almost impossible to obtain, or afford, private lets. On top of this the whole community has suffered from the crisis, for it has meant that only the well-off could afford housing. The shortage has pushed up prices throughout the market, and industrial expansion in the area has been held back by the difficulty of finding accommodation for incoming workers.

The situation has only been exacerbated by the preference given, through the Scottish Special Housing Association (SSHA), to incoming workers. While the District Council has operated a normal points system of housing allocation, people on the waiting list have had to watch while the SSHA, who have their own separate allocation system, found housing for incoming oil workers. Some efforts have been made by the Council to take over the administration and allocation of SSHA houses, but to little effect. In the last resort it is not only the preference system which has been called into question, but the whole system of allocation.

7 Other public services

The effect of the oil industry on other public services in the city has been slightly less severe, and results almost entirely from both the ability of the industry to pay higher wages than those offered in the public sector and the difficulty experienced by the public services in attracting to an area of housing shortage, replacements for labour lost to the oil industry. The Health Service for instance, already hit by reorganisation and a shortage of nurses, has found its secretarial staff reduced to two-thirds its normal strength and its efforts to attract new secretarial and nursing staff founder on the rocks of the housing shortage. This, coupled with the effects of cuts, has led inevitably to increased delays in the 'processing' of National Health patients. In addition an increasing number of 'oil wives' have been seeking psychiatric help at the city's Ross Clinic suffering from the 'Intermittent Husband Syndrome'[2] — that is, an inability to cope emotionally and sexually with the work/leave patterns of their husbands working offshore.

The problems of the Education Service are of long standing and not directly related to the oil industry. There was a small problem about assimilating the children of (often foreign) oil workers, but the American oil community started their own school where the often disturbed children of globe-trotting oil men were directly catered for. There was some small problem too with the shortage of school space, but this has been minor and generally solved, at least temporarily, by the use of prefabricated school buildings.

The Social Services have also had to cope with oil-related problems. In the early days of the boom they had to cope with an increased workload for two reasons. One was that many single men came to the city expecting to find accommodation but did not, and ended up in the city lodging house and on social security, unable to hold down jobs because they were unable to find suitable housing. In addition, evicted families were no longer able to find alternative accommodation. Many were forced to live with relatives in unauthorised Council sub-lets and as a result could not get back on the housing waiting list. There was probably also a more general rise in the case load of individual social workers as families at the lower end of the housing market came under increased stress from overcrowding; but figures are not available for this.

Aberdeen has always been short of community amenities particularly for the young, and during the 1970s this has been exacerbated by the cuts. Even those community centres planned have had to be shelved for lack of public money to finance them, and this contrasts with the provision of many expensive night spots, restaurants and discos, opened to cater for the new rich of the oil industry and quite out of range of the pockets of most young people in the city, who still have to roam the streets in search of entertainment and recreation. During the last two years some oil companies have, as part of their public relations exercise, sponsored various concerts and poetry readings, but these cater for an entirely middle class audience.

8 *Labour market*

Under the capitalist system workers have nothing of value to sell but their labour. Predictably, therefore, those who have been in a position to do so have responded to the changes in the labour market situation by selling themselves to the highest bidder.

Much of the labour required by the oil industry is highly specialised and itinerant, and as a result has had to be imported; but wherever possible the industry has bled the local labour market to satisfy its own needs. We have already seen the detrimental effects this has had in two areas — public sector housing and public sector staffing — but it has also affected any industry employing skilled engineering labour — and most industries do, if only in a maintenance capacity.

The oil companies have no apprenticeship scheme and do not as a rule train their own engineers. These they either import, or lure away from local ship-building, ship-repairing and marine engineering firms. The competition has become more unequal with each successive phase of wage restraint which, while affecting public and private firms in the engineering sector, has not affected the oil industry at all. Coming into the area for the first time oil companies have been able to set starting rates for new employees well above the going rates in local industries. The experience of two firms show how this has worked out in practice.

John Wood Shiprepairing, a large private firm, were able to come to a quick understanding with the unions on wage settlements in 1977. The new rate, and the speed with which it was negotiated, has helped them stem the flow of skilled men. Hall Russells on the other hand (the largest shipbuilding firm in the city and nationalised in 1977) deferred their settlement at the request of the unions until after the publication of the government White Paper on wages policy. When the hoped-for return to 'free collective bargaining' did not materialise the unions were forced to negotiate rates within the ten per cent guidelines. The implementation of the settlement was then further delayed until November because of detailed scrutiny by government departments, and in the interim the firm lost large numbers of skilled men to the oil industry. The size of the eventual wage settlement has not encouraged others to stay.

Hall Russells are now in the anomalous position of having a full order book but not enough skilled labour to fulfil their contracts; and their efforts to import skilled labour from the south have been severely hampered by the difficulty of finding suitable housing. This gradual 'bleeding' of the skilled engineering labour from the area's traditional industries has led to increasing fears that the whole balance of the region's economy has now been knocked askew. If this continues, and if the housing situation does not improve drastically, this can only place the long-term future of the region's economy in jeopardy.

The transfer of labour from other existing industries to oil-related industries has been, with the notable exception of the construction workers, a gradual and cumulative process in Aberdeen. (Elsewhere, such as in Peterhead, it has been far more dramatic.) Generally speaking workers in Aberdeen have stuck to their old jobs until, through recession or redundancy, those jobs have become untenable. Over the past five years there have been recessions and/or rationalisations in nearly all the local primary industries — in trawling and fish processing, in agriculture, some food processing firms and forestry, and in paper making. Now there is even some indication that whisky distilleries will be adversely affected by the latest EEC ruling on whisky pricing. Each industry has then, by degrees, released workers to oil-related industry.

The effects of inflation and wage restraint have also begun to influence the situation. Oil-related work, however unpleasant, has become increasingly attractive, and most oil-related companies receive huge numbers of job applications not only from local people but from all over the country. During the last 18 months the oil industry has moved from the exploration to the production phase, and at the same time UK industrial legislation has been extended to cover offshore installations. This has had the effect of increasing the amount of steady work offshore, and ensuring major improvements in offshore working conditions. Most offshore workers are now paid between £8,000 and £12,000 per annum, which is a very attractive salary for any worker seeing his standard of living gradually fall in onshore employment.

The effect of the oil industry on the labour market has been, then, to unbalance it severely. There is no doubt that the industry forced up wages in some sectors, notably construction, though wherever possible employers have taken advantage of wage restraint and Aberdeen's generally low-wage economy to keep wages down. Those being paid high wages were (and still are) relatively few; and most people in onshore employment have jobs in industries not in direct competition with oil-related industries. In those industries, and particularly in the public sector, wages have consistently lagged behind wages paid in the oil industry; but meanwhile everyone has had to pay inflated oil-related prices.

There has, however, been a steady improvement in the employment prospects for women, either in clerical/secretarial work or in service industries. The College of Commerce has churned out large numbers of secretaries, and the huge expansion in office work has ensured that any qualified woman will find work immediately. Similarly the enormous expansion in the volume of trade in shops, hotels and restaurants has meant that any woman who wants a job in these industries can find one. It may not be very interesting work but it's work none the less, and most local working class women have taken it up gratefully, especially as their menfolk might well be feeling the oil-related or inflation pinch.

Trade union and community responses

Until very recently the trade union/community response to the problems brought by the oil industry has been uneven, uncoordinated and largely ineffectual. There are many reasons why this has been the case. The first we have already mentioned — communication between the Labour Council and the trade unions, and between the Labour Council and their grass-roots support, had decayed almost to the point of non-existence. There was very little active participation by the rank and file in union (or community) affairs. This was usually not so much the result of deliberate paternalism on the part of the trade union officials and stewards but more a reflection of the dominant local tradition of paternal liberalism. Quite simply there was no real tradition of community action and participation in decision-making.

If an individual or group in the community had a problem they took it to their councillor; and over the years local councillors had developed a canny ability to preempt any move to direct action by being present at (and often chairing) protest meetings, making promises and asserting their concern, even if that concern resulted in little concrete improvement.

This dominant tradition places great weight on class and manners (and great power in the hands of a few) and has been deliberately fostered by local schools, media and families. As a result there was a crucial class divide between workers on the one hand and the middle class on the other — a divide which depends on ignorance and prejudice and which the middle class perpetuate by their refusal to recognise that they too are workers. This is reflected not only in the paternalism of the city administration but also in the general paucity of white-collar union activity and membership in the city. Although membership of white-collar unions has been on the increase in Aberdeen as elsewhere, their numbers are still relatively small and those who join do so for mainly selfish reasons -- to protect and improve their living standards rather than to enable them to become actively involved in union and community affairs. This has been unfortunate for the city, especially as its tradition gives this class so much influence in the general affairs of the community.

The Trades Council, for reasons already mentioned, has for the past seven years been swimming against the tide of developments. Until 1975, when a joint Trades Council/Community campaign against the cuts was launched, there was no formal alliance between the Trades Council and community groups. Had there been more active support for, and interest in, the work of the Trades Council it might well have been able to act as a forum for ongoing discussions and joint trade union/community action. Since this was not the case there was in effect no organisational base through which community groups and trade unions could come to any unified view and embark on joint action. This absence of a suitable organisational base undoubtedly contributed to the lack of success which was to mark most community-based campaigns in the crucial years 1972–5.

The strongest unions in the Aberdeen area are the Confederation of Shipbuilding and Engineering Unions, the maritime unions, the TGWU and more recently NALGO. The Confederation unions had made some impact on the life of the city before 1970, and their influence has increased in line with their increase in membership. The same goes for the Seamen's Union, whose membership has more than doubled in the past six years. But their influence was almost entirely confined to the industrial front, and it has taken the recent establishment of the Grampian Association of Health Service Unions, in which NALGO figures strongly, plus the establishment of a branch of the TGWU for workers in voluntary organisations to bring about an improvement in the quality of debate within the unions on more general community issues.

The development of North Sea oil was at first seen by the Confederation unions as a national, rather than simply a local, matter. The North Sea Oil Action Committee was formed in October 1972 by district officials of the Confederation unions to campaign for the full benefits of North Sea Oil coming to Britain. Their campaign document demanded, among other things:

— that pressure be put on the oil companies to 'buy British'
— that British shipyards be given priority and assistance to enable them to build service vessels on a competitive basis
— that companies searching for oil in British waters be registered as British
— that training be provided in the new technical skills required
— that adequate safeguards be provided against pollution
— that rigs and supply boats be unionised
— that planning and control be co-ordinated in the regions
— that local authorities endeavour to curb inflationary house prices and speculation in land.

That these demands should come from an ad hoc Confederation committee rather than from the Trades Council underlines the general lack of credibility given to the Trades Council at the time. Most of these demands were aimed at the Conservative Government which reacted favourably to only one — 'buy British' — and then only after intense pressure from all sections of the business community. Left to itself it would undoubtedly have preferred to adopt a 'laissez-faire' attitude. We have already seen that Aberdeen Town Council took belated steps late in 1974 to curb speculation in land, but to get any response on their other demands the Action Committee had to wait till the election of the October 1974 Labour Government — and action when it did come often fell short of being decisive, partly because of the expenditure cuts and partly because of the minority position of Labour in the Commons.

No great effort has been made by the Government to co-ordinate planning and development in the regions, and workers in the North Sea are still not unionised. On the other hand training facilities have been provided, adequate safeguards have been taken against pollution and the Department of Energy is making an effort to improve safety on rigs and platforms. While companies searching for oil have never been obliged to register in the UK, they have come under considerable pressure from the Labour Government to co-operate with Government policies.

The most publicised failure of the union lobby has been over the issue of unionisation of North Sea installations. From the very start the oil companies have been implacably hostile to organised labour, and in the early days their behaviour was nothing short of outrageous. Men working offshore were fired at an alarming rate (one drilling company produced figures for labour turnover of 600 per cent per annum) and were forced to work to contracts which gave them no say whatever and no comeback in the event of victimisation, which was common. Most contracts, for instance, stipulated that if a man was injured or fell sick his contract was automatically terminated. One union official commented that Scottish workers offshore were being treated as 'tartan coolies'.

The Inter-Union Offshore Oil Committee comprising representatives from eight unions was formed in November 1973 to try to bring about unionisation of offshore installations, but has had very little success beyond persuading the government to extend UK industrial legislation offshore. There is now a unionisation ballot pending on two platforms, but at the time of writing the Committee seems to be tearing itself apart with inter-union wrangles about spheres of influence.

In many ways the visible heating-up of the unionisation issue has been counter-productive for the unions onshore, because it has turned their attention away from their other failures, particularly the failure to mobilise their membership onshore to meet the problems posed by oil-related developments — though in the last resort the two failures are inextricably linked.

On the issue of Old Torry, for instance, the unions were strangely quiet. On the housing issue it is now possible to see in retrospect that the conflict was inevitable and could only have been avoided in the context of a properly conceived overall plan for development spread over a longer period of time than was in fact the case. If communication between the Labour Council and the unions had been better in 1972, or if Labour had been more concerned to protect the interests of the working class, the Council might have responded to the North Sea Action Committee's call for them to take steps to control and co-ordinate developments. But they did not, and the chance was lost. Thereafter the only real chance of averting disaster lay in militant action by tenants and building workers, but since both were poorly organised at the time, that did not materialise either.

It was left to a small group of community activists to make a forlorn attempt to provoke militant action by squatting in an old council tenement early in 1973. Despite active support from the mass media and a lot of sympathy from the working class community, their initiative was very quickly squashed by the Council who used the Criminal Trespass Act to have them forcibly evicted within 48 hours, the main squatters later being fined in court. The housing crisis was not brought up again until April 1975 when Aberdeen Trades Council's secretary spoke to a motion deploring the situation at the Scottish TUC conference. This speech, and the by-now rather desperate pressure from a revitalised Labour District Council (who sensed that their majority was being eroded by their failure to act on this issue) may well have been the decisive factors in persuading the Labour Government to release more public money for Council house building in the city. But as with so much else that the Labour Government has done, it has been a matter of too little, too late.

Airport noise

The campaign mounted to stop the threat of night flights at the airport did not involve the trade unions as such at all. About sixty assorted groups and individuals became involved, including ad hoc residents' groups, a school directly under the flight path, various church and consumer groups, and regional and district councillors for the areas affected. The group running the campaign had no formal organisation, but did manage to collect 2,000 signatures on a petition objecting to the lifting of restrictions which was later submitted to the public enquiry.

Had there been a formal organisation running the campaign, it is doubtful if they would have thought of approaching the Trades Council for support. If they had they would probably have received formal support, but any request for support might have caused problems for the major unions at the airport as a decision in favour of 24-hour use of the airport would undoubtedly have increased the number of jobs and payments for unsocial hours. But as it happened the issue was never tested.

The decisive factor in events leading up to the enquiry was pressure put on the District councillors by the various ad hoc community groups. The councillors were then able to argue in Council that the case could only be fought effectively if the District retained legal counsel. This they did, and at the public enquiry, the legal arguments of counsel for the District proved decisive in the wrangle over who had legal responsibility for planning decisions affecting the airport. Without this legal support it is most unlikely that the ad hoc groups would have been able to offer an argument convincing and coherent enough to counter the often disingenuous sophistry of arguments put forward by counsel retained by the BAA, the CAA and the airlines involved.

Traffic congestion

The issue of traffic congestion on the bridge over the River Dee at Torry was also never brought to the Trades Council. The moving spirit behind that campaign was a Mrs Mary Dalgleish, a local resident. In October 1976 she tried to raise the issue with neighbours, who offered to sign a petition but who were reluctant, at that stage, to take action themselves or become involved in a campaign. Mrs Dalgleish then approached the Torry Action Group for advice. Job Creation workers sponsored by the Aberdeen Neighbourhood Projects Group and loosely attached to the Torry Action Group offered their help in organising a public meeting. About 100 people attended, and a committee was formed, the group being known as the Torry Residents Association.

Up to May 1977 a series of three further meetings were held, at each of which attendance dropped off. The Roads Department of the Regional Council refused to become involved until the last meeting, when officials from the department and from the Police attended to answer questions. This series of meetings culminated in a deputation from the Residents Association being received by the Transport and Roads Committee of the Regional Council at their meeting in May.

In the next few months attendance at meetings of the Torry Residents Association fell off, mainly because the matter was now in the hands of the Council. In the interim the Roads Department, prodded by a local councillor, came up with a plan for a one-way system to relieve traffic congestion on the bridge. The implementation of this scheme would have cost about £130,000, about £100,000 of which was already in the pipeline for the resurfacing of one of the roads involved. When this plan was made public objections were received from businesses along both proposed routes (some objecting to loss of trade and some to loss of parking facilities) and from householders who would lose parking facilities. The local Chamber of Commerce also sent in an objection on behalf of all the businesses involved. The objectors were duly asked to the Roads Committee meeting in February to put their case. The anomaly about this Committee, in fact about the whole issue, was that roads within the city are administered by the Tory-controlled Grampian Regional Council and not by the Labour-controlled District Council. At that meeting the Labour minority asked to have the issue shelved rather than put to a vote which they would undoubtedly have lost. The Tory majority were able to argue that the demand that something be done about the situation had been a 'flash in the pan' and that in the interval between May 1977 and February 1978 support for the original proposal had fallen off. Thus another community campaign faltered because of lack of co-ordinated and sustained support.

Before taking the matter to the Roads Committee the Residents Association had explored the alternative possibility that they might have been legally entitled to insulation for their homes, but this was not possible for various technical reasons. At their original public meeting a proposal had been made to stage a sit-in on the bridge, stopping the traffic; but to do that successfully, requires a good deal of momentum which, over the months of Roads Department delays, was just not there. Part of the reason for the lack of momentum was the withdrawal of full-time support from the Job Creation Project when it terminated in August 1977. The Torry Action Group, which might have lent active support, drew its members from a small corner at the other end of the Torry district, and had little interest in the issue.

Labour problems

The bleeding of skilled labour from traditional public and service industries is now generally recognised in local trade union circles as a major problem, and one that cannot be solved without a simultaneous solution to the intractable housing problem. All the unions most affected have made representations to the various area Councils and to the Government, but nothing has so far been done to solve the problem. In addition calls have recently been made by officials of the Confederation unions and by the Trades Council to channel some of the oil taxation revenues back to Aberdeen in the form of financial support and subsidies for those industries that have suffered at the hands of the oil industry; but the Government's White Paper on oil revenues gives absolutely no indication that they will react favourably to this request.

Demands that might have been made

Most of the problems Aberdeen has suffered at the hands of the oil industry have resulted from the lack of co-ordinated long-term planning and the lack of finance for projects 'in the community interest', most notably housing and amenities. The most sensible solution to the problem would have been for the local Council to have demanded extensive powers to plan and control development and a special fund, financed by the oil companies directly or out of oil revenue, to enable the Council to make good any damage caused to local industries and community amenities.

This is exactly what happened in the Shetlands with the passing of the Shetland Act. This gave the Island Council extensive planning powers and enabled them to set up a special fund, financed by the oil companies, to spend on whatever the Council saw fit. But the Shetlands were lucky — they happened to be the only possible landfall for oil companies who made discoveries in the north North Sea, they had a firm sense of community and a Council firm and decisive enough to extract the required terms from the oil industry. This gave them bargaining power in negotiations with the UK Government and the oil companies which Aberdeen simply did not have.

One of the major reasons for support for the idea of a Scottish Assembly among working-class people in Aberdeen has been the realisation that only a Scottish Assembly (or an independent Government) could have had the power to extract from the oil companies the kind of concessions which the Shetlands Island Council managed to obtain.

Despite its vulnerable position Aberdeen Town Council could

well have made more militant demands than it did, though it would have taken extensive grass roots support to make those demands effective. They might have demanded:

1 Closer co-ordination with other Councils along the east coast to ensure an equitable distribution of oil-related developments, and a minimum of inter-city rivalry.

2 Wider and more draconian powers to direct the speed and location of developments.

3 Far greater rate support grant and a special oil-related subsidy, and a special fund to finance housing, infrastructure, wages in the public sector and community amenities.

4 More stringent regulations to stop speculation, introduced much earlier than was the case.

5 The suspension of normal market pressures on house prices, and the intervention of the Government to hold prices steady.

6 The fixing of a union rate for the job in the construction industry, with the help of subsidies and a special fund.

Nearly all these measures would have required the (at least temporary) suspension of normal market mechanisms, and an unprecedented extension of the Council's powers to intervene in the planning process.

In order to make the above demands the Council would have needed to have extensive and militant support from the community at large. Unfortunately the community was so unused to making demands of this kind that such support would probably not have been forthcoming. But given the failures of the Council, there were other demands and strategies which the community at large might have adopted had there been any viable organisational base through which to make them. Had there, for instance, been a Trade Union and Community Resources Centre in existence in the early 1970s, such a body might well have been able to draw on expertise available in the community and unions to wage a concerted and co-ordinated campaign on behalf of the community. Such a body might, for instance, have been able to organise around the following objectives:

1 to bring about an alliance between tenants' organisations and the building unions to stop all building in the city until finance/subsidies had been made available to ensure the future of the public housing building programme

2 to help in organising a moratorium on office building, and 'green bans' on the demolition of listed buildings and other

developments detrimental to the community at large

3 to foment a work to rule/a token strike/an all-out strike by public service unions to protest against the 'bleeding' of skilled labour and the consequent degeneration of the services provided by those industries

4 to campaign on behalf of (and with the support of) the community for increased finance to be made available to enable public services and amenities to be improved, and more community facilities such as community centres, sports centres and nurseries to be provided

5 to organise and publish research into alternative strategies for development, both in the field of oil and other industries

6 to sponsor a concerted programme of job creation for young people in areas which would benefit the community at large

7 to sponsor a concerted programme of public education in community self-activity and self-government.

Conclusion

We would not like to leave readers with the impression that nothing has been done in Aberdeen to promote joint trade union-community action – it has, but not specifically on problems caused by the oil industry. Aberdeen People's Press, NALGO, the Workers' Educational Association and individuals from other unions have all been active in promoting alliances. Beginning with the joint Campaign Against the Cuts in 1975, and actively supporting campaigns for nurseries and other amenities, this campaign has now developed into an ongoing WEA–Trades Council group to promote trade union education and community action. But the lack of rank and file involvement in union and community affairs remains disappointing, as does the lack of membership and activity of the white collar unions. The size of the difficulty was illustrated by the turnout at a recent march organised by the Trades Council as part of the national campaign being waged by the Scottish TUC against unemployment. While similar protest marches in other Scottish cities drew support from thousands, in Aberdeen only thirty people attended. Unemployment, of course, is not the issue likely to provoke militant action by trade unionists in Aberdeen. However, rank and file trade unionists need to realise that they are also members of the community so that broad campaigns linking workplace and community issues can flourish. Community activists can assist in this process by joining trade unions and becoming actively involved in the struggle to establish those links.

Notes

1   Judy Payne, *Housing Deprivation in Aberdeen*, Medical Sociology Research Unit, 1974.
2   J. K. Morris, 'Intermittent Husbands', *New Society*, 5 January 1978, pp. 12–13.

3 Tate & Lyle: the campaign to save jobs

Keith Hodgson

Background

In August 1973, workers at Tate & Lyle's sugar refinery in Liverpool organised themselves into an Action Committee to fight for their jobs. For some years previous to this date rumours and speculation concerning the effects of entry into the Common Market and the possibility of closure had spread throughout the refinery. These rumours were confirmed when departmental managers advised workers that they had no future at Tate & Lyle and suggested that they begin to look elsewhere for work.

As one worker commented afterwards:

> When all these rumours started to go around fire was added to it and then the new Committee stepped in. Once we heard the whole lot combining, we looked at each other and said 'Oh, this is it'. It's always been a little union here, our own union, different unions always against one another. They're out for their ends and we're out for our ends, but when we see the whole lot getting together you know, staff and all, we really did start getting worried.

In the Company report for 1974, John Lyle, the Chairman of Tate & Lyle Ltd, stated:

> During the course of the last year, we felt obliged to mount an intensive national campaign, featuring Mr Cube, to make the public aware that the Commonwealth imports are essential — so that housewives and industrial customers may buy the sugar they need and for the future of the 6,500 men and women who work in our refineries. The effectiveness of this campaign was helped in no small measure by the vigorous,

independent activity of our refinery employees. (February 1975, our emphasis.)

Yet most of the information that initiated this 'vigorous, independent activity' of refinery employees was provided either directly, or in a disguised manner, by management.

In response to a company document on the likelihood of closure of one or more refineries following entry into the EEC, the workers were advised by management to form Consultative Committees involving management and shop stewards. With General Managers of the refineries acting as Chairmen, these committees first initiated the campaign against the 'threat to the refineries' in 1973 and were set up in all three of Tate and Lyle's UK refineries.

In addition, Aims of Industry, which had two of the Lyle family on its Council, published their first industrial report on sugar in 1973.[1] This report attacked government interference in the sugar industry and the threat to cane refiners' profits with entry into the EEC. Particularly in the early stages, the workers at the various refineries leant heavily on the arguments in this report as the basis for their campaign to save jobs since it was one of the main documents that management supplied the Consultative Committees. However, after only two months of the Consultative Committees, Union district officials in Liverpool called a meeting of all unions. The Divisional Organiser of the AUEW suggested that nominations from all eleven unions involved at Tate's should be put forward and that a workers' Action Committee should be formed, independent of management.

The action committee

With almost indecent haste this new Committee was formed with representation from all the eleven unions, the minutes secretary of the Joint Shop Stewards Committee acting also as minutes secretary to the Action Committee. It was hoped that this new committee would overcome the inter-union differences that had existed previously between craft and production unions and some staff and manual unions, and present a united trade union front to deal with the predictions of disaster being made by management over entry into the EEC. The Committee's formation was also, in part, a recognition of the need for the workers to be able to act independently of management. In a statement to the *Financial Times* (31 August 1973) the public relations spokesman for the Action Committee claimed: 'This is completely non-political. It is not a fight against the Company, the Management or the Government. It is a fight to get a better deal for the Cane Sugar industry in the Common Market', while the *Liverpool Business Post* (5 September 1973) described this early campaign in glowing terms: 'So far the workers have not reacted as have many other Merseysiders caught in a corner: witness the Fisher Bendix factory takeover of 18 months ago. . . . The Committee itself has done much to prevent the more traditional union activities from being manifest at the refinery.'

For many workers, the idea that Tate & Lyle, a company which had always been known for its security and paternalism, might actually close down one or more refineries after over a hundred years of sugar refining was difficult to accept. The majority of workers at Tate's were long-service employees. Many got their jobs in the first instance because their parents or other relatives already worked there. Some workers can trace continuous family connections with the company over four or five generations. According to one woman from the packing floor in the Liverpool refinery, who has well over twenty years' service herself, 'Years ago, when I left school, you know, especially in this area it was a recognised thing — "Oh, I'm going to Tate's, I know where I'm going." ' Or in the words of another worker, 'If you worked at Tate's, my God you had to get a letter from the Holy Ghost to work there. As soon as we were fifteen we were sent down — "And don't forget to tell the Matron that your father works there" — everyone of us came in straight from school, but we were glad of it. It was hard then but the money was still good compared with other places. It's always been called like, from womb to tomb.'

The company has always considered itself a family concern encouraging loyalty through long-service employment from particular families. The paternalistic nature of the company partly accounts for the absence of any major strikes since 1926 and also helps to explain the initial attitude of the employees' Action Committee that the fight was not with the company but with the Common Market.

Yet Tate & Lyle has over the last fifty years moved a long way from its original family origins. The long term investment strategies the company has been carrying through have been towards diversifying into trading, transport, distribution, and investment in production in other countries and away from investment in sugar refining. Two-thirds of Tate & Lyle's profits now come from overseas and the financial returns from speculation in the buying and selling of sugar have both become a considerably more attractive source of income for the company. The growth of large firms such as Tate & Lyle by takeover, diversification and rationalisation, and the lack of social responsibility for the communities they eventually leave behind, when greater profits can be obtained elsewhere, are the main concerns of this chapter.

Tate & Lyle Refineries Ltd

Although the firm of Tate & Lyle is traditionally associated with sugar, golden syrup and that champion of right-wing causes, 'Mr Cube', today it is a massive trans-national group with diverse interests in many parts of the world as well as having a monopoly of cane sugar refining in Britain. The history of the growth and development of Tate & Lyle from its origins in the merger of the two nineteenth-century family sugar firms of Henry Tate and Abram Lyle in 1921, is illustrative of some of the underlying ways in which British capitalist firms are changing.

Tate & Lyle Refineries Ltd is a major United Kingdom subsidiary of the parent Tate & Lyle group and is claimed to be the largest sugar company in the world. This company controls three large cane sugar refineries which are all built near major British ports to minimise the cost of transporting the bulky raw sugar cane brought by sea, mainly from the Caribbean. These refineries are located as indicated (1973 figures).

	Refining capacity (million tons)	No. of workers
Silvertown, London	1.065	3,000
Love Lane, Liverpool	0.675	2,100
Greenock, Clydeside	0.150	450

Essentially there are two main ways of obtaining raw sugar for refining to supply industrial and domestic requirements. The first is the import of sugar cane which is grown in warm countries such as the West Indies. The other way is from sugar beet, a root vegetable which is now extensively produced and harvested in Europe.

It was in an attempt to control the almost monopolistic position of Tate & Lyle over sugar refining in Britain that the Government took control of the refining of home grown sugar beet in 1936, specifically excluding Tate & Lyle from sugar beet production. This was achieved through the government taking a 36 per cent controlling interest in the British Sugar Corporation (BSC) which was formed through an amalgamation of the fifteen small beet refineries which had come into existence mainly in East Anglia. This meant that the whole of the United Kingdom sugar industry was divided into the refining of home grown beet by the BSC, and the refining of imported cane sugar, of which Tate & Lyle had a 75 per cent share. The remaining 25 per cent of the cane refining side was taken up by three small Manbré & Garton cane sugar refineries, also located near the three ports of Liverpool, London and Clydeside. Since then, Tate & Lyle has achieved one of its long-term objectives — a total cane sugar monopoly — with the takeover of all Manbré & Garton refineries, despite a referral to the Monopolies Commission in 1976.

Entry into the EEC

With entry into the European Common Market, there have been strong pressures for a major restructuring of the British sugar industry. The objective of the EEC sugar policy, formulated in 1968 was clearly to make the Common Market self-sufficient by expanding sugar beet production. In following through this policy, beet production was given special consideration to make it profitable even in countries not particularly suited to beet agriculture such as Italy. As the same price had to be charged throughout the Common Market this meant that there were large profits to be made by certain producers, particularly the French, as beet is relatively cheaper to refine in France, because of their more efficient refineries. Such large profits inevitably stimulated the EEC beet-growers and production rose from 5.5 million tons in 1966 to 8 million tons in 1971.

In Britain the sugar industry has traditionally been controlled by national and international agreements to maintain regular supplies of raw cane sugar and steady profits. In particular the Commonwealth Sugar Agreement was a long-term contract for the supply and purchase of 1.74 million tons of raw cane sugar between Britain and the sugar producers of the Commonwealth.[2]

Even before entry into the Common Market the UK sugar industry had a refining capacity which was calculated to be some 65,000 tons greater than the amounts actually processed.[3] Refineries such as those owned by Tate & Lyle were able to refine more sugar than they had raw cane sugar available either through international agreements or through buying on the world market. Consequently, the management of Tate & Lyle Refineries Ltd had long had a desire to streamline the workforce and reduce this surplus refining capacity, and to diversify into other areas of production and investment.

With entry into the Common Market in 1973 these difficulties of over-capacity were brought to a head. Despite assurances that 1.4 million tons of raw cane sugar from the Third World Commonwealth sources were guaranteed access to the EEC, the ending of the Commonwealth Sugar Agreement in 1974 meant that 75,000 tons of Commonwealth raw cane would be lost to Britain. Furthermore there was no certainty that all the 1.4 million tons allowed into the EEC would end up being processed in the British refineries where they had traditionally been refined. In total there was likely to be an overall excess of refining capacity in Britain of nearly 700,000 tons a year, the bulk of it located in the port cane refineries.[4]

In addition there had long been animosity between Tate & Lyle and the BSC. Tate & Lyle resented the monopoly of BSC over the refining of beet and saw the expansion of beet growing in Britain as a threat. In their early pamphlet describing problems likely to result from entry into the Common Market, Aims of Industry made this resentment very clear. Aims of Industry attacked Government involvement in the sugar industry and also the privileged beet-growers:[5]

> Even at present beet prices efficient grain farmers growing beet as a rotational crop, would prosper mightily. At the prices currently guaranteed for the 'Six' under the quota system they could become rich beyond the dreams of avarice.

What had sparked this reaction was the build-up to the final negotiations of British entry into the EEC by Geoffrey Rippon for the Tory Government. The French farmers, as big beet-growers and a powerful pressure group within the Common Market were identified by Aims of Industry as the main opponents. Both sections of the sugar industry, the BSC and the cane refiners, charge the same price for their refined sugar on the market. The price is negotiated with the Government and a 'refining margin' is fixed which determines the profits made. This refining margin is the difference between the cost of the raw materials entering the refinery and the price charged for sugar coming out the other end, and it is a way of controlling the industry to see that it at least receives a steady profit of around 10 per cent on investment. This fixing of the refining margin by the government has meant that there has long been direct government involvement in the affairs of the sugar industry, despite the considerable amount of 'free enterprise' propaganda that has been issued by organisations such as Aims of Industry and the 'Mr Cube' campaigns which have been a constant feature of the company's publicity since the infamous anti-nationalisation propaganda after the Second World War.

With eventual entry into the Common Market the responsibility for fixing the refining margin moved from the British government to the European Commission in Brussels. Before entry the margin had stood at £17 a ton, which provided the refiners with a profit of approximately £2 a ton out of this margin. Britain now agreed to a cut in this margin from £17 to £11.50 a ton. This meant that the port cane refiners would be unable to make a satisfactory profit and would be forced out of sugar refining, leaving the situation clear for the EEC sugar industry to become self-sufficient using home-grown beet.

This then was the context in which the company set about organising its employees as a political lobby and encouraging the formation of campaign committees to fight for a 'better deal for the cane sugar industry in the Common Market'. But while this provides the context to the workers' campaign to save their jobs, it is important to ask what the company itself was doing at this time. What were *its* main objectives?

Tate & Lyle's corporate strategy

Without doubt during the last ten years Tate & Lyle has been trying very effectively to get out of sugar refining in Britain using the profits and government subsidies from the refining side to buy into other areas of investment including transport fleets, shipping lines and warehouses. Like other British multi-nationals, Tate &

Lyle has begun to operate increasingly like a central bank interested in profit from whatever source and withdrawing from direct
involvement in production especially in the UK when greater
profits can be made elsewhere.

As Christopher Hird has pointed out:[6]

> between 1963 and 1972 Tate & Lyle increased its fixed
> assets from £66 million to £114 million. But an examination
> of the accounts of Tate & Lyle Refineries Ltd — the com-
> pany which includes the U.K. sugar refining operations —
> shows that less than £1 million of this was invested in their
> U.K. refining capacity. Throughout this period Tate & Lyle
> were asking the government for help to protect their U.K.
> sugar business against foreign competition. As a report by a
> firm of stockbrokers said: 'sugar refining is to be used as a
> cash cow and divisions in which investment will be particu-
> larly strong are storage, multiple distribution and warehous-
> ing, engineering (particularly in Canada) and specialised ship-
> ping'. All of these activities have a small labour force or are
> outside of Britain.

The massive £40.8m pre-tax profit that Tate & Lyle made in 1974
was assisted in no small measure by the speculation in sugar dealing on the International Sugar market, a form of income that Tate
& Lyle has shown increasing interest in. This was perhaps most evident during the sugar shortage at the end of 1974 when shoppers
hoarded or fought over dwindling sugar supplies in the shops.

In November and December 1974, Tate & Lyle acquired 157,000
tons of sugar at a price that worked out at the equivalent of 15p
a bag. The same sugar two months later, after the sugar crisis and
shortage, was being sold for 30p a bag and according to *The Times
Business News*: 'These deals mean that its trading profits on sugar
have probably already topped the £5 million.' The proportion of
Tate & Lyle's profits actually coming from the category 'storage,
distribution and trading' rose from 18 per cent (£3.9m) in 1973
to a staggering 38 per cent (£17.1m) in 1974. But the published
accounts of the company are not disaggregated to allow more
detailed analysis of the sources of such increased profits.

Not only did Tate & Lyle profit handsomely from this sugar
shortage, it was actively assisted by government aid to the tune of
£120m. The parliamentary Public Accounts Committee reported
in 1977 that the government paid out more than £120m 'under

pressure' to sugar refiners in a bid to boost dwindling sugar supplies after this shortage. In 1975 the government, trying to offset the severe shortages of 1974, had agreed to make up the difference to the cane refiners if they went out and bought sugar on the world market at a rate above that which would be covered by the normal refining margin. This generous government guarantee must have seemed like a licence to print money for Tate & Lyle. Although the Public Accounts Committee did not give any figures for profits made during this time, it did reveal that the Ministry of Agriculture had provided confidential information on Tate & Lyle Refineries' profits for 1970–6. These apparently showed that after adjusting for inflation the home trade profit per ton – in the guarantee period – was higher than the average over the remainder of the six-year period. This improvement followed a period when profits had mainly declined.

Furthermore, since Tate & Lyle now owned the whole chain of sugar production including plantations, the sugar shipping line, cane refineries and an extensive distribution network, it was in a position to offset profitability between its various sectors, either for speculation, political or tax purposes. Without much more detailed access to information the workers employed, and the general public, are at an obvious disadvantage in assessing the company's objectives and the profitability of each sector of operation. One method that Tate & Lyle has used in dealing with profits is in its stock valuation, particularly during the last few years of high inflation and sugar speculation. In Tate & Lyle's 1972 accounts the stock figures included 250,000 tons of sugar valued at £24 a ton but the market price at that time was nearer £200 a ton. Unlike most companies, Tate & Lyle uses a base stock valuation method for its stocks. Any profits made from the rising value of sugar, therefore, do not appear in published profit and loss accounts.

Although such examples are of interest in themselves, if only because of the sheer magnitude of the profits involved, they are included here because they provide some insight into the operation of a company which was very effectively milking its 'cash cow' – the port refineries – to provide resources for investment in other areas while at the same time using its workforce to spearhead a campaign against the beet producers in the Common Market. This campaign, for a while at least, diverted the attention of the workers from the company plans for a widespread restructuring of its refinery interests, and its inevitable desire to substantially reduce its refinery workforce.

Plans for re-structuring

Since before 1970 confidential discussions had taken place between the government and the three sugar refineries in Britain — Tate & Lyle, the BSC and Manbré and Garton. In June 1971 the government commissioned a firm of private consultants, Merret, Cyriax and Associates, to carry out a report on the possible alternatives open to the British sugar industry. Despite its obvious implications for the workers in the sugar refining industry, they were not involved in these crucial discussions and the government pressed on the three companies that these negotiations should be kept secret. The workers have still not seen a copy of the Merret Cyriax report although disagreements between the various interests involved almost certainly formed one of the reasons for Tate & Lyle's political intervention using the workforce in 1973. The root of this disagreement lay in the Government's desire to see a unified industry in both beet and cane with the government controlled British Sugar Corporation in charge, an option which Tate & Lyle totally opposed.

By 17 October 1973 Mr Godber, the Tory Minister of Agriculture, warned publicly that some of the country's refining capacity might have to close. He claimed that even before joining the EEC there were indications that some re-organisation of the refining industry would be necessary.[7] This statement followed a lobby of Parliament the same day by 250 Liverpool workers, with employees from Tate & Lyle's other refineries in London and Greenock, as part of their campaign against the arrangements being made with the Common Market. In the Consultative Committee, which had continued side by side with the employees' Action Committee, the workers had been pressing management to make their position clear and state their view of the situation in the national press. The management continually avoided this issue and were extremely reticent outside of the Consultative Committee.

Since Tate & Lyle management had refused to make their position public the idea came to the Liverpool Action Committee that they could take the initiative themselves and pay for an advert in the national press. Once made this decision began to take on a life of its own. Management were consulted over the contents of the advertisement and eventually, on 23 October, the day before the major 'Sugar Debate' in Parliament, a half-page advertisement was published in a number of national newspapers at a cost of £4,000. The advert claimed that British sugar was at risk and that within two years it would be three times as expensive. It further stated that the cane sugar industry was being sacrificed for political purposes — for EEC membership — and that the French farmers were the interest which would benefit.

Inevitably this advertisement sparked off a considerable rumpus in Parliament, with Mr Godber describing it as 'grotesquely misleading'. The apprehensions of the workers, some of whom were present in the public gallery, were summed up by one Liverpool steward, who said 'it was like creating a monster'. In the Sugar Debate, Godber pressed that 'the essential question for us all — the Government and the industry alike — is how the sugar industry can best organise itself to cope with the inevitable contraction in port refining capacity'. The full text of this speech revealed much of political manoeuvring around the sugar question, particularly the history of complex negotiations on the future structure of the industry following the Merret Cyriax report. Mr Godber was clearly convinced that the management of Tate & Lyle were in part responsible for the campaign over the Common Market issue and were attempting to bring political pressures from all sources (including the workers) to bear on the negotiations.

A similar feeling of suspicion towards the role of management also became manifest among the workers and shop stewards in Liverpool. Essentially, the management had been feeding information to the workers through both the Consultative Committee and the Action Committee, and suggesting who the workers should make contact with. Some shop stewards argued that this was just an example of sensible 'co-operation' between workers and management who had similar objectives. Others argued that they were being led by management. The local Labour MP, Frank Marsden, whose constituency covered the Liverpool refinery, warned the workers in no uncertain manner: 'not to be so involved with management at a time when it may be necessary to fight management. Tate & Lyle will do what is in the best interests of their shareholders. But such action may not be in the best interests of the working people of Liverpool'.[8]

Local community involvement and the role of community projects

By a coincidence, two of Tate & Lyle's three large cane refineries were located within the boundaries of two of the Government-sponsored Community Development Projects (CDPs) which were operational at the time of the workers' campaign. In London, the Silvertown refinery was in the same area as the Canning Town CDP, while the Liverpool refinery was the dominant employer in the Vauxhall CDP area. The threatened loss of jobs in either refinery would have had the most serious consequences for the dependent communities and consequently in varying ways the CDPs became involved with the workers in the Tate & Lyle refineries.

The local communities surrounding the three Tate & Lyle port cane refineries were all built to service the trading needs of capital during the rise of the British Empire. The dockland areas provided both access for the vast quantities of cheap raw materials from the colonies and also an outlet for trade with America, Ireland and Europe. Factories and warehouses had developed in a narrow belt alongside the docks to store, refine and process raw materials. Squalid housing had been crammed in amongst the factories, warehouses and canals, to provide living space for the workers who were to produce and transport the great amount of wealth that was made during the last century. The original communities were formed from migrants from all over Britain who came looking for work. The houses, docks and factories were built up together and working-class communities evolved which were integrated into the docks and related industries.

The decline of such communities, particularly since the war after their useful purpose had been served, is a well-known feature. The problems thrown up by rising unemployment, poor housing and widespread redevelopment undoubtedly formed a central reason for their selection as locations for the national CDP. The decline of the British Empire and changing patterns of trade resulted in the rationalisation of many of the port-based industries including the docks themselves. During the five years between 1967 and 1972 over 20 per cent of the 20,000 industrial jobs in the Vauxhall dockland area disappeared. In Canning Town, CDP research showed that one-third of the area's 40,000 jobs were lost between 1966 and 1972. Traditional firms have substantially reduced their labour force or closed down altogether and sought larger profits elsewhere. This process has been well documented by many of the publications that CDP has published nationally,[9] and was very evident in the economic decline of Vauxhall and Canning Town. The threat to refinery jobs by Tate & Lyle was part of this process.

The CDP in Liverpool had pursued the original Home Office brief with zeal, especially the objectives of attempting to improve local authority social services. The problems of local industry were generally treated as peripheral and beyond the project's terms of reference, although throughout its five year existence different workers did try to affect this direction of the project. However, as the Liverpool CDP became increasingly isolated nationally in terms of its objectives, some concessions were made towards the end of the project and during the last two years of its life, 1974-5, two workers were allowed to work closely with the Tate & Lyle shop stewards committee having non-voting observer status at Action Committee meetings. Although no reference is made to it in the Liverpool Final Report,[10] the shop stewards commissioned the CDP workers to carry out a substantial piece of research, as part of their campaign to protect jobs. The CDP also paid for the cost of publishing the report which had a wide distribution among workers in all three plants.[11]

The Canning Town CDP had, however, promoted the idea that CDPs had a useful function to perform with regard to industry and jobs. It published a report in 1974 which described the job loss taking place in Canning Town and first made reference to the position of Tate & Lyle.[12] It was also one of the sponsors of the commissioned inter-project report, *Jobs in Jeopardy*,[13] which examined a number of major firms including Tate & Lyle. The project in Canning Town had made contact with the shop stewards committee and an offer had been made to provide research and information facilities if these were required. Within the project discussion took place on the political value and benefits that work with Tate & Lyle shop stewards might bring. As a consequence the project provided a series of specific pieces of assistance to the workers and published independently a case study on declining community income which looked at the private decisions of industrial capital, local community interests and public expenditure and which used Tate & Lyle as the central example.[14]

The involvement of the Liverpool CDP with the Action Committee coincided with the growing suspicion towards management by the workers throughout 1973 and 1974. Demonstrations had been organised at all the major political party conferences and at the Trade Union Congress, and on 19 November 1973 a demonstration of over 1,000 workers, including many representatives from the local community, marched through Liverpool to lobby Mr John Davies, Minister for Europe. The Action Committee had written a number of articles for the community newspaper, the *Scottie Press*, which was produced by the CDP. Because of the paternalism of Tates and the fact that the firm had often recruited from particular families, there was a certain amount of local resentment of the Tate & Lyle workers even during the threat of redundancy. According to one female worker: 'Some people take a strange delight in this sort of thing happening. Well, as I said, to work in Tate's you were one of the elite sort of thing, and they like to see you brought down.'

One of the CDP's first roles in this situation was to suggest, through informal meetings and pamphlets, the cost to the whole community of the long term effects of the loss of any more jobs. Canning Town CDP were particularly keen to make some actual calculations of the social costs of closure of the refinery to their community and their pamphlet estimated the direct and indirect costs involved.[15]

While the workers' campaign was geared towards organising demonstrations it was relatively easy to maintain unity and a fighting spirit within the refinery and the community. There were easily identifiable objectives and such organisation involved many people including local residents. However, as the negotiations with the Common Market and the Government developed through 1974 it was felt by the refinery Action Committee that they needed to put their case directly to the European Commission in Brussels. Three times representatives from the Action Committee travelled to Brussels to meet European Ministers and to argue that the 1.4 million tons to be allowed into the EEC should be refined in the UK. These representatives inevitably became highly knowledgeable and skilled in the rarefied atmosphere of high level sugar negotiations but this change of emphasis tended to separate them from the rest of the Action Committee, the workforce and the local community.

The involvement of the two CDPs with the Tate & Lyle workers allowed a valuable insight into the way the company had extracted the surplus of generations of labour from particular areas over

many years. In most important senses, Tate & Lyle was totally un-
accountable to the local communities which it, or its predecessors,
originally created and which have contributed to its profits. Such
considerations did not enter into their corporate decision-making.
For example, when asked by shop stewards at a company conference if they did not accept that the company's policy was adding
to the serious unemployment of depressed areas such as Liverpool,
top management replied that they were hoping to use natural
wastage and streamlining as far as possible but that they felt no
responsibility for the communities in which they operated and
could not carry 'the burden' of unemployment in such areas.

The regular contact between workers on the two CDPs also
meant that there was a rapid and informal flow of information
between at least two communities and shop stewards. This undoubtedly helped to prevent the spread of unsubstantiated
rumours that from time to time tended to threaten the unity of
the Combine Committee (comprising representatives from the different refineries), and the refinery workforces, but it is impossible
to quantify exactly how useful this flow of information was. Much
of the research and information work that was provided by the
CDPs cannot easily be shown to have been effective. Today the
Tate & Lyle workers are still there, but the threat of closure is also
still there and the workers are still fighting. One difference is that
the fight is now more clearly seen to be a campaign against a
multi-national company which is trying to rationalise its refining
interests and perhaps the work of the CDPs helped in this respect
by pinpointing some of the strategies of the company and contributing a critical evaluation of the pronouncements of management. For example, at a conference organised by management to
present the three options of redundancy to the workforce Mr
Clark, the Managing Director of the Liverpool refinery, claimed:
'Any company is in business to contribute towards a better life for
its employees and their families, provide security and a fair return
for the investors, provide customers with products and services at
competitive prices, and be a credit to the community.' The CDPs
were at least able to show exactly how much the company was 'a
credit to the community' and the relative weight given to the
factors listed by Mr Clark.

Another area of potential value was in helping to articulate the
views of the shop floor workers. In Liverpool, as part of the preparation of the CDP report for the Action Committee, extensive use was

made of tape-recorded interviews with a wide variety of shop floor
workers. The transcription of the opinions of workers, who were
not normally active in the union, did prove useful. For example,
although women form a substantial section of the workforce, particularly in the packing section, there were no women sitting on the
Action Committee. Discontent over the dominance of the Committee by men was one very strong view which these tape-recorded
interviews conveyed to the shop stewards. Other shop floor members mentioned the feelings of isolation they felt from the campaign
when it moved away from activities such as demonstrations and
into high-level lobbying in Brussels etc. In response the Action Committee attempted to remedy this by putting out regular leaflets
and organising mass meetings to keep the workforce fully informed
and to try and make the Committee more representative.

But perhaps the most positive aspect of the CDPs' involvement
was that they provided valuable resources to a workforce that
would not have been otherwise available. Having researchers available to check information, dig out facts and figures, and summar-
ise reports can undoubtedly be of great benefit during such campaigning. Also more basic facilities like the supply of printing and
duplicating materials, and publicity through community newspapers or the publication of reports or pamphlets, have a value
which it is impossible to calculate but which can make a considerable difference in a fight to protect jobs. At the same time,
involvement with the Action Committee meant that the Community Development workers in Liverpool had to accept the limitations of their position. As non-voting observers but with access to
confidential and sensitive material, lines of responsibility had to be
spelled out and any trust honoured. Only in such a manner will
community resources become more widely drawn upon by local
shop stewards committees.

The fight continues

By November 1974 agreement had been reached in the European
Commission and the British-based refiners seemed to be guaranteed access to 1.4 million tons of raw cane sugar. The refinery
workers felt some relief that their two-year campaign to avoid redundancy appeared to have been successful and Tate & Lyle
management published another full-page 'Mr Cube' advertisement,
this time saying only 'Thanks Fred' to Fred Peart, the Labour

Minister of Agriculture who had negotiated the deal in Brussels. However, at a follow-up meeting in the Ministry of Agriculture at which workers, management from the whole industry and Government Ministers were invited to discuss the EEC deal, the threat of the Merret Cyriax proposals was raised once again. It was suggested that the sugar industry needed to re-open discussions on this issue and further *private* meetings between the management of Tate & Lyle, Manbré & Garton, BSC and the Government were requested.

For the workers at Tate & Lyle, this was a recognition that the battlefield had now switched from the Government to the company, with the real danger of the re-introduction of 'operation streamline' and the subsequent loss of jobs. It took less than three months for the management of Tate & Lyle to announce their plans in March 1975 for the 'streamlining' of the labour force throughout the three refineries in the interests of 'cutting costs'. Although wrapped up in propaganda to justify their profits, Stage 1, or the main plan as it was called would mean the reduction of 800 jobs in the London refinery, 500 in Liverpool and 80 in Greenock. Stage 2, or the contingency plan, would be particularly disastrous for Liverpool and would virtually mean the closure of all granulated sugar refining and the loss of a further 1,000 jobs in an area of already massive unemployment. The company was particularly vague over the factors that could possibly trigger off the contingency plan and shop stewards justifiably felt that they had a gun pointing at their forehead with the threat — accept streamlining, increase productivity and cut costs or else! It was also becoming clear that each area and refinery would have to compete as to which was the most efficient and profitable and therefore the one to avoid closure.

Although the Action Committee that had been formed at each refinery had come together in a Combine Committee which met regularly and tried to reduce any divisive conflicts by developing a united trade union campaign, there were considerable difficulties in maintaining this unity, in the face of company plans for rationalisation.

The next stage of the company's programme to reduce employment was to submit, in conjunction with Manbré & Garton, a new plan to the workforce and the government to deal with the anticipated over-capacity. This plan listed three new options but once again each proposal simply posed a choice of redundancy between the various refineries. For the management it was merely a question of deciding where such rationalisations should take place. The three options were essentially to close the Liverpool refinery; to close the two Scottish refineries and make reductions elsewhere; or to close one Scottish refinery with bigger reductions elsewhere: each would cost over 1,500 jobs. Tate & Lyle's preferred choice was the third option with 1,560 redundancies including 500 at Canning Town.

The Combine Committee again rejected all these options as politically and economically unacceptable and demanded a new programme. Under this programme, European sugar would be kept out, sufficient cane would be imported, new UK beet refineries would not be developed. Only a reasonable expansion of beet production would take place and one port refinery would be converted to beet refining. Mr John Edmonds, the national officer of one of the biggest unions involved in the negotiations, the General and Municipal Workers' Union, was quoted as saying:[16]

> The Union has already successfully resisted two previous schemes for job reductions in the refineries and Tate & Lyle has no chance of union co-operation unless it produces firm plans for creating suitable alternative work.

The workers themselves could then have had few doubts concerning the objectives of the company. Tate & Lyle has, with considerable skill, attempted to shift responsibility for its desire to streamline its refinery workforces onto the shoulders of the Government, using the threat of unemployment that could result from entry into the EEC (and in the early stages the political clout of the trade union) to extract generous public aid and subsidies to allow it to continue to function as a private industrial concern. This use of public money, extending existing intervention in the sugar industry suggests that a national policy for the industry should do what it did once before — nationalise it completely, though this in itself would give no guarantee that jobs will be maintained. The recent history of nationalisation has less to do with Clause Four of the Labour Party constitution (which states that the most equitable distribution of income is dependent on 'common ownership of the means of production, distribution and exchange') and instead appears more concerned with achieving a massive reduction in employment with the least disruption in certain strategic industries. Coal, steel, shipbuilding and now British

Leyland have all faced substantial redundancies since becoming part of the State-owned sector. The fight-back from the shop floor against unemployment has been tragically weak in many of these industries and nationalisation has thus failed to serve the interests of the working class. Tate & Lyle workers will need to bear the recent history of nationalisation in mind when formulating their campaigns against the ever-present threat of closure.

Recent months have seen an escalation in the number of serious closures in Liverpool. Significantly those high technology industries which were once thought most desirable, and were courted by Governments with financial inducements to come to Merseyside to help 'balance' the declining industries with the growth potential of the 'white-hot technological revolution', are now the very ones shedding labour and closing down. Lucas Management have decided to fight the Lucas Combine Committee over its workers' alternative plan in Liverpool, with the decision to close the Lucas Victor works. This has followed the closure of Plessey's and the decision by GEC to close their East Lancs Road factory in Liverpool. Further, the present Labour Government has recently approved the 'Edwards Plan' for British Leyland including the total closure of the Speke no. 2 Standard Triumph factory, which was only brought to Liverpool because of strong political pressures to relieve the unemployment in the area. It is now to close when unemployment has risen to over 10 per cent.

Today it is no longer a novel approach for workers to lobby MPs or take the train to London to ask for special consideration when a redundancy is announced. The Tate & Lyle workers have over the last years experienced many of the problems involved in fighting redundancy. Their experience has shown the limitations and potential of certain action and has illustrated the immense power of multinational companies like Tate & Lyle. The workers have moved a long way from their early management-orientated attitude to the campaign and have come to realise exactly how 'political' any struggle against redundancy must inevitably be. Their campaign has at least led them to recognise the enemy. The crucial decisions affecting the lives of thousands of workers and their families are those of a handful of men debating in secret who are rarely, if ever, held to public account. Such a situation will only be changed when workers fighting to protect their jobs have developed through their campaign an organisation which is capable of unifying the workforce in multi-plant companies and have extended this unity into the local community and across national boundaries. Perhaps the biggest breakthrough in recent trade union history has been the growth of multi-plant combine committees as a result of shop floor pressure to try to prevent companies trying to play off one plant against another in a competition to avoid redundancy.

Notes

1 Aims of Industry, now called 'Aims of Freedom and Enterprise', is a right-wing pressure group supported by political donations from companies such as Tate & Lyle.
2 *Cane Sugar — the Battle for Survival*, World Development Movement, 1973.
3 *Jobs in Jeopardy*, CDP Inter-Project Report, 1974.
4 Ibid.
5 *Sugar*, Industrial Report no. 1, Aims of Industry, 1973.
6 Christopher Hird, *Your Employer's Profits*, Pluto Press, 1975.
7 *Liverpool Post*, 17 October 1973.
8 *Liverpool Post*, 21 November 1973.
9 See for example the following CDP Inter-Project reports: *The Costs of Industrial Change*, CDP Inter-Project Editorial Team, 1977, and *Gilding the Ghetto*, CDP Inter-Project Editorial Team, 1977.
10 *Government against Poverty*, Liverpool CDP Final Report, University of Oxford, 1977.
11 *Tate & Lyle: the Campaign to Save Jobs*, Liverpool CDP, 1975.
12 *Aims of Industry?*, Canning Town CDP, 1974 (revised with new postscript, 1977).
13 *Jobs in Jeopardy*.
14 *Declining Community Income*, Canning Town CDP, 1977.
15 Ibid.
16 *Guardian*, 29 March 1977.

4 Redundancy, worker resistance and the community

Tom Clarke

The first casualty of the major restructuring of western economies from the mid-1960s has proved to be the employment security which was the most cherished achievement for the working class of the post-war period. The single-minded search for enhanced profitability has involved a reassertion of the commodity status of labour and ushered in a new era of large-scale redundancy and mass unemployment. Despite the active support of Labour Governments for such rationalisation, and the tacit compliance of some trade union officials, workers confronted with the stripping away of their livelihoods, skills and living standards have accurately perceived this as an overwhelmingly irrational dismantling of the economy. The imposition of mass redundancy as an easy expedient of management control was checked only when it encountered significant working-class opposition. Thus the fatalism and resignation of workers towards redundancy was replaced in the early 1970s by frequent determined resistance, encompassing strikes, sit-ins, work-ins and other forms of industrial action. In the last resort, factory occupations have proved among the most viable means to combat redundancy and factory closures, check the arbitrary property rights of capital, and pose the basic question, 'To whom do jobs belong?'

If workers take up occupation, their weakness when faced by an employer who simply wants to get rid of them is overcome. The duress in negotiations is neatly reversed: before, workers want to negotiate but management refuse, now management are often forced to request negotiations (though this does not represent any balance of power between the two parties). One shop steward, engaged in a factory occupation commented: 'We have occupied because management refused to negotiate. They laughed at us in talks last week, and since then have ignored us. Well, they can't

ignore us now, can they?' Though formally illegal, factory occupations consistently have enjoyed great public support and sympathy, and management action often has been viewed as irrespons-
ible and damaging. The media itself has been in quite a quandary:
having proclaimed constantly that the British working man was
work-shy, how could it condemn him for fighting for the right to
work? The strength of this shop floor resistance movement developed from Upper Clyde Shipbuilders (UCS) onwards, to the
extent that it was directly instrumental in diverting the 1970–4
Conservative Government away from its destructive lame duck
policy, and undermined the political credibility of monetarist
policies in general.

Hence, the success of some factory occupations has slowed the
frantic pace of capitalist restructuring; translated the rhetoric of
the right to work into a practical reaffirmation; and prompted
government to shore up the law on employment protection to prevent the worst abuses. Indeed a measure of the respectability of
the occupation tactic is that it has now secured official Trade
Union Congress General Council endorsement:[1]

> The relevance to industrial democracy of sit-ins and similar
> actions lies in the way in which imminent closures and similar
> events can be challenged at local level. They are local defen-
> sive reactions to decisions on investment, closure and mergers
> taken elsewhere. The challenge to their unlimited property
> rights to do this that an occupation represents is an import-
> ant consideration. . . . The use of sit-ins and work-ins is an
> appropriate trade union tactic in certain circumstances.

But first it is imperative to attack the rationale of redundancy at
its roots.

Conflicting rationalities: redundancy and resistance

There is a profound contradiction between employers' use of
redundancy and unemployment to reduce labour costs and increase
profits, and the central importance of the work ethic to the capitalist value system. The fundamental problem is that in capitalist
society employers adopt an exploitative approach toward employment: labour is used and disposed of in a manner conducive to the
highest immediate profit. In a new study of redundancy, Greenwood maintains that workers' attempts to protect employment are

wholly understandable and justifiable on both economic and welfare grounds. Whatever the short-term advantages for companies
that impose them, in terms of economic effects on the labour
market, large-scale redundancies are unnecessary, wasteful and haphazard; together with being financially damaging and personally
demoralising for the workers concerned. It is clearly established
by Greenwood that the demand for labour in expanding industries
could be satisfied from new entrants to the labour market alone
(in the UK new entrants amount to 800,000 per annum); when
combined with the millions of workers re-entering the labour force
or voluntarily changing jobs, this destroys the monetarist myth
that wholesale redundancies are necessary to provide labour for
new industries. In contrast to popular conceptions of the reasons for
closure — non-viable factories with labour troubles — most closures
are caused by short term problems such as temporary illiquidity,
lack of investment, and management failure in product development and marketing. In short, redundancy is a crude and irrespons-
ible economic tool of unpredictable effects and dubious benefits.[2]
Closures are often only rational in the context of narrow, profit-
oriented company accounting and do not coincide with the wider
interests of the economy or the working population: employers
may deceive with elegant logic and urbane manners, but factory
closures frequently amount to little more than economic vandalism. (It is interesting that an EEC proposal to invest public authorities with the power to prevent unnecessary 'mass dismissals' by
private companies was rescinded, and replaced by a milder measure
of public constraint.)[3]

For workers the implications of redundancy are serious, and
usually involve a downward slide in their job and living standards.
Workers already made redundant once, are the most prone to
future redundancy since the problem is concentrated in particular
regions and occupations. This pattern of compound or 'galloping'
redundancy means repeated periods of unemployment, a gradual
degrading of skill, a considerable loss of income, and a deterioration of working conditions. In fact, resort to redundancy is often
a deliberate part of employers' attempts to erode terms and conditions of employment, and undermine the strengths of trade
union organisation. When faced with unemployment workers are
often reluctant to move from their communities to find work
elsewhere. This attachment to the working class community is not
simply sentimental, but is economically sound: some dispersal of

capital and other resources permits their most effective utilisation in the economy as a whole; the congestion which has resulted from the concentration of new industries in the South and Midlands is not conducive to an expanding economy or a stable society; moreover, it is both economically wrong, and personally insulting to tell Clyde boilermakers that there are splendid openings as bistro waiters in Belgravia, which is effectively what official policy on redundancy implies. Therefore workers are acting eminently rationally when they demand to work where they are, instead of meekly complying with the instruction to pursue employment wherever it may be: that it is capital that should be moved to sources of labour, rather than labour moved to capital.

Despite the protests of workers, the dimensions of the problem have not been fully appreciated. As Fryer has observed: 'For some phenomenon of social life to qualify as a social problem requires that someone should both pick out and identify it as undesirable and, further, be able to mobilize public policy with a view to mitigating the "harm" caused by the problem.'[4] The tragedy of redundancy has not been fully impressed on the public consciousness and insufficient effort has been directed toward preventing redundancy and developing more rational, humane and democratic methods of labour deployment. It is an ironic paradox that today individual dismissal is officially protected against, whilst mass dismissal is not. Trade union officers, themselves, have frequently failed to oppose redundancy seriously, and as an official investigation of the effects of redundancy indicated, seem largely to have accepted managerial explanations of the problem: 'About half of the officers thought that the redundancies among their members were "entirely unavoidable" both in the short and long term', and that most of them only thought that there 'were some circumstances in which workers were justified in opposing redundancy'.[5]

The failure of workers to impress *their* interests upon public policy is clearly *not* due to any lack of rational and convincing argument justifying the importance of secure employment on both economic and social grounds; nor is the adoption of employers' interests and priorities by the state a result of the excellence of their economic analysis. On the contrary, the issue is decided on the basis of who is presently in control of industry and the wider economy. As individuals, redundant workers are dispirited and defenceless, and where redundancy remains unopposed it becomes a ready management option to sack labour, as the most easily varied factor of production, even to deal with temporary problems. However, when organised together in resistance to such arbitrary dictates of management, workers can wield considerable power.

The historical relevance of factory occupations

There is a long history of international experience of factory occupations as a method of working-class struggle. It is possible to distinguish two general types of occupations by workers which have occurred this century: firstly, occupations with revolutionary overtones; and secondly, more limited occupations which are militant extensions of conventional industrial action.

A number of occupations have had revolutionary overtones such as those in Russia in 1917, in Italy in 1920, in France in 1968 and most recently in Chile and Portugal. Most occupations, however, are extensions of conventional industrial action and tend to be restricted to particular areas or factories; make limited demands concerning wages and conditions, often related to the right to trade union organisation; and normally entail a preparedness to return to work for the same employer under similar conditions upon the resolution of the immediate problems. Despite these limitations, the militancy displayed in such confrontations should not be underestimated: many workers were unionised for the first time in a series of 'sit-down strikes' in the United States steel and motor industry in 1936-7, though they encountered fierce opposition from the company and civil police.[6] Anti-redundancy defensive occupations also fall into this category. Hannington has described vividly how unemployed engineering workers in Britain carried out a sequence of bold 'factory raids' in the early 1920s, protesting at the imposition of overtime working, and thus helping to stimulate trade union rejection of overtime agreements.[7] More recent redundancy struggles in this country have often formally denied any political commitment beyond the fight to save jobs. For example James Airlie, the chairman of the UCS co-ordinating committee, once declared, 'Our only purpose is to save the jobs of the men. If, as a by-product, a new form of protest or control comes about then that is welcome – but it is not our aim.'[8] This equivocal approach is partly to avoid employer-inspired charges of 'political motivation' (which of course, are themselves politically motivated). The 'right to work' is an important and powerful principle, which should not be interpreted as the right to be wage slaves to any capitalist employer; there is little evidence that workers' leaders are so short-sighted, though the failure to recognise and discuss the political implications of industrial action is often a significant strategic weakness, which leads to unsatisfactory compromise.

British experience is composed of these more restricted forms of occupation: all have been settled without serious political disturbance or change, and even the TUC acknowledges that 'In most of the cases analysed there was no lasting structural change achieved in the enterprise as a result of sit-ins or work-ins.'[9] However, in practice the distinction between offensive and defensive occupations may not be so clear: the implicit threat to property and authority rights presented by this embryonic form of workers' power is usually sufficient to worry both management and trade union officials.[10] Invariably factory occupations display a critical potential to escalate into more profound demands and questioning of the existing economic and political structure.

The evolution of contemporary occupations has derived essentially from the shop floor struggle. The post-war achievement of workshop bargaining enhanced the autonomy of rank-and-file workers from national union-management negotiations; and the attempt to suppress unofficial action made in the Industrial Relations Act of 1971 served to heighten political consciousness and resistance, which was successful in effectively neutralising the Act. The experience of workers on the continent and students at home of the use of occupations, meant that they were readily adopted by workers as a weapon to combat the mounting redundancies of the early 1970s. In Britain occupations have taken place primarily in well-organised industries: more than half the occupations have been confined to branches of the engineering industry, vehicles, mechanical and electrical engineering; and a further quarter of all occupations have occurred in construction, metal, printing and publishing, and shipbuilding industries. (Though occupations are more widespread in France where there is a lower level of unionisation.) In this country the frequency of occupations increased up to a maximum of about one a week in the mid-1970s, thus as the uniqueness and news value of individual occupations diminished, they became collectively a more potent check upon management power. By July 1975 it has been calculated that there were forty-four factory occupations in progress in the UK, and between two and three hundred in France; between July 1971 and December 1975 it has been estimated that nearly 150,000 workers took part in two hundred occupations in the UK.[11] Though the level of activity has varied since then, due to familiarity with the tactic, it is probable that occupations have become a permanent addition to the repertoire of workers' industrial action.

Factory occupations to prevent redundancies are acts of desperation and reveal the weakness of trade union organisation, since redundancy should not be allowed to occur in the first place. There are few effective alternatives to occupation, since strike action permits the accelerated run-down of the factory. Typically, companies announce closure or mass redundancies at very short notice, requiring an immediate response to prevent the removal of products and machinery. In the past workers have been made redundant with as little as one day's notice; the Employment Protection Act will curb this practice a little, since employers are required to give minimum periods of notice, depending on length of service, though it is possible they will find ways of violating these regulations. Occupations develop the confidence of workers that more positive and radical action is feasible, and may develop the political awareness of workers that the workplace and their jobs should be under their control, not the employer's. Employers themselves are not immune to such considerations: 'Some employers seem to take the view that if their employees were prepared to enter the boardroom then they were quite capable of taking over the business as a whole.'[12] The common threat of redundancy forges unity between white collar and manual workers, and this solidarity strengthens trade union organisation. Moreover, it is easier to defend a factory with an occupation than with picket lines: employers are concerned about the potential damage to property and products, as well as their reputation, if there is violence; thus the sit-in or work-in makes it easier to prevent the use of blackleg labour and the dismantling of the factory. Occupations normally avoid the clash with police common on picket lines, though recent changes in the law of trespass could exacerbate the problem. The convenience and comfort of workers in occupation is greater, compared to strikers, since essential services are usually maintained for safety, maintenance, and security. Finally, an occupation permits workers to find out much more about their company from the accounts and files, than they would ever learn from management. (Indeed at times of mass redundancy and closure, management is particularly prone to feed workers misleading and distorted information.)

Often factory occupations have proved immensely dramatic and emotive events for their participants, who, in contrast to their normal sense of powerlessness, have experienced a euphoric increase of their knowledge and control of their daily lives, stretching their imaginations towards conceptions of workers' control which would have been dismissed as Utopian dreams beforehand. A number of dramatists have assessed these cathartic events, and in turn, have contributed to the intensity of the experience undergone.[13] However, the euphoria and enthusiasm induced during occupations, whilst invigorating to the workers concerned, simply cannot alone secure any release from their problems beyond the purely temporary. If occupations are to rise above the level of symbolic gesture, then the political understanding and commitment of workers must be focused, and only this will prevent a gradual relapse into resignation and defeatism. Political mobilisation during factory occupations has two dimensions, internal and external. Internally it is imperative that workers are allowed to be fully involved in the conduct of the occupation: this demands democratic organisation, including participation in the committees, meetings and visits; and open debate of the major issues at regular departmental and mass meetings. The success of participation is in turn dependent upon the full communication of all information to the workers, rather than a select group of shop stewards. Otherwise occupations can degenerate into demanding *less* activity on the part of the rank and file than strike action, leaving the stewards to perform organisational tasks in a quasi-managerial role. This has proved consistently a problem, even with the well-known and successful occupations. Moreover, without such involvement, workers are inclined to drift away from the occupation; the temptation may be slight in areas of high unemployment, but redundancy payments may be an enticement hard-up workers find difficult to resist. The normal management practice is to wait till exhaustion sets in before attempting legal eviction or some apparent compromise. To resist this ploy effectively and maintain the pressure on management, workers must generate and extend external support. Successful occupations have very actively publicised their dispute externally, using the plant as a centre for the organisation of widespread political, financial, and practical support from both trade unions and other sections of the working class. In particular, it is of paramount importance to obtain the active support of local union branches and the neighbouring community. The fact that the largest occupations were surrounded by loyal working-class communities, was directly instrumental in dissuading the authorities from taking imprudent action.

Organisation and strategy of occupations

The variety of defensive occupations that have occurred may be defined as sit-ins, work-ins, collective bargaining sit-ins and tactical sit-ins. The first two entail workers taking over the whole plant; whereas collective bargaining sit-ins and tactical sit-ins may achieve the desired effect when only one section of the plant is occupied such as the shop floor, office block, accounts department, telephone exchange or computer room. Redundancy struggles usually adopt sit-ins or work-ins; the work-in is a rarer form due partly to the difficulty in effective operation. The UCS workers accomplished a protracted work-in since the technology of shipbuilding meant a long time scale before completion. Workers engaged in individual occupations in other industries such as the motorcycle industry, would have had to rely upon constant supplies of components and regular receipts from sales, together with banking facilities; none of which could be depended upon, given the presence of a dispossessed management. Therefore most occupations have assumed the sit-in form, which allows workers considerable time and opportunity to promote their cause.

The strengths and weaknesses of different forms of occupation are best illustrated by a brief examination of some important occupations. The first attempt at an occupation against redundancies was at the General Electric Company (GEC) in Liverpool in 1969, which failed, but signalled the obstacles to be overcome. The GEC–EEC Government-sponsored merger of 1968 led to 12,000 redundancies by late 1969, 3,000 of which were announced, without consultation, on Merseyside. In the absence of a combine committee able to mobilise a concerted effort against GEC redundancies, the Liverpool stewards gained acceptance of a resolution, at a mass meeting of the workforce, in favour of occupation and the demand for public ownership. However, little effort was made to involve workers in the stewards' plans or to communicate and explain them, with the result that the decision to occupy was revoked later at a confused mass meeting involving representatives of management.[14]

The Government-aimed blow at the Upper Clyde Shipbuilders workforce in 1971 was so severe, amounting to a loss of 6,000 jobs out of a total of 8,500, that it may have been designed to induce paralysis. Fortunately though, the tradition of class combativity and resilience on Clydeside permitted the rapid organisation of opposition. A work-in was decided upon since a strike might have aggravated the bankruptcy and given an excuse for the media to attack the workers. Moreover a long dispute was anticipated, and with four scattered yards it was thought that a work-in would be easier to maintain than a sit-in. The first aim of the co-ordinating committee of shop stewards was to gain the broadest support for their campaign possible. With the loss of thousands of indirect jobs, the heartland of Clydeside was threatened with industrial collapse and the local community was totally behind the workers' action including unions, local authorities, MPs, churches, civil and community groups, political parties and the Scottish Trade Union Congress. The workers' case was that the Heath Government was pursuing a 'thoroughly disastrous line of policy with malignant determination'.[15] The prosperity of the yards had declined due to a long history of neglect of investment and poor management. With the formation of UCS, the unions had negotiated mobility and productivity agreements but contracts remained unprofitable due to management failure in pricing policies; these contracts had been worked and were about to be replaced by profitable contracts when the government decision to close UCS was announced. The government report contained the deliberate misrepresentation that UCS itself had wasted £5½m of public funds, when £3½m of the money went to pay off losses on existing contracts, that is to compensate the former private owners, and £1m investment went to Yarrow's Yard which was returning to private ownership. The Government's open hostility to UCS was countered not only by the work-in, but by massive strikes and marches in Scotland, with a climax on 18 August 1971, when 200,000 people, one-quarter of all Scottish workers, took strike action and 80,000 marched in Glasgow.

The work-in consisted of assuming control of the gates of the yards, and refusing to accept any redundancies. Men who received their notice handed their insurance cards to the shop stewards who paid them from the fighting fund. The fund was collected from a

50 pence weekly levy on all the UCS workers, and donations from the labour movement, and amounted to nearly half a million pounds in total. The work-in was organised by daily shop stewards' meetings; a shop stewards' bulletin was published regularly to inform the workers, and contained wry analysis of the problem, 'OK, lads, with retraining, you'll be unemployed in two skills!' Large numbers of speakers were sent to address union conferences, trades councils and other working-class audiences throughout the country. Observers were consistently surprised at how well orchestrated and orderly the campaign was. However, herein lay the central weakness of the UCS work-in. It has been claimed that the shop stewards' organisation was bureaucratic, precluding the involvement and encouraging the passivity of rank-and-file workers; the action itself was largely limited to a publicity exercise, with stewards controlling the men, but, only to a limited extent, production in the yards.[16] It is reported that only 400 commenced the work-in and this number gradually dwindled.[17] Meanwhile, with the active compliance of the media, the leading shop stewards were built into heroes, which effectively diverted attention from the men themselves: as an early analysis of the phenomena lamented: 'This power of initiative, this sense of responsibility, the self respect which comes from expressed manhood, is taken from the men and consolidated in the leader. The sum of *their* initiative, *their* responsibility, *their* self-respect becomes his.'[18] The UCS campaign was diverted from the demand for full public ownership of all yards, and accepted the compromise of a private American owner for Clydebank, with a 'no strike' clause, and the overall loss of the 2,000 jobs of the workers who had already left the yards by 1972. However, the stature of the UCS achievement should not be underestimated: whatever its shortcomings, UCS promoted the idea, throughout this country and abroad, that unemployment and redundancy need not be tolerated, and that working men had it within their power to defend their basic rights.

A number of occupation struggles which took place simultaneously with UCS suggest other possibilities of action. At Plessey Alexandria, also in Scotland, the workers took up full occupation, firmly ejecting the management until an agreement not to close the plant was made. The workers at Briant Colour Printing in London showed that even a small plant with a scattered workforce could organise an influential occupation if sufficiently committed: they contacted every branch of every print union in the country, supported and advised other occupations, and provided printing services for other workers in dispute. A study of the North-East experience of occupations reveals how the struggles galvanised the local labour movement into unaccustomed activity. At Coles Cranes 2,500 workers took up occupation when management announced an immediate reduction of the workforce, all redundant workers to be off-site by the end of the week (which contravened their contracts of employment). The occupation lasted three months and built up considerable support in Sunderland, putting new fight into the town's trades council; to the extent that the occupation was entirely successful, all demands being acceded to. At Propytex the workers returned from their summer holiday to discover that, despite a full order book they were to be made redundant due to a cash flow problem. Most of the workers had experienced multiple redundancies before and were not prepared to be subject, yet again, to the experience; besides, the factory had been open for less than two years so they did not qualify for redundancy pay. The occupation caught the sympathy of Hartlepool:[19]

> With an area already marked by high unemployment, and with a threat constantly hanging over the Steel Works, the work-in at Propytex seems to have had an uplifting effect on the whole community. Local townsfolk for instance, held a variety of fund raising events to aid the work-in. Clubs, pubs, and institutes throughout the town involved themselves in holding free dances, entertainment nights, 'teddy bear' raffles, and even sponsored walks. . . . The local Steel Workers Action Committee sent a £20 donation and local ratepayers and tenants associations also sent donations.

At Fisher-Bendix in Kirkby the workers were threatened with redundancy in 1972 by Thorn Electrical Industries; they prepared a sophisticated information bulletin of all Thorn products in advance, and upon taking up occupation issued this to dockers, airport workers and other transport workers, to secure the blacking by the labour movement of the products. The occupation of 1972 was total and the factory facilities were employed to encourage the support of families, friends and the local community. Open visits, talks, meetings and shows were arranged which proved highly popular, especially with wives and children who are normally excluded from any dispute, though they equally suffer the consequences of failure. The pressure on Thorns was sufficient to make them arrange for an alternative employer to maintain the full workforce. However, a weakness of the occupation was senior steward domination, and when an occupation proved necessary again in 1974 the senior stewards and sympathetic Labour MPs settled on the co-operative alternative, with the workforce rather bemused bystanders.[20]

The lengthy work-in at the French watch factory of Lip showed that workers could complete production of small consumer goods and obtain widespread sales from a sympathetic labour movement, the proceeds of which could be used to finance the campaign to keep the factory open. The eventual eviction of the Lip workers only served to strengthen public support which sustained the workers' action for over a year until a settlement was reached.[21] The redundancy dispute at C. A. Parsons shows the interpenetration of employment with other trade union issues. Management sent out hundreds of redundancy notices which were defiantly returned by DATA members. However the management action was part of an attempt to break a closed shop agreement in return for the withdrawal of compulsory redundancies.[22]

The sad dispute at Strachan's van bodies plant in Hampshire in 1974 began with workers being given one and a half hours' notice of closure. For four and a half months they fought the press, police and employers, only to be intimidated into accepting redundancy payments by their full-time trade union officials.[23] Thus even when trade union officials are fully sympathetic their assistance may prove equivocal, as Greenwood notes:[24]

> There is more than a suggestion in many sit-ins of determined intervention by higher level trade union officers to limit the scope of such conduct by directly elected committees. That this should be so need not indicate ulterior motives on the part of union officials. Rather . . . this may stem from their perception that a compromise will need to be made at the most favourable time and on the best possible terms, whereas the dynamics of a participative shopfloor movement lead those directly involved to believe that all is possible. Relationships, therefore, between stewards and officials in such circumstances, tend to be, at best, in the nature of a wary coalition. . . .

A final example of an occupation was that at Imperial Typewriters in 1975, which also failed due partly to familiar problems. Imperial Typewriters was 'beheaded' by Litton Industries which took their prestige and markets but abandoned production in this country. The divisiveness between the Hull and Leicester factories led to them being played off against each other and the Hull occupation received little assistance from Leicester. Shop stewards, engaged in negotiations in London, became divorced from the workforce in Hull and the attendance at the occupation gradually deteriorated; though workers in their homes were still sympathetic to the struggle, this made the occupation easy prey for legal eviction when it seemed that the possibility of resuming production had disappeared.

It would be useful to conclude with a brief analysis of the central problems facing workers who embark upon factory occupations in opposition to redundancy. The first problem is to prepare in advance by anticipating management action and preventing sudden announcements taking workers by surprise. Further information and assistance may be necessary to ascertain the extent of the problem; however it is important to alert workers and unions to build up support and the promise of sympathy action. Once an occupation is commenced it is critical that participation of everyone is encouraged to maintain morale. The work of the occupation may be delegated to various committees: finance, to raise and administer a fighting fund; security and safety to preserve order internally and secure the factory from the outside (though it is probably unnecessary to patrol the perimeter fence with a pet Labrador as one worker did); publicity, to ensure that the workers involved are informed about and understand the issues and that the world outside hears the workers' interpretation of the dispute: it is helpful to escape from the phenomena of workers 'learning' about the progress of their own dispute primarily from the television; entertainment, to relieve boredom; and education and training, to provide the opportunity for personal development normally precluded in the factory routine. Particular problems of internal organisation include the conduct of mass meetings, which sometimes tend to be dominated by the platform, and may not provide an opportunity for informed discussion; though the level of debate at mass meetings will reflect the democratic participation in the occupation generally. Another problem concerns the participation of women workers. In the past they have often proved an unexpected source of strength when they are not deliberately excluded. The media emphasis on the 'men' is both chauvinistic and divisive, given the present proportion of women workers in industry. Husbands and wives should be encouraged to attend, as one woman commented in reply to the question, 'Do you think we are going to be successful?' . . . 'Well, when I am at home I don't think so, but when I am here I think we *are*.'[25]

A problem not yet touched on is that of the law. In the past, particularly with the failure of the Industrial Relations Act, employers have been reluctant to introduce the law into industrial relations, as its use fosters acrimony to little purpose, and often only brings the law into discredit. The police have frequently been loath to become involved in what was regarded as a civil matter. Normally in disputes workers are presented as the transgressors, but when management declare major redundancies the responsibility for the dispute is more clearly their own. Occupations are usually well disciplined and orderly; and the effort to dislodge workers in a major occupation could prove counter-productive. In the past writs have been issued, but difficulty was encountered in delivering or enforcing them. Moreover, the recognition that isolated sit-ins in defence of the right to work pose little direct threat to the established order, encourages official tolerance. Large companies have uniformly refrained from the occasional vindictive application of the law attempted by small employers; however, as the implications of the spread of the occupation tactic emerged, and as the tactic was applied in various subsidiaries of most of the major multinational corporations, it is likely that pressure for sterner legal measures issued particularly from this quarter.

Previously trespass was a civil offence, but the Criminal Law Act 1977, creates new substantive criminal offences relating to trespass: it will be an offence to use or threaten 'violence' to secure entry to premises, which could amount to slight damage to property, or a caretaker feeling that he has been intimidated; numbers alone entail 'violence' in the opinion of the police. Second, when on the premises it is an offence to have a 'weapon of violence' which in a factory could be a set of tools. Finally if the court sends in the bailiffs and the occupiers peacefully refuse to move then they can be convicted of obstructing an officer of the court. In all these offences police officers are given the power to enter, search and arrest without warrant. The new offences carry prison sentences of up to three to six months and fines up to £1,000; and in none of the offences can you elect for trial by jury. The law effectively undermines the immunity of trade union-ists from legal action taken in furtherance of a trade dispute. In recognition of this the TUC carried a resolution calling for changes in the law which would enable factory occupations to be treated as an acceptable form of industrial action; and in 1977 the TUC passed a motion rejecting the introduction of criminal law into the law of trespass and the exposure of trade unionists legitimately engaged in occupations to criminal sanctions by employers through the courts.[26] This law represents a medieval return to a vicious defence of property rights. It is highly unlikely that it would be successfully applied against a large-scale occupation backed by industrial strength; however, as with the Industrial Relations Act, it will be used against small occupations, to victimise individuals, and to intimidate those workers contemplating occupations. The Campaign Against A Criminal Trespass Law maintains further that[27]

> Another factor which will determine the way in which the police react to workplace occupations is the degree to which they have managed successfully to use this law against other forms of occupation. Their strategy is likely to be to use it in the first place against weaker sections of the movement (students, squatters and community groups, as well as ill-organised workers) and then later, having thus 'legitimised' the use of the law, feel freer to increase its use against workplace occupations. (It is thus important that we make sure that *any* attempts to use this law are opposed, whether it be in the workplace, in the community or in colleges, in order to block attempts to legitimise its use in general — which will affect us all.)

The active support of the local community is again the critical ingredient which could decide whether the law is used or rejected; and the presence of this alien factor in future lays stress on the importance of adequate publicity and communication to counter-act the erroneous impressions the authorities might foster. Thus the playwright John McGrath in the introduction to his drama of a factory occupation in Liverpool refers to the sinister explanation of an army expert of how to defeat political resistance; taking up Mao's analogy of the party or front as the fish and the population as the water through which it moves, the brigadier argues:[28]

> If the fish has got to be destroyed, it can be attacked directly

by rod or net. . . . But if rod and net cannot succeed by themselves, it may be necessary to do something to the water which will force the fish into a position where it can be caught. Conceivably it might be necessary to kill the fish by polluting the water. . . . The first aim of those involved in counter-subversion is to gain control of the people, because in most cases this is a necessary prelude to destroying the enemy's forces — and in any case it is the ultimate reason for doing so.

Redundancy occupations, as with other forms of conventional industrial action, are an extension of collective bargaining by other means, and remain often within the limitations of collective bargaining. Some workers who have engaged in factory occupations have maintained the tactic is too limited, particularly as the element of surprise has been lost — most employers making large-scale redundancies today anticipate some form of occupation. Therefore more militant alternatives have been considered: occupation of neighbouring subsidiaries of the same company, which the management want to remain open; occupation of company headquarters; and, in at least one instance, the occupation of the bank responsible for putting the company into receivership. It is possible that the occupation tactic will develop in the future in these and other directions. The limitations of the aims of redundancy occupations are also clear: many occupations direct their energy exclusively at an immediate redundancy problem, rather than simultaneously contributing to the effort to change the economic system which constantly reproduces such problems.

The recent experience of Merseyside in particular has shown that within the present system respite from mass redundancy is of a very temporary nature. Indeed the most disturbing recent development in the approach of employers and government toward redundancy has been the 'buying' of large-scale redundancies in areas of high unemployment. The closure in 1978 of the British Leyland Triumph TR7 plant in Liverpool, and the closure of several British Steel Corporation plants including East Moors in Cardiff was facilitated by the offer of increased redundancy payments, which were exaggerated by the media and undermined the attempt at resistance. Workers are enticed by the vision of paying off debts to accept these payments, in the hope that other work will turn up later. But the tragedy is that these working class communities are in a state of gradual decline; once such large numbers of industrial jobs are removed it is unlikely they will be replaced and workers will be left fighting for the few jobs available. Thus the coldly obsessive rationality of capitalist managers is being constantly applied regardless of the social consequences in the regions: centralising production in neighbouring capital-intensive plants to maximise volume, destroying locally based militant trade unionism in the process. If these insistent pressures are to be effectively resisted, combine committees must assert the interest of the company workforce as a whole in maintaining employment against management attempts to promote sectional interests.

Although public ownership and a democratically planned economy remain the only permanent avenues to employment security, yet the existing nationalised sector is modelled on the private sector, and subservient to its needs, and therefore displays some of the worst features of capitalist industry. What is essential is a fundamental rehabilitation of nationalisation, and the only force capable of performing this is the organised working class. Hence a study of Allende's Chile contrasted the democratic and participative control of those factories where the workers themselves had seized control, with the retained oligarchical management control of those companies nationalised by decree, which 'froze' existing authority structures.[29] Only an active, militant and politically conscious rank and file can effectively defend their jobs and communities. Promoting this activity is the crucial long term task for those interested in the removal of the insecurity and waste of capitalism.

Notes

1   TUC General Council, *Industrial Democracy*, 1974, p. 31.
2   J. Greenwood, *Worker Sit-ins and Job Protection*, Gower Press, 1977.
3   Ibid., p. 7.
4   R. H. Fryer, 'Redundancy, values and public policy', *Industrial Relations Journal*, 4(2), 1973, p. 3.
5   S. R. Parker *et al.*, *Effects of the Redundancy Payments Act*, HMSO, 1971.
6   W. Linder, *The Great Flint Sit-Down Strike Against GM 1936-37*, Solidarity Pamphlet, 1969; A. Preis, *Labour's Giant Step — Twenty Years of the CIO*.
7   W. Hannington, *Unemployed Struggles 1919-1936*, Lawrence & Wishart, 1936 (reprinted in paperback by Gollancz and E. P. Publishers, 1977).

8   A. Buchan, *The Right to Work*, Calder and Boyars, 1972, p. 144.

9   TUC, op. cit., p. 31.

10 Literature advising management what to do in the event of an occupation includes, Institute of Personnel Management, *Sit-ins and Work-ins*, IPM, 1976; C. Thomas, 'Strategy for a Sit-In', *Personnel Management*, 8(1), 1976.

11 These estimates are derived from the most comprehensive empirical study of occupations in the UK, North-East Trade Union Studies Information Unit, *Workers' Occupations and the North-East Experience*, TUSIU (5 Queen Street, Newcastle), 1976. Also from J. Hemingway and W. Keyser, *Who's in Charge?*, Metra Oxford Consulting Ltd, Oxford, 1975.

12 D. Elliot, 'Sit-ins', Open University Management Consultancy, typescript, 1972, p. 24.

13 Contemporary plays on occupations include Jim Allen, *The Big Flame*, a percipient study of a (fictional) insurrectionary occupation of the Liverpool Docks by the dockers; Trevor Griffiths, *Occupations*, a gripping examination of the contradictions of the 1920 Turin factory occupations and the role of Antonio Gramsci; John McGrath, *Fish In The Sea*, a humorous musical look at a Glasgow factory occupation, though set in Liverpool; Chris Bond, *Under New Management*, another musical comedy based on the Fisher-Bendix saga from its origin in 1960 till 1975; and David Edgar, *Events Following the Closure of a Motorcycle Factory*, an investigative documentary drama of the Triumph Meriden occupation. Factory occupations have also attracted the attention of film-makers, and films include: British Film Institute, *Fakenham*, a documentary of the struggle by women to keep open a small leather works in Norfolk; Marin Karmitz, *Blow for Blow*, a dramatised documentary of a continental occupation, again by women; and Gael Dohany, *Occupy!*, British Film Institute, a dramatised documentary of the Fisher-Bendix occupation incorporating parts of Chris Bond's play.

14 Institute for Workers' Control, *GEC–EEC Workers' Takeover*, IWC Pamphlet no. 17, 1969.

15 W. Thompson and F. Hart, *The UCS Work-In*, Lawrence & Wishart, 1972, p. 12. Further studies of UCS include A. Buchan, *The Right to Work*, Calder & Boyars, 1972, and R. Murray, *UCS: The Anatomy of Bankruptcy*, Spokesman Books, 1972.

16 Critical analysis of UCS and other occupations from a revolutionary standpoint is contained in 'Sit-ins: the Experience', *International Socialism*, 53, 1972, pp. 8–11, and J. Deason, 'Redundancy, Closures and the Sit-in Tactic', *International Socialism*, 73, 1974, pp. 8–25.

17 Greenwood, op. cit., p. 161.

18 Unofficial Reform Committee, *The Miners' Next Step* (first published 1912). Reprints in Labour History, no. 4, Pluto Press, 1973, p. 19.

19 North-East Trade Union Studies Information Unit, op. cit., pp. 42–3.

20 T. Clarke, *Sit-in at Fisher-Bendix*, IWC Pamphlet no. 42, 1974, and T. Clarke, *The Workers Co-operatives: a Social Experiment*, forthcoming.

21 Greenwood, op. cit.

22 'The Redundancy Dispute at C. A. Parsons', *International Socialism*, 73, 1974, pp. 19–23.
23 D. Peers, 'Sold Out at Strachans', *International Socialism*, 73, 1974, p. 24.
24 Greenwood, op. cit., p. 100.
25 M. Marks, 'The Battle at Fisher-Bendix', *International Socialism*, 73, 1974, p. 14.
26 H. Levinson, 'Criminal Law Act 1977', *Labour Research*, January 1978, pp. 9–11.
27 'Campaign Against a Criminal Trespass Law', *Workplace Occupations and the Law*, May 1978, p. 3. Also see CACTL, *Trespass Laws: an Attack on Direct Action* and the *CACTL Newsletter* (CACTL, 35 Wellington Street, London WC2).
28 McGrath, op. cit.
29 A. Zimbalist and J. Petras, *Workers' Control in Allende's Chile*, IWC pamphlet no. 47, 1975, p. 5.

5 Race, community and marginality: Spiralynx

Peter Morris

This chapter describes attempts to organise the workforce of a small company in East London. The company, which was strongly resistant to any union representation of its workers, is far from untypical of many small firms in the inner city. With the decline of long established industry in these areas, a new low-wage sector is emerging. Operating on low cost margins, their image is, in the words of the managing director of Spiralynx, of 'good solid firms that don't normally go bankrupt'.[1] They survive. But their survival as often as not, depends on paying their workers well below the agreed minimum rate for their industry. The average wage levels in many of the older industrial areas are the result of the struggles of generations of workers; these rates now are being undermined and reset by a new generation of sweatshop employers.

Companies like Spiralynx set up, or move into, areas of industrial decline because premises in derelict factories or vacant sites are cheap. In addition they are increasingly being given incentives to set up or move into these areas. Local authorities, concerned about their declining rate base and rising unemployment tend to encourage any new industry, regardless of its employment practices. They are reinforced in this by a succession of recent Government policies, which give a central role to small firms as the key economic generator for the industrial revival of the inner city. Furthermore, in the Department of Employment, Mr Harold Lever is currently discussing raising the exemption limit of certain provisions of the Employment Protection Act and other protective legislation so that small firms and their employees are excluded. A countervailing strategy, in which trade unions are strongly represented on the relevant bodies to enforce agreed pay and conditions as a condition for aid has scarcely begun to emerge. It is vitally needed.

By themselves, the law and planning procedures are not very effective in these matters. Where labour is weak, they can do a little, but not much, to regulate the conditions of employment. The starting-point for any strategy for dealing with low wages must be the organisation of the workers concerned.

Trade union organisation has traditionally been weak among low-paid workers. This is partly for obvious reasons; it is extremely difficult to organise workers in small and isolated 'shops', who have close relations with employers who are themselves strongly hostile to unions. But it also reflects a failure of the unions to recognise the relevance of the demands of groups of workers whose interests may coincide only partially with their own. For example, workers who are recent immigrants, once they have acquired some sort of job, may be more concerned about getting adequate housing, or defending themselves against racialist attacks than about improving the quality of that job. Where such workers *have* organised themselves — as the women at Trico, or the Asian workers in a succession of strikes at Courtaulds', Woolf's, Mansfield Hosiery, Imperial Typewriters or Grunwicks — unions have all too often been slow to respond. Without union support, these actions may be bold and spontaneous but they remain limited, one-off events. At the same time, by failing to respond, trade unions cut themselves off from a potent source of working-class action for, as noted in relation to the Asian working struggles in the early 1970s: 'their strikes . . . threatened the system as few strikes did — for they were subsidised and supported by the community, united across divisions of labour, and possessed of a genius for organisation and obstinacy against all odds'.[2]

In the case of Spiralynx, a small furniture factory in East London, the union (the Furniture, Timber and Allied Trades Union, FTAT) has been trying to organise workers in the company since the early 1960s. This chapter is primarily an account of an approach to organising that concentrated outside the factory in question, after a dead end had been reached while using more conventional means. The campaign involved immigrant workers' organisations, the Furniture Union, the Trades Council and a number of workers from community agencies. It was part of a wider strategy aimed at linking factory and community struggles, and in particular, at linking black workers' struggles with the local labour movement. The campaign to organise Spiralynx failed, though there were partial successes. But in the process of organising, important links were forged, particularly between Asian workers' organisations and the Trades Council. These Asian workers were faced, for example, with damp and overcrowded accommodation, and unresolved issues of immigration status. These issues had a direct bearing on organisation at the factory and it became clear that an approach based solely on wages and conditions was an insufficient defence of these workers' interests. The approach was not new, but it had for a long time been neglected by the trade unions. Long hours, low wages and poor working conditions have always been a feature of working life in Newham. The Royal Docks, the factories alongside them, and later the Stratford rail-yards were built in the last quarter of the nineteenth century. As part of the same unregulated development, 'noxious trades' such as tallow soap and glue-making, which by-laws excluded from London, were set up in small workshops to the east of the River Lea which then formed the metropolitan boundary. There were numerous other badly paid trades too, for example, in many homes the women took in clothing work.

The major battles for the rights of organised labour to security and an adequate wage centred on the docks and the heavy manu-facturing industries. But alongside the struggles for a decent wage at work, the community organised itself to deal with the problems of an overcrowded and insanitary environment. There was no clear division between the two arenas and many activists, such as Will Thorne, were prominent in both. Through direct action, demon-stration and marches on the Town Hall, and finally through the formation of one of the first socialist municipalities, they fought for better control of the environment, including the regulation of small sweatshops. Although many workers were still paid low wages, the low wage sector, the small un-unionised shops, became marginal to the local economy, as a result of these struggles.

By the early 1970s, however, massive withdrawal of investment had left Newham an industrial graveyard. The large companies moved out, shedding 30,000 jobs in ten years. As they went, a succession of small industries moved in, taking advantage of the old premises and a changing labour force. Many were from older areas of East London bordering on the City. They included clothing, furniture, plastics and cosmetics factories and short-term-lease warehousing.

Spiralynx

The management

The firm employs around 200 workers. They make beds, mattresses, divans and domestic furniture. Although the work involves a variety of journeymen trades, almost all the workers are classified as unskilled. Management claims to have taken a leaf out of Ford's book:[3]

> our system is broken right down, so that each person is taught one little skill which would be of no use to him whatever, if he went out into another factory . . . we work very much on the principle that one individual does one job, but he adapts easily if we shift him into another job. We break the jobs right down.

Most workers were recent immigrants speaking little English. Management were clear about who they recruited. They did not want workers made redundant from the large factories: 'they come round the door, "I've been working for Fords, BUT" — you know, we often get this "but" — and we say, "Well, we'd like to employ you, you know, you're a nice looking fellow, look like a good hand, but we can't get anywhere near the wages that Ford can offer you. And we'd rather we didn't employ you because you'll only be unsettled." ' Instead they looked for immigrant workers: 'one and a half men looking for a job . . . they were prepared to work, do anything . . . they were a bit of the debris left after Ford's had picked the cream.'[4]

Spiralynx wages are low. The Furniture Union told a local newspaper that 'our latest figures show that people are being paid 12 to 20 pence (an hour) below the nationally agreed rate. This means they are anywhere between £5 and £12 a week down.'[5] A local authority investigation carried out by the Careers Office concluded with serious criticisms of the conditions at the factory, which were referred to the Factory Inspectorate as being in breach of the law:[6]

> I can only say I was shocked and disgusted by the conditions in this factory which were seen to constitute definite health and safety hazards. All the machines were archaic with no

proper safety guards, e.g. guillotines, spring-making machines, and other similar machines with a cutting edge, had no automatic stopping device. In the metal and spring-making department, the floor was littered with pieces of metal, coils of wire and shavings; the surface of the floor was greasy, the premises generally filthy. The machines in the spring-making department gave off choking fumes and a grey pall seemed to hang over the department; the noise here was deafening. I noticed pungent fumes coming from the spray painting and lacquer booth, which were often situated in the middle of an area with workers around them; the men working these booths wore no masks or overalls; paint and lacquer residue formed thick globules and stalagmites.

Bad as conditions were, it was management's attitudes that figured most strongly in workers' complaints about the factory. Any questions were treated as insubordination. Harassment featured in account after account, extracts from some of which were quoted in the local press. These accounts were in direct contrast to the management's claim: 'we don't have bad labour relations . . . I have no concern if they are in the union, I don't pry into their private life'.[7]

Organising the factory: the Furniture Union

FTAT[8] first became involved with Spiralynx at their Whitechapel factory in 1963. They were approached by a young black worker with a claim for non-payment for the Bank Holiday. They found in addition that he was being paid at half the rate laid down in the bedding agreement. They lodged a claim on his behalf. On the following day, he was dismissed. When the union District Officer went to see the managing director he was told that there was nothing to discuss. Further attempts to process the claim, which now included dismissal without pay in lieu of notice, were unanswered. Registered mail was returned and management refused to meet the union. The matter was referred to the Ministry of Labour. The Ministry's intervention came to nothing, but the company did, finally, agree to settle as a result of an embargo by the

London Co-op (this in itself, the result of protracted negotiations) on all trade with Spiralynx, until the claim was paid.

The first claim brought to light a whole series of malpractices within the factory. In May 1964 the union began a campaign of recruitment outside the factory gates. By June some sixty-two workers had joined the union. But the following month a leading member denounced the union. Within days, management knew the names of all union members and within weeks the union organisation had collapsed.

Unable to regain a foothold within the factory, the union sought compensation for its members through the courts. There was a steady succession of cases. Once, a redundancy claim on behalf of four fitters, went to the Court of Appeal, where their Lordships found for the union, without requiring to hear their case. In 1970 an industrial tribunal granted redundancy payments of £682 and £216 respectively to union members. As the union's District Secretary wrote, in a letter to the company's solicitor (the company having failed to reply): 'I suggest they settle this claim and avoid the course that takes us along the well trodden path to the courts. If that is the only means we have to secure a just settlement we will take it.'

But the law at best could only offer retrospective compensation; it could provide no protection to workers inside the factory. So the union continued to try and organise outside the factory. It was a rough business. On one occasion, for example, the gates were shut during the lunch hour, on the pretext that they had jammed, and workers were told that they could not leave the premises. Pressure outside the factory ensured that no one would openly join the union.

Community organisation

A further approach was evolved from a number of different sources. In December 1974 three Pakistani women signed on at the social security office. They were unskilled and spoke little English. They were offered jobs at Spiralynx at 50 pence an hour. One of their fathers knew some one who had been sacked from the factory for trying to join the union. The women told the office that they would not take the job. As a result their benefit was cut off, on the grounds that they had turned down 'suitable employment'. They appealed against the ruling to the Supplementary Benefits Tribunal and went to a local advice centre for assistance. The Tribunal upheld their appeal and in their decision accepted that 'the firm is notorious for its low wages, and under these circumstances the turning down of the job was reasonable'. In preparing the case, the advice centre had contacted FTAT for information on Spiralynx and the result was widely publicised. One result was the investigation, referred to earlier, by the Newham Careers Office.

At the same time, a small group of community workers and lawyers were meeting to look at the issue of black workers in relation to employment and the problems of low pay. Spiralynx was one of a number of firms that stood out with a reputation for repressive management. It was thought that the development of trade union organisation in one 'notorious' firm might have an encouraging effect on unorganised workers in other local factories. It was also hoped that connections with Trades Council and immigrant organisations might provide the basis for a successful campaign. Meetings were arranged with FTAT and with the organiser of a comparable campaign in West London. Over a period of six months hundreds of visits had been made to workers in their homes, because conditions in the factory had made direct organisation at work impossible. The union was now recognised at this factory and the union rate paid.

A similar strategy was adopted for Spiralynx. The first contacts were made with workers known to an active Pakistani trade unionist at Ford's and to an interpreter in Malayalam and Tamil (southern Indian languages) from the Social Services Department. Several early evening visits were made each week with an interpreter. Information was sought about the firm (jobs, wages, hours, working conditions) and the workers themselves (previous jobs, British language ability, trade union experience, special grievances, length of time at Spiralynx). The aim was to recruit members to the union and (it was hoped) to generate independent discussion about the need for local organisation.

The first visits gave a clearer picture of the composition of the workforce. The firm employed between 180 and 200 workers. Of these, 50 per cent were Tamils or Malayalees from southern India. Many of these had worked in the British Naval Dockyards in

Singapore before its closure in 1970; some of them had been members of the Dockers Union and involved in a major strike. Altogether 80 per cent of the workforce were of Asian background. Around twenty-five women, mostly from northern India, were employed at the time.

Lack of facilities was frequently mentioned — for instance, no canteen, cold tap frequently broken, lavatories not stocked with paper. But the major grievance was the attitude of management. The workers felt they could say nothing about their work or pay without risk of the sack. Most had heard of the earlier sackings of suspected trade union members. These fears were compounded by the fact that the workers were split along ethnic and language lines and unable to communicate freely among themselves. Several workers mentioned that they worked in 'shops' where only one other person spoke the same language, which militated against the development of organisation among the workers. Malayalees and Tamils, the main groups visited at this stage, wanted assurances that Gujrati, Punjabi, Pakistani, West Indian and English workers were also being approached.

It was also clear that, no matter how long they had worked at the factory, most workers looked on it as a temporary job, a stepping-stone, while they learnt enough English and established themselves, before moving on to Fords or the railways. Yet, in reality, with unemployment in the area at 12 per cent, the actual prospect of their finding other work was remote.

It should be mentioned that many of the workers lived in very bad housing. Overcrowding was typical, with husband, wife and two children living in one room. Some of the workers lived in single rooms in a redevelopment area where damp ran down the walls, the paper was peeling and there was scarcely room for a bed.

Most workers, despite their precarious economic position and the possibility of dismissal, said they were prepared to join the union. They were extremely hospitable to the organisers. Some, though, questioned what the personal motive was in persuading them to join the union. One of the community workers noted: 'At this stage, it is fair to say that we weren't, ourselves, clear about our interest. We talked only in terms of improving the situation for Spiralynx workers.'

By the early summer of 1975 it was decided (for reasons which included the difficulty of making further contact and the inter-preter going on extended holiday) to publish a leaflet which out-lined the major grievances, and set out the case for joining the union. In order to meet workers' anxieties that only certain groups were being approached it was necessary to provide simultaneous translations in Tamil, Malayalam, Urdu and Bengali. Some of the problems of translation only emerged later: the Urdu script, for example, though beautifully written, was in a classical style, more or less incomprehensible to Pakistani workers of a peasant back-ground. Other difficulties were the result of tautological or un-clear constructions in the original. The leaflets were distributed to the households that had already been visited; they were also given out at a bus stop used by many of the workers, on their way home.

On the basis of the leaflet and further discussions with Pakistani workers, a meeting was arranged in a hall not far from the factory. It was agreed that there should be no open moves, that might set management on their guard, until there was a sure basis for organi-sation among the workers. Leaflets advertising this meeting were distributed at the bus stop. Twelve workers turned up, only two of whom were familiar from previous visits. A well-known Indian socialist and the District Organiser of FTAT put the case for the union. Two active trade unionists at Fords (one Pakistani, one Tamil) interpreted. After one and a half hours, the eldest Malayalee stood up and spoke briefly. He said, 'Please, no more speeches, just give us the forms, and we'll sign up and be on our way.' In the following weeks, further members were recruited to the union.

The aim was to recruit between forty and fifty members (which was seen as the breaking-point for organisation within the factory) before going campaigning openly outside the factory gates. Never-theless, by mid-September, management had learned of the cam-paign and were, by all accounts, angry. They did not appear to know how many workers had joined the union. It was decided to go on the offensive and picket the factory gates.

Pickets were arranged on three evenings between 5.00 and 5.30 pm, the time when workers left the factory. They included representatives from the Trades Council and the FTAT. Leaflets, the union's recruiting literature and the Asian language leaflets, were distributed. On the first evening, management tried to direct workers out through a back entrance, on the pretext that the main gate had jammed. By the third time, the workers were showing signs of increasing defiance. Whereas before, many had been reluctant to accept a leaflet, most were now taking them and some were stopping to talk. A fortnight later, at an early morning picket, two officers from FTAT, a few community workers and several dockers from the TGWU were outside the gates with the Trades Council banner. The police (who had been informed of the picket by the union) had contacted the management who had then drawn up all their lorries (two with Alsatians in the cabs) along the length of the road, to restrict access to the gates. The manager, general manager and five staff came out to guide the workers in. They tried to prevent the leaflets being handed out, and when the general manager grabbed one of the union posters, there was a brief skirmish with fists flying. Workers watched from the windows, shouting support. Management attempted to take photos of those on the picket. They called the police and statements were taken.

Following this demonstration, the District Organiser wrote to the company informing them that the union had members within the factory, and requesting a meeting to discuss rates of pay. He received no reply.

Confidence was growing. Regular contact between the union and the workers was maintained through a van (placarded with posters in Urdu, Malayalam and Tamil) parked round a corner from the factory. A second meeting was organised. An Indian community relations official (who had been active in a recognition dispute in a South London factory involving Tamil and Malayalee workers) was invited to speak. There was an attempt to regularise the collection of dues (largely to the exclusion of any discussion on how organisation in the factory might be extensively extended). In the end, by a somewhat haphazard process, a worker was selected as shop steward, mainly on the basis of his ability to speak English. More workers joined the union.

Some weeks later, when the shop steward was visited to discuss membership, he seemed resigned and fatalistic, and mentioned, in passing, that, before the last meeting, several workers had been sacked for suspected union activity. He could identify only one name from the list of union members. The fact that nothing had been mentioned at the meeting demonstrated, at the very least, that there were serious problems in communication. It was agreed that it was important to act quickly, but concrete information was needed. A week's hard work came up with the facts about three dismissals, two of them concerning union members. One member had moved to Birmingham; another had walked off the job after an argument with the foreman about being constantly shifted from one job to another; the third, who was not a union member, had been supposedly sacked for trade union activity but he could not be contacted. Thus there was no legal case, and the trade union organisation in the factory was not strong enough to take action. It is not certain that these were the only cases.

The inability to respond effectively to the sackings undermined the campaign. In the absence of a clear initiative from the workers it lapsed. In the winter, union members were visited to find out what was happening and what they thought should be done next. They reported that most workers had received rises in wages, which they compared favourably with the wages in other factories in the area. None thought it was time for action. One member was sure that management had had spies at the second meeting.

In the early summer of 1976 there were important developments resulting from the upsurge in racial violence. For the first time militant Asian workers' organisations combined with the local labour movement. This alliance, both inside and outside such organisations as the Trades Council, provides the surest basis for organisation in the future. For one clear lesson from the Spiralynx campaign is that though the defeats matter, the gains from these previous struggles can be built upon.

Review

Much more could be done by trade unionists to regulate the development of sweatshop employment by using their position on various local and national bodies. But there are limits to what planning regulations and protective industrial legislation can achieve. Industrial Tribunals have shown themselves reluctant to order the reinstatement of workers, unfairly dismissed. On the other hand, managements like Spiralynx have been prepared to go to the highest court in the land and pay out thousands of pounds, rather than allow any encroachment on their right to employ labour at the rate they think fit. Though recognition procedures have been improved, the dispute at Grunwick demonstrates how limited legal sanctions are, in the face of determined opposition from management. The defence of workers' rights is, first of all, a matter of organisation at the workplace. Spiralynx is but one of thousands of small employers who resist the most elementary expression of trade union rights. A new approach is required by the unions. The implications for a long-term strategy for the unions have been discussed elsewhere.[9] But one element in such an approach is a readiness to draw on resources beyond the workplace. For most workers, and particularly for those in low paid jobs, the division between work and home is not as complete as the divisions between trade union and community organisations imply. Issues of housing, or racialism, or child care constantly impinge upon the place of work. Linking struggles that straddle workplace and the home may prove institutionally untidy, but this is a necessary first step to effective organisation.[10] Furthermore, such an approach necessarily raises questions about the total political system.

The campaign over Spiralynx illustrates the formidable problems that these small firms can present. But despite its failures it also indicates the possibility of a trade union strategy that links the workplace with community agencies, such as law centres or local research projects, Trades Councils and other community organisations. Using a geographical as well as a trade basis for organisation, provides the starting-point for a new and more effective approach.

Notes

1 Recorded discussion with Mr Goodman, Managing Director of Spiralynx, January 1975.
2 A. Sivananden, 'Race, Class and the State', *Race and Class*, 17, spring 1976, no. 4.
3 Discussion with Mr Goodman, op. cit.
4 Ibid.
5 *Stratford Express*, 26 November 1976.
6 Newham Careers Office Report, 17 October 1975.
7 *Stratford Express*, 26 November 1976.
8 Furniture, Timber and Allied Trades Union, formerly National Union of Furniture Trade Operatives.
9 See for example Alan Fisher and Bernard Dix, *Low Pay and How to Fight it: a Trade Union Approach*, Pitman, 1974.
10 e.g., see historically: Leeds clothing workers in 1890s, E. P. Thompson, 'Homage to Tom Maguire' in *Essays in Labour History*, vol. 1, ed. Asa Briggs and John Saville; agitation by Jewish anarchist workers' organisations at the beginning of this century: W. W. Fishman, *East End Jewish*

Radicals 1975-1914, Duckworth, 1975; some of the 'Wobblies' (industrial workers of the world) campaigns; not to mention contemporary struggles by Asian workers at Imperial Typewriters, Mansfield Hosiery, Courtauld and Grunwick.

6 The London homeworking campaign

Joe Noble

Introduction

For nearly a century the problems presented by homeworkers have caused concern both to the trade union movement and to community and voluntary organisations. In the past these activities have tended to be independent of each other and sometimes hostile. The key difference with the present series of campaigns has been a conscious effort to develop close links between the trade union movement and community work. This has necessitated a great deal of preliminary work by the campaign – work which needs to be explained in this article to give a thorough perspective to the campaign.

A homeworker has been defined as a 'person who is employed directly by a firm to carry out work in his or her own home not directly under control or management of that employer'.[1] Typical work includes machining garments, making toys, addressing envelopes, clerical work etc., and is, of course, almost exclusively carried out by women. Women who work at home are bedevilled by the same problems that women face at work in general – problems of low pay, unskilled work, difficult hours, job insecurity etc. But not only do they suffer the exploitation of women workers in general and usually in a more severe way, they also suffer in turn from working in their own homes. There is none of the spontaneous solidarity of working alongside other workers as in the factory or office nor the possible concrete gains that can be won through trade union membership from which home workers have, until now, been virtually excluded. Thus historically homeworkers have been excluded from the legitimate ranks of the national work force and it is therefore no accident that in this twilight world between work and home it is community workers who have played an important part in such recent initiatives as the London Home-working Campaign and many others across the country.

History

It was seventy years ago that the famous *Daily Mail* 'Sweated Trades' exhibition took place. Many organisations of varying political and religious shades have taken up the issue since. In the early days the women's trade union league fought for strict control of all forms of home working, organising in the sweated industries, lobbying for legislative reform and successfully focusing public attention on this historically hidden sector of workers.

Their approach to the issue was not the only one. At the same time other groups launched their own campaigns against what they saw as the health hazard presented by garments produced in insanitary conditions and in fact this concern became reflected in the factory and workshops bill which was subsequently introduced in 1900. Under this legislation all unwholesome processes were proscribed and the use of infected premises for the purposes of homeworking was clearly prohibited. In addition the bill stipulated that the names of all out-workers were to be entered on a list and provided with the particulars of the jobs so that they could calculate their wages. In 1909 trades boards were set up and given the task of establishing and supervising minimum wages in a variety of low paid industrial sectors.

These activities marked the end of any further action until after the Second World War when the TUC in 1947 carried out an investigation throughout the trade union movement. But, with the boom years of the 1950s and '60s the matter lapsed yet again. Brian Bolton in his pamphlet *An End to Homeworking*[2] provides an excellent historical basis for a number of more recent initiatives. Interest has again also been taken by the TUC who set up a new working party in 1976 to report to the 1978 TUC. This recognised the present impossibility of calling for the complete prohibition of homeworkers, the need to improve social provision, as well as the organisation of homeworkers. Further a resolution was passed at the 1977 TUC Women's Conference moved by the National Union of Tailor and Garment Workers and seconded by the Union of Shop Distributive and Allied Trades on the question of improving the conditions of homeworkers. This was carried overwhelmingly.

Nature of the problem

Although there are no precise figures of the number of home-workers (despite the fact that employers are required by law to make half yearly returns to the local authority), recent studies suggest a figure in the region of a quarter of a million. In one London borough, for instance, there are extremely large numbers of home-workers (particularly in the rag trade) clearly visible in their front room windows and further identified by the dozens of advertisements in the local paper yet only the following returns have been made over the last two years: February 1976, 162; August 1976, 345; February 1977, 284; August 1977, 176. (This lack of precise information is one of the major reasons for the necessity of large-scale research into the whole problem of homeworking.) When a short article appeared in *Woman's Own* recently mentioning the London Homeworking Campaign and asking homeworkers to contact us for further information, over 100 replies were received. Unfortunately all but one were requests for work. Not only are existing numbers of homeworkers large but clearly there is still a massive untapped workforce behind them.

The trades in which homeworkers are prevalent are many and varied although key areas include the garment trade, clerical work such as typing envelopes and, especially at Christmas time, toy-making. In fact the trades listed by the Secretary of State to be classified as homeworking for which legislation has been passed range from 'making of iron steel cables and chains, making of iron steel anchors and grapnels' to 'packeting buttons, hooks and eyes, pens and hairpins'. Trades covered by homeworkers are certainly wide and not all are covered by wages councils. In Marie Brown's pamphlet[3] a sample of homeworkers was studied which found that very low rates of pay indeed were being received. The sample of homeworkers was studied by making contact through the Jimmy Young radio programme and included many types of home-work, from making plastic pants for babies to mascara brushes. Table 6.1 gives a breakdown of the hourly rates of the fifty women interviewed, but despite the fact that most of those concerned were covered by wages councils only one woman in the sample earned above the already low statutory minimum rate. One home-worker from another study in East London was found to be actually paying her employer money after all her overheads had been taken into account. Why then do women choose to be homeworkers?

Table 6.1

Hourly rates of pay (p)	Number of workers
Up to 3	3
4–5	8
6–10	6
11–15	9
16–20	8
21–25	4
26–30	2
31–35	5
36–40	1
41–45	1
46–50	2
72	1
Total	50

At first glance the answer appears to be simple because there would seem to be many advantages in working at home. A woman can work the hours that suit her best, she can fit in activities such as housework, shopping, fetching the children from school, looking after under-fives more easily around the work schedule that homeworking imposes. But in reality, for most women who work in their own homes, there is no choice. It is either a 'take it' or 'have no work at all'. Women need the money either because their husband's income is far too low or else social security benefits for single parents are totally inadequate. They are unable to leave the home because they need to care for young children, handicapped parents or elderly relatives, or they have school-aged children and need to fit in with the school day. In the ethnic communities extra pressures are put on women from both religious and cultural reasons against them leaving the home to work.

Often advertisements for homeworking are put in misleading ways so that an impression is given that it is very convenient to work at home. With the unemployment situation in general, and women being squeezed out of the job market at a faster rate than men, homeworking again seems to be the sole possibility. It is only with plenty of jobs available, and full social provision for child care etc., that homeworking will in any sense become a real choice for women and even that begs the ideological question of why it should be women who face such a choice.

For the employer who hasn't the investment potential to capitalise on large-scale production homeworking is an obvious answer. The employer saves money by paying low wages, not paying holiday money, or contributions to pension funds, national insurance and training schemes. Further, by not having factories or premises he pays no rent, rates, power, lighting, canteen and insurance costs which the homeworker has to meet. He also avoids such annoying legislation as redundancy payments, health and safety legislation, etc., etc. But for more detailed analysis of why homeworking continues the position of the employers needs much further careful research.

The problem is well put by Maria Macciocchi, writing about Naples.[4]

These women, for the most part, are not housewives at all which is the way they are officially registered by the Bureau of Statistics — but underpaid labourers. They are labourers and they do not even know it, and they also do not know that, working at home, they received from industry (which hires them on the sly) a salary five times lower than that of a regular female worker. They have no welfare benefits at all, no insurance, no social security, no pension. The women of the back streets sew shoe uppers, gloves, umbrellas, trousers; they are the workforce of the 'shadow factories' against which it is impossible to organise a strike or any kind of struggle since the bosses have no faces. The women are not signed up in the unions even as artisans since, among other reasons, they cannot indicate who it is that hires them — they do not even know his name. . . . I do no more than draw out the conclusions from what the women themselves have said: I explain to them that far from being housewives, they constitute a very real part of the Neapolitan economy. Indirectly, the European Common Market reaches all the way down to the twisting narrow streets of these neighbourhoods in the sense that gloves sewn for ten lire a pair by Anna Astuto sell in Paris or Brussels — with the label 'Made in Italy' — for 5,000 lire. It is the same story for shoes. So too for the umbrellas of black silk which go, for the most part, to London. . . . The problem of identifying the bosses of these industries is a very difficult one. As soon as someone threatens to go to the unions, the bosses change intermediaries. Moreover, the boss who controls this mass of underpaid workers will only admit, officially, to ten to twelve employees at most. Once in a while the truth comes out, but it usually happens purely by chance.

Homeworking in London follows the same pattern, it is concentrated in trades that are marginal to capital. The basis of their survival is competition with the sweatshops of Hong Kong, South Korea and Portugal. Their poor performance is the result of years of neglect by the majority of owners. Despite these facts homeworkers are still in existence in such large numbers that they are quite clearly an integral part of the total economy of Britain and need to be treated as such.

Campaigns

Macciocchi writes:[5]

> The problems are these (a) organise these women in unions as categories of workers, which of course, they are; (b) transform their sub-salaries into salaries with all the rights that go along with real salaries; (c) organise the women, at the same time. Politically, teaching them the rudimentary elements of how labour-power is exploited and hence the reasons for the political battle against capitalism.

Now the scale and nature of the problem are such that specialised campaigns are needed even to begin to tackle the problem.

Toward the end of 1975 a number of groups mainly in the East End boroughs of London started small local initiatives on the question of homeworking. A group in Newham produced a leaflet on homeworkers' rights. A group in Hackney started meeting to discuss the basis of a local campaign, and over in Pimlico a women's group had already started to do some organising. These groups, along with other interested individuals, started meeting together and in 1976 the London Homeworking Campaign was formed and had its official inaugural meeting in October that year.

The aim of the campaign was to bring home work out of the twilight world of semi-legality where women frequently worked long hours for little money under bad if not hazardous conditions. The priorities were for the recognition of homeworkers or employees with the same rights as factory and office workers, and for the establishment of decent social conditions which would end the necessity for taking in homework. These aims were contained in the homeworkers' charter.

The Homeworkers' Charter
HUNDREDS OF THOUSANDS OF PEOPLE, MAINLY WOMEN, HAVE LITTLE CHOICE BUT TO WORK IN THEIR OWN HOME FOR OUTSIDE EMPLOYERS. HOMEWORKERS WORK FOR POOR PAY UNDER BAD WORKING CONDITIONS. WE AIM AT FULL PROTECTION FOR THOSE WHO WORK AT HOME. WE ARE CAMPAIGNING FOR CONDITIONS THAT MAKE HOMEWORK A REAL CHOICE RATHER THAN A FORCED NECESSITY.

We pledge ourselves to agitate and organise for

Decent Pay and Conditions for Those who Work at Home
1 Full status of 'employee' for homeworkers, and the extension of existing protective legislation to cover homeworkers (for example, Health and Safety at Work, Employment Protection Act).
2 Extension of trade union organization to cover homeworking, and the full involvement of homeworkers in Trade Unions.
3 Full information on homeworking and the rights of homeworkers to be widely publicized.
4 Enforced obligation on employers to provide statistical details of homework to the Department of Employment. Lists of homeworkers should be available, through a responsible local agency, to Trades Unions and others concerned to ensure the rights of homeworkers.
5 Pay equal to rates of unionized factory workers, plus a homework premium to cover overhead costs.

Decent Social Provision to End the Necessity for Homeworking
6 Improved local authority provision for
   — Daytime care of young children, pre-school and school-aged children (after school and during school and during school holidays)
   — Day care of handicapped and elderly dependants
   — English language training for immigrants.
7 State benefits (Family Allowance, Family Income Supplement, Supplementary Benefit) to be raised to realistic levels to end the financial necessity of taking in homework.

8 Extension of Government training programmes with pay.
9 Enforcement of employers' disabled workers quotas.

It was the activities of local groups doing research, gathering information, advising homeworkers on their existing rights, pressing for legislative change and, most important, organising homeworkers which was to be the main test of the London Homeworking Campaign.

In order to achieve the objectives set out in the Charter, the campaign needed to work through independent affiliated organisations and homeworkers themselves, hopefully co-ordinated on a borough by borough basis. The campaign contacted all trades councils, women's groups, community relations councils and law centres in London and many others with their literature. Immigrant associations in particular areas as well as the relevant trade union organisations and other groups were also contacted.

The basis for the campaign has been the trade unions, where the campaign has built up credibility with the National Union of Tailor and Garment Workers, The National Union of Hosiery and Knitwear Workers and the General and Municipal Workers Union. It has also made some input into the proceedings of the TUC working party on homeworking. Besides this about half a dozen trades councils in London have affiliated to the campaign. In general there has been little direct success in bringing women's organisations and women's groups into the campaign, although discussion on the very real organising problems which homeworkers present has been raised.

Pimlico Women's Group

The Pimlico Women's Group was one of the first affiliated organisations to become involved on a direct basis with trying to organise homeworkers. They became involved through contact with a woman employed by a pregnancy testing agency to assemble urine sample bottles at the rate of £1.64 per thousand. It took her and her two children approximately three hours to assemble a thousand bottles which were then used for pregnancy tests at £3 each. The homeworkers were not informed of the need for care in handling the bottles and as a result of the haphazard methods of assembly the bottles were often contaminated, leading to wrong results in pregnancy tests.

The group determined to expose this double exploitation of women. With little or no experience they set about getting information on the company and advertised in local shops and on local and national radio to find other homeworkers. One of the group worked inside the laboratory for several days but unfortunately, just as they finished their research with evidence of low safety standards and wage rates the firm upped and moved. Clearly the sort of approach taken by the Pimlico Women's Group was one of the more concrete ways in which homeworkers could be contacted and organised.

Fitzrovia Neighbourhood Centre

The Fitzrovia Neighbourhood Centre carried out a similar campaign in North Soho among garment workers mainly Chinese, Bangladesh and Greek Cypriot women who all spoke very little English. Workers from the centre carried out a general survey from which a pattern emerged of low wages, uncertain employment and haphazard arrangements made through agents. It was usual for those already engaged in homeworking to pass on the names and addresses of employers to those interested. Very little information was given in these interchanges and pay was only alluded to by the remark that 'they pay well and you can have as much work as you want'.

The only contact these workers had with the firm was through the driver who delivered and collected the materials. If they were able to speak English then they could state how much work they required, if not then they simply took what came along. For the majority of homeworkers the workload did vary very greatly. The looseness of the transaction between employer and employee whilst on the one hand giving the worker a degree of independence also served to generate a feeling in some that her job was not a proper one. It is not surprising that many felt that their workload and wages came about by quite informal dealings between the driver and themselves. Project workers in fact accompanied immigrant working women to small factories and enquired about work and rates on their behalf. While there, they were able to note points about working conditions, etc. They found, however, as they became increasingly well known, that it was difficult to continue with any credibility.

Torrington and Morley GMWU

Trade unions have found incredible difficulty in organising home-workers. The main obstacle to trade union protection of home-workers is the immense difficulty of organising this sector of the workforce due to lack of information as to who they are, language difficulties, isolation of the individual workers, and fears of victim-isation. These difficulties are compounded by the fragmented structure of the industries in which the homeworker system oper-ates and the consequent difficulty of unionising even the factory based workforce. Despite the difficulties some workers have joined trade unions. Last year the General and Municipal Workers Union founded its first homeworking branch in the glove-making industry at Torrington, Exeter. Within three months increases totalling 41½ per cent had been negotiated for homeworkers as a step towards bringing their earnings up to the level of factory based workers. Negotiations are planned for holiday pay, electricity allowances, etc.

The initial success, although in a small area, proved that joining a union can bring immediate benefits to homeworkers. Perhaps more important, they realised that through the union not only will they be involved in negotiations affecting pay and conditions, but will be members of an organisation that can fight on a national level both politically and industrially to ensure that action is then taken against the evils inherent in the homeworking system.

The success of that piece of organising might well be put down to the fact that it took place in a fairly closed community in a rural area. A more realistic example would be that of a group of homeworkers in Morley in Yorkshire who also joined the GMWU. Though successful in that the employer agreed to increase their wages, the understanding was that they would leave the union and in fact the most militant woman amongst them, who had led them into the trade union, was herself sacked.

Lambeth Homeworking Campaign

A number of Lambeth organisations were contacted and invited to an initial meeting, including locally-based trade unions, immigrant groups, women's groups, community agencies, relevant educational organisations, and local information and law centres. They out-lined the many obstacles, lack of information on homeworkers

and their employers, the difficulty of contacting isolated homeworkers and the lack of protective legislation, and acknowledged
the slowness that the campaign would have. The group have been
effective in getting publicity in the local press and raising the
issue through a number of channels, including the distribution of
a 'homeworker's rights' leaflet in eight languages.

Their first concrete attempt at organising homeworkers arose
out of an article in the South London press when two homeworkers contacted the Lambeth Campaign. They had both previously worked for a local firm and complained of the low wages.
Leaflets were produced in conjunction with the GMWU stating
the minimum rates decided by the relevant wages council. While
handing out the leaflets they had discussions with the homeworkers who had to collect their own work. They were paid 89p
for fixing a thousand buttons on cards in groups of six, which was
just the legal minimum rate. But in reality it actually took them
between five and nine hours to complete a thousand, making the
hourly rate pitifully low. Although there was initially a good
response, it gradually became more hostile as the management
interfered and after a time it was felt to be no longer productive
and the initiative ended. The people in the campaign felt very
deeply the need to make the necessary legal changes that would in
future facilitate such efforts.

What is to be done

Research into employers is needed to establish where control lies
within the company. Whether for example it is the small factory
that puts out work directly to the home or whether the small factory is at the end of a long chain of intermediaries from a firm
with a household name. This information would largely determine
the way in which a local campaign is organised — for example at
what point pressure could be brought on to the company, where
propaganda will be most effective, whether the organisation to
improve wages and conditions will extend to include the middle-
men and small factory owners, against the large retailers.

The first step in finding this out is to look at how the trade is
organised, how far it depends on intermediaries, where the markets
are for the products. Britains, a well-known toy factory in Wal-
thamstow, puts out work direct and it is worth checking out the
links with other companies and finding out the rate of turnover

and profit in a large company of this sort. But it is more important to find out comparable wages inside the factory, the number of homeworkers employed, and whether there is any possibility of joint action by the unions between home and factory workers. In the Rag Trade, on the other hand, the structure is characteristically highly fragmented and the marketing arrangements very complicated at the local level, where someone may acquire several machines one moment and have to trade them in the next. It is often difficult to decide who is and is not a homeworker and who is a minor capitalist.

The pattern varies from trade to trade, but intervention without and understanding of the structure of the trade in local situations could lead to a loss of jobs and the undermining of family economies that are already precarious. But not only is there a need to research into employers; there clearly needs to be a great deal of research on homeworkers themselves and, despite a number of small-scale studies that have been carried out, there is still a need for comprehensive study to be undertaken.

At the present time most homeworkers are outside employment protection legislation. They tend to be regarded as self employed and have no rights to National Insurance Benefits, holiday pay and training. Legislation is needed to make them employees in the normal sense with all the accompanying rights. The attitude of the trade union movement has changed from one of outright condemnation to one of condemning the exploitative system under which homeworkers operate rather than the homeworkers themselves, and is slowly moving to cover homeworkers more fully. It was partially recognised at the TUC Women's Conference in 1977 which said in the first paragraph of its report:

> Conference notes that the incidence of homeworking among women has tended to increase. Conference reaffirms the terms of the 1976 TUC Women's Conference resolution and requests that action be taken to ensure that all existing regulations are fully implemented and for a comprehensive review and strengthening of the legal status of homeworkers.

In West Germany and France comprehensive legislation on homeworking is already in existence and it would seem a justifiable demand that another EEC country such as Britain should adopt comprehensive legislation. At the first national conference of groups involved in the homeworking campaign held in Birmingham in November 1977 a working party was set up with the precise aim of establishing some model legislation for Britain.

Although some contact has been made with individual home-workers and some employers, the size of the problem remains. The dimensions of the homeworking economy are still unknown, employers remain secretive and homeworkers themselves remain difficult to contact. Clearly the problem which still remains to be tackled is that of organising homeworkers around their employment situation. More successful has been the raising of public consciousness around the homeworking issue, the renewal in interest of the trade union movement, the increase in research projects and the possible legislative changes that are envisaged. Clearly from the Lambeth experience and others, the ability to organise is greatly hampered by the current legal position of homeworkers and the need to lobby and campaign for such changes has increasingly been seen as a key aspect in the totality of the project. Whether these developments would have happened without the community based intervention taking place is an open question, but to be effective in the long run there must be a coming together of community based interests alongside sizeable trade union support.

Notes

1   Emily Hope, Mary Kennedy and Anne de Winter, 'Homeworkers in North London', in *Dependence and Exploitation in Work and Marriage*, ed. Diana Leonard Barker and Sheila Allen, Longman, 1976.
2   Brian Bolton, *End to Homeworking?*, Fabian Pamphlet, 1975.
3   Marie Brown, *Sweated Labour*, Low Pay Unit, 1974.
4   Maria Macciocchi, *Letters from Inside the Italian Communist Party to Louis Althusser*, New Left Books, 1973, p. 45.
5   Ibid.

Part III Nationalized Industries and Public Services: the Need for Social Accountability

7 The National Coal Board: what price consultation?

Ken Coates

Introduction

A secret document

In the autumn of 1976 I received a telephone call informing me of the existence of a complex plan for the phased closure of all the collieries in the Ashfield area of Nottinghamshire, together with a number of others which were scattered along the western fringe of the county. This plan was based upon data furnished by the National Coal Board to the Structure Planning Unit of the Nottinghamshire County Council. My informant wished to know whether the Miners' Union had been informed of the sweeping transformation which would one day overtake them. Apparently the plan anticipated the exhaustion of coal reserves across a wide area, resulting in serious concentration of shut-downs bunched towards the mid-1980s. I took my caller seriously and began to check what he had told me.

I have for some time been convinced that some earlier closures in our broader area were profoundly mistaken, notably that at Clifton, where power station coal could have been deposited in a power station yard for a considerable while to come if the Board had not, largely unsuccessfully, tried to push its labour force into moving to Cotgrave. In the event, the pit closed and many miners left the industry altogether. For this reason I believe that the fullest consultation is necessary from the very earliest stages if the Board is to avoid such mistakes by profiting from the experience and advice of the mine-workers. So I asked leading members of the NUM whether they had been notified of the Ashfield proposals. They had not.

I then asked a County Councillor who is employed in the mining industry, whether he had been informed. He had not. Further enquiries revealed that the document in question was 'confidential', and was not even to be shown to County Councillors.

So it seems a public body, the NCB, accountable to us all, prepares a secret document and gives it to another public body, accountable to us all, on condition that our elected representatives are not allowed to see it.

This paper looks at the key importance of the NCB's future plans in terms of their effect on Nottinghamshire's employment situation and their implications for existing mining communities. The paper shows how the NCB hid behind the false myth of the technical inevitability of pit closures and thereby avoided consideration of the social costs and the wider implications of their investment decisions. The paper explains the failure of attempts to bring these issues out into the open. It concludes by emphasising the importance of developing democratic pressures so that miners and mining communities have a real say in planning the NCB's investment programme which determines the future of their work and mining villages in which they live.

The myth of the technical inevitability of pit closure

During my attempts to bring the proposals out into the open for public discussion I was able to dig out a considerable amount of information on the secret document from various published documents which formed the industrial inputs to the structure plan.

The structure plan, as subsequently revised by the planners, revealed that future mining employment in Nottinghamshire was expected to fall by 6,300 between 1976 and 1986 and by a further 6,400 between 1986 and 1996. However the NCB was not perturbed by how it was going to lose this labour. The age structure of the mining workforce is such that 63 per cent of those presently employed are over forty years of age, so only 37 per cent would be available for work in 1996. Therefore, although total employment was likely to fall, recruitment into the industry needed to continue. The problem was rather one of recruiting sufficient young men into the industry.

The NCB's annual report for 1975–6 stated that 'the low voluntary wastage and the substantial recruitment of ex-mine workers in the last two years mean that this source of already trained manpower is now much smaller and recruitment in future will increasingly require to be from men and boys new to the industry. It is expected that recruitment will become more difficult as the economy recovers from the recession of 1975.' Writing on this matter in the *Sunday Times*, Roger Eglin pointed out at the time of the miners' ballot on the question of implementing their bid to reduce retirement to fifty-five by 1980, that this would mean 80,000, one-third of the labour force, retiring in the next three and a half years: 'NCB officials pale at the Herculean prospect of recruiting some 40,000 to 50,000 men a year to maintain the labour force. Some regions would be harder hit than others.'

It was clear from the structure plan documents that the NCB secret document contained a detailed grid giving the age structure, colliery by colliery. For the employment report that accompanied the structure plan broke the coalfields into four zones. The report stated that in some of the zones containing older miners, where reserves would eventually be exhausted, the age structure of the miners was such that only a remarkable success in colliery recruitment would enable them to operate fully. In the Erewash zone 69 per cent of the existing labour force were over forty. In the Ashfield region 41 per cent of the labour force would retire before 1986 and 26 per cent between 1986 and 1996. And it was in these two zones that mining employment was expected to fall most rapidly. In Erewash the plan stated that employment would fall from 34,000 in 1976 to 1,150 in 1996, while in Ashfield the decline was from 9,100 jobs in 1976 to 2,300 in 1996. This decline was also to be concentrated in the middle of the next decade.

The reason given for the rapid decline in employment is the exhaustion of coal reserves. However, despite the plan's emphasis on the exhaustion of coal reserves, the evidence suggests that estimates about the life of available reserves have much smaller weight than those of the residual life of an ageing workforce. The first kind of estimates may be variable and contingent, while the second constitute extremely hard facts which rigorously imply that pit closures will become necessary to redeploy a shrinking manpower.

In this situation it may well appear logical from the NCB's point of view to close the least productive pits in the Erewash and Ashfield region, particularly since labour would be required for some new pits in the Vale of Belvoir in the east of the county where the NCB had discovered coalfields which would produce more coal with fewer men. Thus, in the words of the employment report, 'the magnitude of the labour deficit will be reduced by transfer of miners from collieries whose reserves are likely to become exhausted over the Plan period to existing or new workings where labour is required'.

As a boy I worked in the three-quarter seam in Silverhill and I would be the last man to wish those conditions on anyone else; given a choice between thin seams on the Notts-Derbyshire border and thick ones (say at Belvoir), one would be bound, in the abstract, to prefer the new coalfield. The fact remains that we are not talking about these decisions in the abstract but in their given community context.

The implication of such a massive employment loss in the Ashfield and Erewash regions, concentrated in the middle of the next decade as implied in the plan, would have major repercussions on the area. The background papers to the structure plan made it clear that what constitutes 'exhaustion of reserves' is not a simple inevitable technical question but is open for discussion and dependent on several factors. The information contained in the NCB's secret document should have been available to the miners and county councillors so that all could have been involved in the discussion. Instead the board argued that since the pit closures depended solely on the exhaustion of reserves the information supplied to the county council officers were long-term predictions which were bound to be unreliable and, as such, not to be divulged since they would only arouse unnecessary fears.

Having pointed out the fallacy in this argument I now want to look briefly at the implications of the NCB investment decisions and the effect of withholding information.

What were the community issues involved in the NCB's decision?

The NCB is Nottinghamshire's main employer. While the coal industry has declined substantially naturally since the war, both in employment (from 780,000 in 1951 to 315,000 in 1973) and in output (from 209 million tons to 118 million tons per annum over the same period), there were still 45,000 NCB employees in Nottinghamshire in 1973. Nationally, output is now planned to remain at its present level until 1985. Consequently NCB employment will continue to be vital for the area. However, the people of Nottinghamshire were being kept in the dark about investment plans and merely being told that 12,700 jobs were to be lost in two decades.

The plans of the NCB were bound to have a major impact on the local economy. The fact that a scheduled statement dealing with this crucial sector of the economy was withheld from councillors and the public meant that it became impossible for them to comment on the economic future of the area.

Not only did the secret document impede the planning of the local economy and throw doubt on the whole structure plan consultation but it also showed how the NCB, despite being a nationalised industry with some public accountability, took investment decisions with no regard to social costs. For the plans of the Board did have enormous social implications. If the Board is going to sink not one, but three or four pits in the Vale of Belvoir, from where will the miners come to staff them? If they come from Ashfield, will they be asked to commute in order not to offend the local gentry by their presence during the hunt? If that happened, how long would the journey take? Or will they be invited to move? If so, will they be able to take Gran and Grandad, or will Teversall or Stanton Hill become old people's ghettoes? Will there be jobs for miners' wives in the Vale? Will the new houses be built as part of a self-contained mining settlement, or will they be scattered round existing rural villages and townships? I do not know the answers to these questions but it is clear that the social consequences of such a migration would be enormous and they are certainly not confined to problems of jobs and rehousing. We live in a community where old people help younger ones, where each depends on the other. Most of the time we don't even notice it, it is so familiar. But it will hurt very much on the day it isn't there.

Yet despite these major social implications, the Board never considered asking the miners and their wives and their aged relatives and children what they thought about the proposed closure of pits. There has been recent legislation since 1974, the Industry Act and the Employment Protection Act, both of which guarantee trade unionists 'the right to know'. Employers are bound to reveal information for collective bargaining purposes and the Government recognises, in principle, the right of workers to bargain about investment decisions, questions affecting closures, and a variety of other major economic matters. Nevertheless, the NCB were taking decisions in secret which ignored the spirit of this legislation and the social costs of switching production from one pit to another. Even though it is a nationalised industry the NCB was no different from a private firm which planned its future on grounds of profitability alone, without considering the social implications of redundancies.

The attempt to bring the issue into the open

Given the importance of the secret document I hoped that the Council and the National Union of Mineworkers (NUM) would take swift action to ensure that the documents were released. I wrote several letters to force the issue into the open.

Soon after the news became generally known, the Labour Group of members on the County Council met and resolved to approach the National Coal Board to request their permission to release the Topic Report to Council members. But permission was not forthcoming and once this became understood, leading members of the Labour Group changed their public position on the question. However, some rank-and-file councillors continued to insist that the Report should be released.

Meantime, the Mansfield District Council had officially resolved to ask for access to the Report and the Ashfield Constituency Labour Party unanimously agreed to approach the Secretary of State for Energy, Tony Benn, to secure its release to councillors. In spite of this it soon began to look as if the leaders of the County Labour Group were anxious not to press too hard in order to allow their council members permission to unlock the filing cabinets of their planning department.

The County Labour Group chose four councillors to approach the NCB in order to secure the raising of the embargo on the circulation of the Topic Paper. These councillors accepted the NCB's rejection of a proposal for a meeting. Various lame excuses were given including firstly that much of the information contained in the original Topic Paper was given to the Council before the trial borings in the Vale of Belvoir and was subsequently out of date and, secondly that because Tony Benn had been involved by myself and the Ashfield Labour Party, the Coal Board was having to review the whole procedure of releasing information to County Councils up and down the country. The Labour Group were not prepared to tackle the problem of a prominent industrial interest giving information to employed officials under conditions of secrecy which prevented even elected councillors from access to it.

Meanwhile, early in 1977 the NUM Area Council requested an early meeting with the two Area NCB directors in order to discuss 'future employment prospects'. On 15 March the NCB issued a press release on this meeting, extracts of which are given below:

> The Executive Committee of the Nottinghamshire Area of the NUM and the Directors and supporting staff of the two Nottinghamshire Areas of the NCB met recently to discuss anxieties about future employment prospects in the mining industry.
>
> The chairman, NUM President Mr Len Clarke, explained that the meeting had been called as a result of questions about security of employment arising from comment on the Nottinghamshire Draft Structure Plan and references to a report allegedly forecasting a large reduction in local mining jobs.
>
> Mr Ian Dowson, South Notts Deputy Director, explained that the report referred to — a 'Topic Report' on the mining industry — was prepared by County Council officers as one element of the build up to the Draft Structure Plan. He said the mining manpower estimates provided by the Board reflected the situation as it then appeared two years earlier. Similar estimates provided for an earlier planning study had proved to be about 50 per cent wrong as a result of changed circumstances, such as oil price increases and improved mining methods.
>
> On this occasion projections up to 20 years into the future had been requested but the published Draft Plan had, in fairness, noted that the figures were only projections and were subject to continuous review. In fact, they were now already out of date.
>
> Executive member Mr Vic Lloyd said the County Council had to try to anticipate replacement job requirements so it was important that their information was regularly brought up to date.
>
> This was agreed and the meeting also felt it might be beneficial for Union and Board representatives to jointly meet County Council members prior to the Council meeting to approve the Structure Plan. Mr Whelan, the union's Financial Secretary, said he was satisfied that local NCB

management were not keeping secrets from the union and saw no point in getting alarmed about long term predictions which were bound to be unreliable. The Union Vice President, Mr Neville Hawkins, agreed, pointing out that fears of the closure of Harworth Colliery a few years ago had proved groundless.

Summing up, Mr Clarke said the meeting had confirmed that there was unlikely to be any serious contraction in the period up to 1986 but it was accepted that the following decade could see some exhaustion of reserves although this was likely to be offset by expansion at existing long-life collieries and the possible development of new ones.

The meeting agreed to the issue of this joint press release summarising the discussion.

Various things are missing from this report. First, although the Topic Report was handed to the NUM chairman, it was not circulated to members of the Executive. In May 1977 some of these members have still not seen the full report. What the Board spokesmen did at the meeting was to project various slides onto a screen, illustrating some matters which had been covered in the Report and some which had not. When Jack Grainger tried to raise the vexed question of the social consequences of closures, he was ruled out of order by the union chairman, on the grounds that the meeting was called to consider employment prospects, not social consequences. Other members of the NUM team found apparent errors in the arithmetic of the evidence which was furnished to them. Vic Lloyd pointed out that if the figures were 'out of date' this would invalidate parts of the structure plan. One member asked that the final decision be not minuted as unanimous. The joint press release, therefore, is not quite as informative as it might have been, and it does some of the members of the union side less credit than they deserve.

The fact remains that the document is painfully obscure at precisely the points where it needs to explain. Which figures, we must ask, are 'out of date'? It has always been understood that figures about reserves are subject to serious fluctuation. But are the figures about the age-structure of the work-force also so subject? Of course not. For the existing labour force, these figures are entirely accurate. Mr Dowson would have been far more persuasive if he had given these figures instead of vaguely querying the validity of those already furnished by his own colleagues to the structure planners. Even then, the $64,000 question would remain: what guarantees are to be given to this intake of new, predominantly young, workers, that they have any real or acceptable security in an industry which can apparently plan major upheavals in its structure without any prior consultation with its employees?

Reading between the lines of the NCB's statements, some members of the NUM Executive told me that they thought we had gained a qualified victory, in that first, the Topic Report was no longer flatly denied; second, the Board seemed to have modified its time-scales for certain closures, giving a limited stay of execution for some pits; and third, it would be more difficult to hatch plots like this one again.

I would like to think this true, but I have an important reservation about it. If the Board is varying its timescales, this proves they were nothing to do with geological reserves, which would be invariable if that argument were valid: and everything to do with manpower, as I have suspected all along. The simplest explanation of the 'reprieve', then, is that the older collieries were to have been used as 'refrigerators' in which to store labour for a development of the Eastern area of the old Notts coalfield. Now they may refrigerate a little longer, to store labour also for Belvoir, the development of which will take longer, since work cannot begin until extensive enquiries and other formalities are complete.

Conclusion

In this story, the industrial relations problems of consultation have necessarily been highlighted, and the procedures of the National Coal Board are bound to be faulted.

Faulty, too, have been the consultative procedures of the County Council, because, in spite of a real attempt to discuss general planning questions, councillors themselves have been consistently denied access to a key source of information.

Some leading trade unionists have now given the impression that they are satisfied with this state of affairs. Some councillors, too, seem to agree that it is all quite tolerable. Why, then, should the rest of us complain? The truth is, in a nutshell, that about one-third of the miners of the large condemned area are young enough to be compelled, within a relatively short time, either to uproot themselves, or to commute for unreasonable distances, in order to be able to carry on their chosen jobs. First, they have a right to know what to expect. Second, they need to know in time to be able to put up any alternative proposals which seem sensible to them. Third, and crucially important, they have a right to insist that any new mining developments will avoid the dreadful and callous mistakes of the Robens era, and that redevelopment will be planned for and with *communities*, rather than concerning itself simply with the adjustment of a pay-roll.

This means that we need to develop democratic pressures to ensure that miners and miners' wives, and all the senior and junior members of their families, all have a real say in what is to happen, how investments are made, and to what use the industry's resources are put.

Subsequently, the Labour Party incurred heavy losses in the 1977 County Council elections, and control passed to the Conservatives.

The Revised Draft Written Statement of the Structure Plan appeared in the autumn of 1977, with quite new estimates of the potential contraction of mining employment. Now, we were informed, the decline would involve 7,900 jobs, only 600 of which would disappear in the first half of the plan period.

Welcome though these figures were, I was curious about their provenance, since we had previously been informed that the NCB were reluctant to speak to councillors or liaise with the County Council, after the news of the Topic Report had broken. I enquired about this matter, and was informed by the planners that the new data had been gathered from 'a press release issued by the Coal Board'.

Meantime, a newly elected Labour County Councillor, Mrs Stella Smedley, put in a written request for a copy of the scheduled report. She was informed that she could not see it until the NCB approved its release to her, although negotiations about this matter are apparently still going on.

Such pressures will exert themselves through the NUM, through the deputies' and managers' unions and through local government and local political parties. But, as the failure to publish the secret Topic Paper showed, 'such pressures' are not disembodied processes, boiling up willy-nilly whatever we do or don't do. We shall get the consideration we fight for and not a ha'p'orth more. Enough has been written here to show that there is a case for concern, and that something should be done. Will it get done?

8 Resisting the run-down of docklands

John Connolly

Introduction

In early 1976 the Port of London Authority (PLA) decided they
wanted to close the West India and Millwall group of docks in
Tower Hamlets, one of the last two operating docks within London itself. This was part of the PLA's strategy to concentrate
cargo handling in its docks 20 miles downstream at Tilbury and
eventually at the new port of Maplin, if it was built. As part of
this strategy three dock systems, St Katharine's, the Surrey and
the London Docks, had already been closed in the late 1960s and
early 1970s, releasing for development large and valuable areas of
land close to London's business centre.

The PLA justified the move downstream by pointing to the
increasing size of ships, the declining amount of conventional (as
opposed to containerised) cargo, and the extra distance that ships
had to travel to reach London's upstream docks. The West India
and Millwall docks can take only medium-sized ships and special-
ise in conventional cargo (especially fruit). They do not have a
large amount of 'back-up' land essential for a major container
base.

The PLA was therefore confident that it would win general
acceptance for its closure plans during the three month consultation period. In fact, however, it met a concerted resistance campaign, which brought together the docks' trade unions and many
community based groups in the surrounding area. The campaign
argued that the closure of the West India dock was against the
interests of the dockworkers, the port of London as a whole and
the local community. Thus closure would cut back labour-intensive,
conventional cargo-handling in favour of the highly capital-
intensive container traffic. Yet much of world trade will not be

139

containerised, and closure would therefore mean the further diversion of ships to other ports. London would also be less able to take advantage of the burgeoning short sea trade with Europe, which would increasingly use the East Coast and Channel ports. This in turn would mean more lorry traffic and larger roads from these ports to London. Instead, the campaign argued, the upstream docks should be developed for this trade, bringing ships to central London, thus minimising the social impact of moving goods.

More immediately the campaign pointed out that the docks are at the heart of the economy of East London. Their disappearance would further undermine an area which had lost over 30,000 jobs in the previous fifteen years and whose unemployment rate was well over twice the national average. The campaign argued that rebuilding of the docks would provide an important core for industrial revival.

These demands thus linked workers in the docks with the area's community and trade union groups which were anxious to stop further industrial decline. Organisation was based around the dock shop stewards and the locally based Tower Hamlets Action Committee on Jobs, whose membership spanned local trade union branches, the trades council, churches, tenants' groups and so on. A vigorous campaign involved extensive leafletting, lobbying, local meetings and a march on Parliament. This mobilised considerable support which brought in the Borough Council and local MPs. In mid-1976 the West India and Millwall Docks were given a reprieve. The campaign went on to demand a general programme of industrial development in the area, and the Council established an employment working group (with campaign representatives) to implement it. But in the event progress has been extremely slow. In this interview, John Connolly, one of the leading West India dock shop stewards, discusses the campaign and its aftermath.

Resisting the run-down of docklands

What was the effect when the Port of London Authority announced the closure?

Traffic using the West India Dock immediately started to look elsewhere. What's more, shipping companies saw this as a continuing trend, part of a PLA policy to run down the facilities and they started to look at other ports, nearer the coast, places like Sheerness. And so the threat to the West India was seen as a question of running down London as a whole. Even closures of a berth often means the shipping line using it leaves the port altogether. They don't want to go anywhere else within the dock; they would sooner go somewhere they can see ten to fifteen years of continuity of service. The dock trade union committees, which covered London as a whole, not just the West India Dock, knew the question was really the future of London as a port. Tilbury would be the only place open for ships coming to London. We already had full capacity working at Tilbury, so that any upstream closure meant a loss of traffic and revenues and a further rundown of the Port of London.

One of the PLA's main arguments for moving downstream was the tight schedules that shipping had to keep. There is a lot of laid-up shipping not carrying any freight, so competition is fierce. Travelling up river an extra two to four hours would add to their turn-around time. But this argument is not borne out by experience elsewhere. Ships are prepared to travel past ports where they could be accommodated and go further on in order to get a particular service.

To underline this point, in 1974, the West India Dock was expected to contribute £800,000 to the PLA's central fund. In fact the income from traffic in 1974 was finally estimated at £1.6 million, so it was making money.

Another PLA argument for closure was the impact of increased containerisation. In fact that had already largely happened, and much of the West India's import traffic had already been lost to Southampton. The threat to the West was more a consequence of the decasualisation of dock labour, when everyone was made a permanent man and was paid, work or no work. Containerisation took the work away from dockers and put the process out of gear: no one knew it would happen so quickly. There wasn't enough conventional traffic to go round, stuff going 'over the quay' (where the PLA makes money) rather than into barges.

The dock closure then was part of the strategy to reduce the number of registered dockers working on conventional cargo. So although there was no direct threat to registered dockers, closure of the West India would have certainly meant a loss of jobs. Dockers would not transfer to other areas because they would have increased costs and travel times. In addition there would have been a much greater job loss among staff and maintenance men.

What was the Government's attitude to the PLA's plans?

The PLA are to some extent responsible to the Government.
They get government loans to finance severance payments to
dockers and staff and they were given £8 million of government
money towards the development of container facilities at Tilbury.
All this was conditional on some rationalisation and contraction
elsewhere — though how this took place was up to the PLA. They
could close a dock or close down some berths in both upstream
docks. Some grants to private industry are for expansion but the
ones to the PLA were for streamlining. The Government weren't
prepared to support the Port of London in its present situation, or
to improve facilities in the upstream docks.

How was the opposition to closure organised, within the docks?

To begin with, it was very parochial. The men in the other
docks talked about supporting the West India Docks in their fight
but there wasn't too much practical support. After all, if we were
successful, the other upstream group of docks, the Royals, would
come under threat of closure. We attempted to involve the shop
stewards in the Royal Group and some who could see the danger
to the port of London as a whole did get involved. We then looked
at alternatives. The Transport and General Workers Union Docks
Group tried to broaden out the issue industrially and a committee
— the Liaison Committee for West India Dock — was set up to
look at the effect of closure on *all* the trades involved. It did a lot
of work but eventually, because of pressures on the staff side
(staff could see a chance for redundancy which quite a lot of them
were looking for), they didn't fancy a fight and the Liaison Committee lost much of its initial push.

Is that when you decided to look for support in the community?

We could see that we may not have got the support required
from the people working in the West India Dock and that made
us think there was a need to involve ourselves in broader issues
and get the support of the community, especially those involved in
other factory closures that were taking place — Bryant & May's
and Far Famed Cakes. It was seen to be a broader issue than just
the closure of a dock — it involved the whole community. Remember we'd seen it all before, in the Surrey Docks and the London
Docks, where shops and firms that relied on the docks went out of
business. It's said that three jobs in the community depend on
every dock job, and the West India employed three thousand
people.

Some dockers felt we should take up the issue on our own but in fact there was a much greater chance of success by involving people and directing the community to pressure the PLA, letting them say to the PLA, 'You've got some responsibility to us as well, not only to the people you employ, but to the people in the area. What you've done in the past has only taken away something we had.' A number of us saw that as the right way to approach the campaign, not on a purely selfish basis but taking account of the fact that closure would have a very drastic effect on the area as a whole. A number of shop stewards therefore got involved in the work of the Tower Hamlets Action Committee on Jobs.

Was there any opposition from the dockers to this approach?

Not at all. We went to the men and told them what we were planning to do. We said it could mean a fight, even industrial action at the end of the road. At the Liaison Committee we laid that on the line at the first meeting we had. We got a few grunts and moans from people about being involved in organisations that were not closely connected with work. Nevertheless the complaints disappeared. We didn't kid anybody. We told them that as we saw it the docks were not going to close and that, if necessary, we would have to take some industrial action in the future, but we said we could see the issue being overcome if we involved the people in the community who were going to be affected anyway – initially with the effect on jobs, then the effect on shops and rates, etc. We got their support. There may have been a query as to whom we were going to involve ourselves with but as long as we told them that the Tower Hamlets Action Committee was involved in unemployment and jobs only they were satisfied.

How did the Council come to support the campaign?

I don't think for one minute they became involved because they believed it was the right thing to do. It wasn't voluntary. They saw what was going on in the area; the general decline of industry and the pressure of the campaign, and they could see they would have to come to terms with them. The Council also became involved because the closure would have meant a loss of rate revenue of about £300,000 a year. Already they had no major industry left apart from the docks. So this was another pressure, on top of the activity of the campaign – the meetings, the leaflets and the march. In the end though the Council was an important ally, in keeping up the pressure in Parliament.

How important then was the community support in stopping the closure?

The trade unions were convinced the docks weren't going to shut and they acted accordingly but there's no doubt we would have had a much harder fight if we hadn't been involved with the groups outside the dock gates. The build-up of the campaign and the real fight put up by outside groups certainly stopped the closure of the dock. The PLA was surprised at the general reaction of people — they expected a reaction from people in the dock, of course, but not generally. It also raises the question of the support the Resource Centre could supply. This was something you couldn't do without in a campaign of this sort; contacting people, writing letters, telephoning, leafletting, printing, generally bringing groups together and straightening out what people think into some form of policy and direction, backed up by facts and statistics. The campaign had eventually to take that form to have a chance of being effective.

Why did the joint campaign keep going?

After the initial reaction to the announcement there was a lot of activity to involve the other groups and to involve the men in the West India Dock. The community were aware of the broader issues involved in the dock closure because they could see closures taking place in other industries, outside the docks. These closures were not necessarily because of the closure of docks but just generally because the East End was becoming an area of decline. Firms did not want to stay here. There were rationalisations going on within those industries and they didn't choose to stay in the East End, or even London. Eventually when the dock closure did not happen there was still a general threat of closure and this helped to sustain the campaign. In fact by the time of the Tower Hamlets march on Parliament we had moved away from the particular issue of the West India Dock and got into the whole question of unemployment and the prevailing situation in Tower Hamlets. It had taken off in that way — we had moved into the whole question of bringing back industry and bringing development into the area. As a result of that sort of pressure we were invited to take part in the working group the local Council had set up on the employment problems of the borough.

What has been the effect of the Council's Employment Working Party?

When the Council set up the Working Party, they wanted the involvement of people from outside the Council to give direction in their employment policy. But in practice their emphasis has not been on long-term industrial development. Look what's happened during the last 18 months over the proposed development of the riverside — the emphasis has been on providing nice houses, not on jobs.

What then are the lessons and long term benefits of the campaign?

First, the fact that we took on the PLA, that's the main issue. In the past, once there was a policy decision taken, that's what came about. No one questioned it. No one said, 'We're not accepting that.' People would say, 'They've made a decision, what can we do about it, they're the people with the money?' Now it seems a campaign, properly supported, can change the minds of the decision-makers. How long for, that's another question. If, for example, the financial inducements for transfer to other docks had been higher we might not have got the mandate to go ahead so easily.

Second, we know how to organise a campaign, what has to be done to get it on the road if we are faced with that situation again. We know the organisations and people are there, ready to be involved. Third, we've developed our ideas. We know for example there are still smaller ships being built. Much of the new traffic is in small ships built for the Middle East fruit trade which need a quick turn-around and these can be accommodated in the West India Dock.

Fourth, I think if they try to close docks again, the debate is now set up right. It won't be seen as an attempt to close a particular dock, but about the prospects for the port of London as a whole. After all there are only a certain number of jobs at Tilbury. We can't all be employed there, so there is a good opportunity to get something going between all three docks on a common issue.

9 Direct labour: goodbye to contractors

Linda Clarke

Its origins

In theory 'Direct Labour' has referred to any work undertaken directly by the public sector without the intervention of a private contractor. However, as it has become accepted that more and more local authority services, such as rubbish collection, road maintenance, etc., cannot be carried out by the private sector and have therefore become functions of the local authority, the term direct labour has come to apply specifically to building work. Much local authority building work, which includes housing, schools, public buildings, and so on, is still done by private contractors.

Until the 1890s, the main function of local authorities was to act as rate-collecting agencies for paying the accounts of private contractors who were employed for all work. Direct labour organisations (or direct works, as they are also known) were originally set up in order to check the exorbitant tenders of these contractors, to prevent the formation of 'rings' and to provide good quality work. They were seen as a more positive solution to unemployment than public relief works and as a means of combating the bad conditions, casual employment and lack of unionisation in the private building industry. The campaign for direct labour, which coincided with the growing strength of the labour movement, became a focus for the 'Fair Wages Movement' fighting for trade union conditions, for the agitation over housing to remedy slum conditions and homelessness, and for the municipal socialists seeking to extend local authority services.[2] It became one of the main platforms of the Progressives who gained control of the new London County Council (LCC) in 1889, defeating the Moderates who represented the interests of local contractors and private companies. One of their first acts was to bring in a clause enforcing trade union conditions and pay on all contracts given out by the council. The contractors retaliated by putting in outrageously high tenders. To break the monopolistic position of the contractors, the LCC set up their own Works Department, whose first task in 1892 was the building of the York Road sewer. The lowest estimate received for this was £11,000 — the Works Department completed the work for £6,854.[3]

The lead given by the LCC was soon followed by Battersea in 1894 and West Ham in 1896. Their work was varied — from the building of a power station in Battersea to the LCC's contract for all school furniture. To undertake this, the departments were equipped with a large number of workshops: the LCC even owned its own brickworks. Interestingly enough, the idea of cost efficiency which has come to be one of the main issues today concerning direct works was not then of paramount importance. For if outside tenders were lower than direct labour estimates this was taken as an indication of scamped work and poor wages and conditions. As Mr Williams, architect, explained:[4]

> The profit and loss fallacy is not indulged in at Battersea. I gathered that it was quite understood in Battersea that good materials, good and expeditious workmanship and proper conditions of labour were the points to be aimed at, and whether the eventual cost came out above or below the estimate the community benefited thereby in the end.

With the increasing number and growing success of direct labour departments, contractors launched their first full-scale campaign, making direct works one of the main issues of the 1908 LCC elections. The Moderates in the name of 'municipal reform' claimed that it was costly and took away local employment, and when they subsequently gained control of the council they proceeded ruthlessly to destroy the Works Department and to sack its 3,000 workers.

The development of direct labour[5]

So began the repeated threats to direct labour made by private contractors anxious to ride through their own crises by seeking public sector work, of little interest to them during booms in the private sector. In spite of these threats the number of direct labour departments has steadily risen. Between 1919 and 1920, with growing unrest over housing conditions, seventy new departments were set up.[6] Direct labour was seen as the only way to get housing built in the face of the excessive tenders submitted by private contractors. Both working conditions and wages in the departments were better than those in the private sector, including a 44-hour week and payment for 'wet time'.

Again, after the Second World War, many direct labour organisations were set up as building prices soared and local authorities needed a method of checking the prices quoted by contractors. By 1949 the number of departments had doubled compared with 1939, coinciding with the emergence of new labour strongholds. Many of these, for instance St Pancras direct works, included advisory committees of trade unions. The expansion of the private sector during the 1950s, however, following the Tory return to power in 1951, reduced the supply of labour available to direct labour organisations (DLOs). Local authorities were forced to pay only trade union rates at the lowest local level with bonus schemes limited to 20 per cent of this. Private contractors operating with no such constraints were able to draw labour away from direct labour departments. The experience showed just how important it was to keep wages high for the protection of direct works departments. On top of this, in 1959, the Government suddenly imposed the requirement that direct labour must win every third contract in competition with local and national firms before they would be given loan sanction. Not only did this jeopardise continuity of employment in direct works, but it contradicted demands by private industry for selective tendering and negotiated contracts and even 'package deals'[7] — demands which were increasingly reflected in government policy. On the one hand then the industry was arguing and continues to argue, that direct labour could only be efficient in competition; on the other, that private contractors could operate more efficiently if they were not tendering in open competition.

Another obstacle to the expansion of direct labour forces was the growing use and encouragement in the 1950s and 1960s of industrialised systems, not often employed in DLOs, with some notable exceptions. Many authorities were either too small and therefore lacked the resources to break away from traditional techniques, or were unable to build up sufficient plant because of repeated closure threats. (Birmingham direct works, for instance, was closed down in 1969 and plant sold off to remove competition from private builders in the area. The closure resulted in such a great disruption to the house-building programme that it was re-opened in 1973 and now again, along with the GLC, is under threat of a complete shut-down.) Manchester direct works did, however, take part in the initiative to form a consortium of local authorities, pooling the resources of direct labour departments, in order to produce schools with industrialised systems. This scheme, known as CLASP, became what is probably the only relatively successful example in this country of systems building. However, none of the work was undertaken in the end by direct labour. Manchester's proposal for a direct labour department to manufacture building components for other authorities was nevertheless accepted with the passing of the Manchester Corporation Act of 1965, in spite of opposition from the National Federation of Building Trade Employers (NFBTE).

The enquiry triggered by the Manchester proposal led the government to revoke the restrictive 'one in three' tendering requirement and to encourage direct labour 'to play a full part in the house-building programme'.[8] Direct labour departments had continued to expand in number even under the earlier constraints, but, under these more favourable conditions, they reached their peak, employing nearly 200,000 in 1967. But in 1969 the 'one in three' clause was restored. With the boom years for construction of 1970 to 1974, the costs of new construction increased by 80 per cent and, as the private sector abandoned municipal housing, only the building programmes of those councils which had promoted powerful direct labour organisations were largely unaffected. The end of the property boom in 1974 was followed by a marked down turn in the construction industry. Private contractors again turned to local authorities for contracts and direct labour came under renewed attack.

The advantages of direct labour

Many of the problems which now face DLOs can be traced back to local authority reorganisation in 1972, when functions such as Transport, Police, Fire and Highways came under different authorities. The DLOs of the old authorities lost their right to construct new premises relating to these functions, since the Local Authority Act did not permit one authority to provide new

construction to another. Twenty-five authorities received dispen-
sation from this, but the General Powers Bill which was intended
to allow direct labour to tender for the work of another authority
was defeated in 1976.

There are now, out of a total of 717 local authorities, 537 with
DLOs, employing 172,581 operatives. These constitute 12 per
cent of the country's construction workforce. Some departments,
such as Manchester, Lincoln, Newcastle and Sheffield are very
large, on a par with the big contractors. Others confine their work
mainly to maintenance and have only a very small workforce. The
Greater London Council (GLC), for instance, until recently did 90
per cent of all maintenance on its 205,000 dwellings at a cost of
some £40m per annum. In 1976 they managed to save £3.5m on
the estimated cost of this work. 'If the work currently carried out
by the direct labour force in the maintenance branch was placed
with the lowest tender term contractors, the additional cost to the
GLC would be over £8m per annum.'[9] More typical than the GLC
is Lambeth, employing over 1,000 operatives and with capital
assets of £145,000. In 1975-6 for example, it carried out nearly
£19m worth of work, saving nearly £1½m on tenders.[10] The best
known, perhaps, of all DLOs, and one of the largest, is Manchester,
which employs over 5,000 workers and 630 apprentices, of whom
5 per cent are disabled, and undertakes a wide variety of work
from schools to manufactured components with the necessary
plant and workshop back-up.

Manchester epitomises the better working conditions in DLOs
compared with the private sector. Workers receive superannuation,
holiday pay, sickpay, and long-service bonus, none of which is normally paid by private building contractors. These extra benefits
cost £1.3m in 1975–6 and added 12½ per cent to on-cost rates and
6 per cent to tender price (compare this to the estimated 5 per cent
net profit margin of contractors).[11] Considering that apprentice
training in Manchester covering fourteen different crafts costs
£650,000 per annum and adds another 4 per cent to on-cost rates,
wranglings by private contractors over the cost efficiency of direct
labour become a nonsense, for the departments have consistently
shown savings on top of these additional costs. In contrast, relatively few private contractors pay a training levy to the Construction Industry Training Board (CITB) and even this is much lower
than the cost to DLOs of training, since they are not eligible for
CITB grants. In addition, accident rates in DLOs are very much

lower than in the construction industry generally, which has the worst safety record of any industry in terms of fatalities and injuries. Wandsworth direct works, for instance, has a full-time safety officer and apprentice supervisor and its new depot at Falcon Wharf contains all modern welfare facilities.[12]

There is then no comparison between conditions for workers in direct labour and in the private sector. This does not mean that conditions for direct labour workers are by any means satisfactory but, being a decasualised labour force, they do not suffer from the instability of employment, the bouts of unemployment, long working hours and lack of safety standards and compensation which are an inherent feature of the private construction industry. In 1977, 214,000 building workers were unemployed − 66,000 of these skilled craftsmen − giving a rate of unemployment for construction of 16 per cent or three times higher than the level in the economy as a whole. If all those working for the industry in one way or another (e.g. architects and building materials workers) are included in this, then total unemployment was 300,000.

Proposals for decasualisation of the industry have been made regularly since the 1919 Foster Report with the most recent, in 1977, being the Labour Party's proposals.[13] For the 'lump' in the building industry (the system whereby work is subcontracted on a labour-only basis) is particularly notorious. The system encourages skimped work and lack of regard to safety regulations and, because it involves no commitment to training, is destructive of skilled labour whilst at the same time functioning to attract it. In 1973 it was estimated that nearly half a million were working on the 'lump'. The last major survey of labour in the construction industry, the Phelps Brown Report of 1968, showed that instability of employment is a permanent characteristic and that estimated labour turnover in construction is about twice as high as the average for all employment. Among large contractors only about 25 per cent of employees are regarded as permanent. Compared to this situation in the private sector, turnover in local authorities is very much lower − the Phelps Brown report found that 81 per cent of workers had one year's service or more.

A decasualised direct labour force with continuity of employment as well as benefiting workers also has great advantages for tenants. It reduces organisational problems on site, thus increasing output at the same time as improving the quality of work done. The costs to tenants of subsidising the defects and inefficiencies of private contractors are now astronomical, as reflected in both rents and rates. Maintenance work carried out by direct labour is both less expensive and longer-lasting. For instance, the Association of Metropolitan Authorities estimated that to service a lift costs £500 p.a. with a private contractor and £260 p.a. if done by direct labour.[14]

Defects in private sector work are now a major element of maintenance costs. Islington Council, for instance, estimates that it needs to spend £750,000 each year for the next five years on unplanned major defects. Further upheaval to tenants is caused by the infamous time overruns by private contractors, which have often disrupted the housing programme and delayed rehousing. Wandsworth Council estimated that 75 per cent of the contracts given to private contractors had taken longer than they were supposed to. It is extremely difficult for a local authority to take legal proceedings against contractors' cost overruns: first, because most contracts contain fluctuation clauses; second, because contractors simply go into voluntary liquidation or threaten to stop work, disrupting the completion of the scheme even further and involving greater cost.

The crisis in the construction industry

In the light of the clear advantages for local authorities of using direct labour for all work, both maintenance and new construction, it is hardly surprising that private contractors see the departments as a great threat, which are expressed in the continual diatribes against direct labour in construction journals and pamphlets. In 1977 the NFBTE poured £250,000 into a campaign against direct labour. These concerted attempts by contractors to remove a potential competitor reflect the general crisis in the building industry. During the boom years of the early 1970s many local authorities set up DLOs because they had difficulty in getting private tenders for work. The situation now is reversed as contractors scramble for public sector work to ride over their crises, and seek to remove the check on their tenders given by direct labour departments.

The decision to run down Birmingham direct works completely was taken explicitly because 'private contractors were short of work and were quite capable of carrying out the contracts' according to the new Tory leader. Yet, when it was closed down in 1969, the department had consistently shown savings to the local authority. In 1975–6 these were £178,000 over costs, with a turn-over of £5.5m. It is similarly scandalous that the GLC should attempt to close down its DLO when private contractors have been such an unnecessary burden. In 1974, the authority handed over £1.6m in ex gratia payments to cover losses in private contracts and in 1976 committed itself to providing £4.5m to ten different building firms engaged in contracts.

Enormous subsidies to large contractors have also come from government: in 1976 French Kier, for instance, received a gift of £9.5m and a £4.5m loan; another company, Cubitts, was given government aid to the tune of £1¾m in August of that year. With this record, it is hardly surprising that the larger contractors now fear nationalisation and in June 1978 another extravagant propaganda campaign was launched to fight the Labour Party's proposals for nationalisation.

Output in both the construction industry and the building materials industry has dropped considerably since the early 1970s: in 1977 it had declined over 25 per cent compared with 1973. The National Economic Development Office (NEDO) estimates that average yearly output for 1978–80 will be 28 per cent lower than that for the years 1970-6. This has not necessarily affected the profitability of large firms employing over 600 (who by 1975 accounted for one-third of all output), but has meant that many medium-size firms are operating on narrow margins and cut-price tendering. In contrast, output in the public sector which constitutes half of all construction work, has not fallen so dramatically. The consequent increased dependence of the industry on public sector work has also resulted in the private sector making attacks on the traditional direct labour domain of repair and maintenance. Repair and maintenance is of crucial importance to the industry for it employs 40 per cent of the construction labour force. Remedying the 'mistakes' now revealing themselves in 1950s and 1960s estates can involve very large contracts, as well as new skills. Though acquiring these skills (e.g. masticking, false work, etc.) often requires a minimum training commitment many contractors have obtained a monopoly over them simply because DLOs have often confined themselves to traditional crafts.

The tendering procedure

As described earlier, government policy has increasingly been directed towards an insistence on DLOs tendering for work and an acceptance of the lowest tender submitted. With the tendering system, work is usually put out to tender to selected contractors, a procedure which in itself encourages the formation of 'rings'. In theory local authorities are supposed to be able to decide whether or not their DLO must tender in order to obtain work. In practice, however, it is difficult to obtain loan sanction from the Government unless the DLO has tendered for the work. The procedure that the local authority must accept the lowest tender and that DLOs must compete on these criteria is illogical, since DLOs are in a totally different position from private contractors. They have, after all, only one client which is the local authority, and they are publicly accountable. The effect of this absurdity, which amounts to the local authority tendering for its own work, is, however, to place DLOs in an extremely vulnerable position. For in times of crisis, contractors are prepared to tender at a loss in order to obtain work, or even in order to force DLOs to close down.

There can be no direct comparison between private contractors and DLOs, yet the tendering procedure assumes that there is. The tender prices of private contractors reflect the short-term market situation in the industry rather than the intrinsic value of the work. They do not reflect: direct subsidies to the industry to compensate for inefficiencies; speculative ventures; hidden subsidies through government support to the labour force through unemployment, either seasonal or caused by casual employment, and through sick pay and compensation; payment of professional and construction staff employed by local authorities to work on developments carried out by private contractors; and, support through government training schemes. Nor do they reflect the cost to the local authority of skimped work.

The effect of subjecting DLOs to tendering procedures is to undermine the principles on which direct labour is based and to subject it to the swings and starts of the market. For if a direct labour tender is refused the department may have to close down until another tender is accepted, thereby removing all the advantages of continuity of employment, etc. To overcome this some local authorities, for instance Castleford DLO after the war, have refused to put out to tender. At other times, when private contractors have refused to tender for work, as happened in Wandsworth (over Tooting Swimming Pool and Burhop Road housing) work is automatically negotiated with direct labour. Similarly, in

Newcastle, when the design of one new scheme was altered to industrialised methods, the work was given to direct labour because it was impossible to line up firms for the job. There are numerous other examples of DLOs undertaking difficult schemes which contractors will not tender for.

Attempts to undermine the principles of direct labour

It seems in fact common sense to avoid all the pitfalls involved in giving private contractors public sector work through having a planned local authority building programme and giving all work to direct labour, organised as a service and not on the same lines as a private contractor. In 1959, forty-one local authorities were building by direct labour alone but government tendering constraints now make this difficult. Rather than removing these constraints, attempts are now being made to undermine the service basis of DLOs by turning them into trading organisations and even semi-private firms in the form of building co-operatives, as in the case of Haringey. But DLOs are based on entirely different principles from private contractors: they have to be accountable to local people; they do not operate in order to make a profit; they do not thrive on speculative ventures; they are decasualised and ensure good working conditions; they are intended as a service, to provide good quality housing and other public building for the benefit of tenants and the community in general. The implications of turning DLOs into semi-private firms or trading organisations are: first, for workers, that continuity of employment would be threatened — particularly during periods of slump and consequent cut-price tendering by the private sector; second, for tenants, that there would be no guarantee of good service — departments would be encouraged to undertake only work which was commercially viable (e.g. not awkward repairs) and to skimp work as in the private sector; third, that local authorities would lose control over their own operations.

A Department of the Environment working party was established in 1978 to consider ways in which to 'rationalise direct labour' by defining what DLOs can and cannot do, and to formalise their accounting procedures. Recommendations for such procedures for new construction and maintenance work have already been produced by the Chartered Institute of Public Finance and Accountancy.[15] These recommendations, based on such criteria as 'Is the undertaking competitive?' will impose constraints turning DLOs further away from service departments and towards trading organisations. Wandsworth's difficulties should be seen as a 'warning light' against attempts to turn DLOs into trading organisations. They have found that these procedures do not take account of special conditions on each project and cannot take full account of on-going cost variations. For instance results based on the conversion of acquired houses have to be applied to quite different works in offices, baths, parks and depots. Indeed Wandsworth's DLO was put in jeopardy precisely because one project, which it was admitted was not a viable proposition for a private contractor, could not be seen as a 'commercial undertaking'.[16]

Manchester direct works has also severely criticised the 'Value for Money' approach:

> Being immeasurable in financial terms, the standards of service provided by direct works, its prime functions, are ignored when value for money appraisals are being given. Meeting standards and completing work programmes on scheduled time, which for Manchester are of high order, does cost additional money from the more mundane and contractual approach and is therefore accountable when cost appraisals are around.

They cite the costs saved in maintenance and time, for instance that they have reduced the period of completing modernisation from ten to four to five weeks per house. What is strange about the 'value for money' measure is that no such regulator applies to any other municipal service. Direct labour departments have of course to be accountable in financial terms but then they can be on the basis of valuation and cost, and through showing savings. They have a long record not only of achieving large savings in comparison with private contractors' tenders but also in reducing their cost below the original valuation. Manchester has, for instance, over fifteen years up to 1976 achieved total savings of nearly £4m. In this time not only have they built 17,500 low- and high-rise dwellings, 56 schools and other educational buildings, and 17 other major buildings, but also built their own large workshop in Bessemer Street (valued at £2m), employing 419 workers. The workshop produced in 1975-6 manufactured and bespoke joinery to the value of £1.5m, saving 17.8 per cent on manufactured window frames alone.

It is contractors who have, in the national construction press, persistently argued for turning DLOs into trading departments. To conform with this they have also argued that the existing departments be divided into separate sections. Some of the most successful DLOs (e.g. Sandwell), however, are those in which all services are combined — from repair and maintenance to improvement and new construction of schools and houses. This has advantages for workers in that it allows great flexibility for transfer from one scheme to another and from one type of work to another and thereby facilitates continuity of employment. Dividing DLOs into separate sections will place direct labour in an even more vulnerable position. This applies particularly to repair and maintenance work which has traditionally been undertaken by direct labour rather than by contractors or subcontractors precisely because it is a 'service' to tenants.

The attack on council housing

Behind the attempts to undermine the service nature of direct labour lie the threats to council housing generally. For council housing is itself a service and an answer to the inability of the private sector to house those in need. It is now being attacked in similar ways by either passing it totally into private hands through owner-occupation, housing associations and housing co-operatives, or making it semi-private in the case of tenant management co-operatives.

It is a sad reflection on the confusion in housing policy that attempts to undermine the basis of council housing are being made in the name of 'tenant control'. 'Tenant control' cannot mean that councils cut down on all repairs and make tenants sub-landlords, as proposed in tenant co-operative schemes. Not only would this have obvious consequences for poorly organised tenants and those in substandard estates, but it holds the prospect of the elimination of direct labour and the encouragement of 'lump' labour.

What 'tenant control' should mean is that councils respond effectively to tenants' demands and not abdicate from their responsibilities altogether. It should also offer opportunities for tenants and building workers jointly to exercise greater control over the quality of the housing service. Too often stagnant, stifling bureaucracies have been placed as an expensive wedge between tenants and direct labour workers, leading to great time delays and endless paperwork for the smallest repair. In Camden, for instance, every request for a repair put in by a tenant has to pass through an obstacle course before it reaches the works department. This is partly to decide on whether it should be done by the tenant on the do-it-yourself policy — a policy which not only costs as much to administer as actually to do the work, but also directly encourages the 'lump'. If the repairs are still not done, tenants may through their tenants' association have the matter brought up at their district management committee, consisting of councillors and tenants' associations' leaders (though not building workers) and involving yet another obstacle course through the various committees. Similarly, building and repair programmes have been drawn up with no consultation. Making DLOs completely separate departments divided into different sections only increases the distance between tenants and direct labour employees. Only Manchester employs a tenant liaison officer in its direct works. In a few other local authorities, such as Camden, tenants are encouraged informally by the direct labour shop stewards to contact them directly about frustrating delays over repairs.

It is clearly necessary that councils should be accountable to tenants, rather than pursuing policies against the interests of both tenants and building workers. One step in this direction has been taken in Hackney where, with a DLO of 1,000 and a council stock of 25,000 dwellings, the building unions realised that unless the building programme was stepped up by 200 buildings a year workers would be made redundant and housing need in the area could not be met. As a result, they succeeded in getting agreement on a five-year rehabilitation programme which removed the immediate threat. A Joint Working Party was then set up to investigate the building programme and to put forward union proposals for ways of bringing in work to compensate for the severe drop in house-building. These included an adequate programme of acquisition in preference to financial support for housing association activity.

The possibilities of direct labour

If direct labour were properly organised as an integrated part of the local authority service, then their potential is enormous. There is no reason why all local authority building and repair work should not automatically be done by direct labour. Contractors are not able to undertake public sector work partly because the industry has thrived on speculative gains and because it has remained in many senses backward and inefficient, dominated by small firms. It has practically abdicated responsibility for training apprentices, and perpetuated casual employment and poor working conditions. The defects in buildings which this system produces are now only too apparent, for instance maintenance costs are about double those on new building by direct labour. In contrast, DLOs, many of which are of comparable size in terms of plant and workforce to large contractors, could expand their activities (particularly training) providing further employment to the benefit of the whole community. Acting in consortium with other authorities they could provide up-to-date workshops for the production of building components and fittings for all public sector buildings from schools and offices to houses and recreation facilities, as well as (as suggested by Manchester's Director of Works) include training cells for apprentices to operate in full liaison with the CITB.

It is important not only to defend DLOs as they are from attack, but also to fight for their potential for improvement and expansion. There has been a long history of struggle by the labour movement for direct labour: in the 1890s, particularly in Battersea and the LCC; immediately after the First World War e.g. in Liverpool; again after the Second World War, for instance in St Pancras following the trades council's initiative; and now in the directions taken in Sheffield and Hackney and in the examples of Manchester and Sandwell. In August 1977 a campaign was launched in Manchester by direct labour stewards from departments all over the country calling for expansion of direct labour and agreeing on a nine-point programme. Local action groups of tenants and workers have also been set up, for instance in Tower Hamlets. Direct labour is of vital importance, involving as it does a large number of issues of relevance to tenants and ratepayers and building workers. It highlights the nature of the building industry, and particularly the problems of unemployment and training. It illustrates the potential quality and extent of local authority services. Above all, it points to ways in which those housed by local authorities can begin to make contacts with building workers and exercise increasing control over the provision of housing.

Notes

1 *London*, 6 January 1898, p. 3 — a paper which later became the *London Municipal Journal.*

2 For some of the details of the activities of the municipal socialists, see *John Burns*, Royal Historical Society, 1977 — particularly for his fight against contractors.

3 For more details of early direct labour work, see *Direct Building* published by the Labour Research Department in 1929 and still one of the best accounts of direct labour. See also the official trade unionist report by Bradford Trades Council, *London, Battersea and West Ham Municipal Works Departments*, of 1904 in Battersea Local History Library.

4 See *London*, 27 January 1898.

5 For a general background to the development of direct labour, see *Direct Labour: the Answer to Building Chaos*, North-East Trade Union Studies Information Unit, June 1977 and *Building with Direct Labour*, CSE Housing Workshop, 1978.

6 Labour Research Monthly Circular, Local Government Notes, November 1920.

7 'Package deals' are arrangements made with contractors to do all work from design to build.

8 Government Circular 50/65.

9 H. Graham, 'Getting the Best out of your Directly Employed Labour', Institute of Building Management Report on the most appropriate methods of accomplishing the expansion of municipal direct labour departments for new construction, building and civil engineering (Press release, November 1976).

10 Lambeth Construction Services, Chairman's report 1975–6.

11 Manchester C.C. Direct Works Department: 'Value for Money and Service', in Institute of Municipal Building Management Press Release, 1976.

12 J. Tilley, 'Building with Direct Labour: a Fresh Assessment', London Borough of Wandsworth, November 1975.

13 'Building Britain's Future: Labour's Policy on Construction', a Policy Background Paper, Labour Party, October 1977.

14 'Report to the Policy Committee of the Association of Metropolitan Authorities', November 1973.

15 CIPFA, *Direct Works Undertakings*, 1976.

16 District Auditor's Report on Wandsworth, January 1978.

10 Fighting for better health services: the role of the Community Health Council

Jane Leighton

By the summer of 1977, Liverpool's health service was on the verge of collapse. A dramatic announcement of cuts involving the closure of wards in 14 hospitals and the loss of 500 jobs brought an explosion of protest. It also brought together the trade unions and the patients' representative, the Community Health Council, in a determined effort to stop the cuts. Their action prompted an official enquiry into Liverpool Area Health Authority — the first enquiry into the operation of the health service at a local level since the reorganisation of the health service in 1974.

The lid blew off Liverpool's health service in May 1977, but from its inception in 1974 Liverpool Area Health Authority (AHA) had serious problems in maintaining an acceptable standard of health care in the city. This massive organisation, employer of 12,500 people, has a budget of £70m a year to provide a service to half a million Liverpudlians, and because of its renown as a teaching centre to nearly as many people from all over south-west Lancashire, Cheshire and North Wales.

To the people of Liverpool it seemed as though the AHA was determined to bring the local health service to its knees by a process of attrition. In the twelve months from August 1976 two-thirds of Liverpool's hospitals came under threat of closure, partial closure or change of use. In the same period the AHA, with the uneasy agreement of the trade unions, vigorously employed a policy of non-filling of vacancies, a policy which, from August 1976 to December 1977 resulted in the loss of 230 nursing, 119 ancillary, 16 administrative, 4 professional and technical and 3 medical posts.

Staff were demoralised but lacked organisation. Those workers in trade unions began to take action against the cuts. In particular the National Union of Public Employees (NUPE), the largest union with 1,700 members, side-stepped agreed negotiating procedure in favour of lightning strikes. The state of industrial relations in central Liverpool between 1976 and 1978 was later described by the Committee of Inquiry as 'guerilla warfare'.

Through information 'leaked' to newspapers, Liverpool people began to have some grasp of the implications of national and local cutbacks. The general knowledge though, was very low and the Community Health Council, the consumers' representative in the health service, had its work cut out trying to inform the community councils, residents' associations, and other local groups of the crisis in Liverpool.

Slowly with knowledge of the underlying causes of the crisis, the fragmented discontent began to fuse. Sparks of opposition in the form of local action groups were just appearing when, on 24 May 1977, the sudden announcement of £1m cuts electrified the health service in the city. Patients and ancillary, medical and nursing staff were unanimous in deploring the cuts. Consultants, nurses, junior hospital doctors, family doctors, porters, cooks and patients, with one voice declared that the health service in Liverpool was near to collapse.

Never before had the health service seen such unanimity between workers at all levels in the health service. Solidarity in mutual adversity triumphed over the seemingly impregnable elitism which dominates the service.

The unified protest is popularly viewed as one city's action against cutbacks in public expenditure. The crisis in Liverpool, and within the National Health Service generally, is rather more complicated but essentially problems are rooted in national policy — a policy which has consistently denied the NHS adequate finance, staffing or equipment.

Within the NHS itself the division of resources has been uneven, with the large teaching areas (mainly in London) commanding most of the finance. The decision of a national working party, the Resource Allocation Working Party (RAWP) to facilitate a more equal distribution of resources by reallocating money from the 'richer' regions to 'poorer' regions was a major blow for Liverpool.

In terms of resources, Liverpool is always accused of being 'over-funded' for its population. It has more beds and staff per head of population than many other areas but it also treats people from all over Merseyside, so its true catchment area is very large. Liverpool also has a high incidence of illness, particularly respiratory diseases. It has the second highest rate of lung cancer in Great Britain. The greater use of hospital beds can also be accounted for by Liverpool's extreme deprivation and poverty. Liverpool is an area with an unemployment rate of 12 per cent, which is double the national average. In the inner city unemployment currently stands at 30 per cent and between January and March 1978, eight thousand people in Liverpool lost their jobs or were threatened with redundancy. It is not surprising that people under such severe economic and social stress have a greater-than-average need for their health service.

The criteria which RAWP used were insensitive to these important factors. In 1977 Liverpool commanded 2 per cent less of the Region's budget than it had in 1974 and the cutback was too great for the health service to absorb. Liverpool also had other serious problems. The city had a tradition of spending its money on hospital services rather than community services. One of the legacies of this policy was a 'primary care' sector in desperate need of development. Primary care involves general practitioners, district nurses, health visitors — the community health services. In 1974 10 per cent of Liverpool GPs practised from health centres — half the national average. And in January 1978 the Committee of Inquiry said: 'The key to success in Liverpool lies in the development of primary and community services. . . . The plans for primary health care offer no way out of the Liverpool dilemma within the next decade.'

The pressing need to develop primary care services became greater with the imminent completion of the Royal Liverpool Hospital. The hospital had become a national scandal. 'An appalling fiasco', said the Chairman of the Public Accounts Committee, commenting in March 1978 on the seventeen years of building and the rise in its cost from £12m to an estimated £56m. The hospital was built to replace five local hospitals and to run efficiently would work on a fast turn-round of patients. If community services were not developed so that people could convalesce in small community hospital units in the area, or at home with good care from district nurses, then the hospital would quickly have a thrombosis through 'blocked' beds. Standing in one of the most desolate areas of the city with no natural catchment area (the people were rehoused long ago) the hospital also threatens to cripple other health services with its enormous running costs — the latest estimate is £12.5m per year. The irony of Liverpool sporting an enormous hospital for some specialties while the majority of its other services barely limp along is not lost among local people. 'Around here there's nothing, it costs nearly £2 return to get to that hospital on two buses. What we need is a small injuries unit, and a local health centre. Out here we feel like second-class citizens with a second-class health service.'

John McVoy lives in Speke, a large corporation housing estate of 22,000 people on the outskirts of Liverpool. Resentment and antipathy towards the new hospital is understandable when you think of families cracking up because neither the health nor the social services can help in looking after an elderly relative with senile dementia; when you consider elderly people in constant discomfort because they can't get their feet done — the NHS chiropody service is so overstretched. While there remains a screaming need for these basic services, the new Royal Liverpool Hospital, a monument to high technology, will engender little affection among the people of Liverpool.

The remaining problems result entirely from poor management. To the dissatisfaction of local people must be added the uncertainty and discontent of staff who, in each of the hospitals to be closed, have evolved their own traditions and team spirit. Staff in these hospitals were not told that their jobs would be secure until March 1978, seven months before the official opening of the new Royal Liverpool Hospital. On visits to the hospitals, nurses frankly told the Community Health Council (CHC) that they had no faith in the Health Authority. A doctor at one of the local hospitals said, 'Anyone with an ounce of initiative will leave Liverpool.' And a nurse who had given twenty years of her life to the health service in Liverpool wrote to the CHC:

> Democracy they call it, isn't it? I must have the wrong understanding of democracy. To my mind, matters are decided and no matter how many discussions, very few of which we so foolishly have been involved in, they will not alter the decisions one iota. The goings on of the last few months have been very salutary for me — I can now have more sympathy for other people's frustrations and maybe understand their behaviour.
>
> I shall now quietly fade out of a lifetime's work, unnoticed, unappreciated, and thoroughly disillusioned for having wasted my life.

Overspending was the major precipitative factor in the cuts proposals. Liverpool AHA overspent its 1976–7 budget by nearly £1m. The health authority did not consider a deputation to the Regional Health Authority to state the impossibility of keeping to its budget. Nor did it examine the scope for economy in a proper, planned sense. Instead the few members who attended meetings became mesmerised by the Treasurer's balance sheet and allowed the officers to attempt to claw back revenue by a series of panic measures which would clearly jeopardise the standard of health care in the local population.

Perhaps the clearest illustration of Liverpool AHA's self-inflicted problems is the 'single district' proposal. Liverpool's approach was 'disastrous' said the Committee of Inquiry and 'should stand as a warning to other AHAs contemplating similar structural changes'.

The 1974 NHS reorganisation left Liverpool AHA, in common with eighty-nine other AHAs, to contend with a new and cumbersome management structure. Staff were uncertain of their new roles and desperately needed a period of tranquillity. Instead of this they received yet another massive blow – Liverpool AHA decided to reorganise itself again, by streamlining its two districts into one.

During the whole of this extraordinarily difficult 'settling down' period following the 1974 reorganisation, Liverpool's health managers spent most of their time debating the 'single district' prospect. Hospital staff, who were already unsettled, became increasingly discontented and suspicious at the prospect of yet more changes. A large number of managers fled the city for more agreeable jobs in more settled areas. By the time the Secretary of State approved the single district area, there were fourteen senior management vacancies in Liverpool AHA. So, although this Authority had special problems – in the face of a cutback in budget it had to get a new, massively expensive hospital open and develop much neglected community services – the Authority had itself irretrievably damaged the morale and loyalty of health workers and alienated local people.

This then was the background to an unprecedented uproar of protest which confronted Liverpool AHA in May 1977.

The main body of opposition emerged from an unusual and important alliance between the trade unions and the CHC, which proved for many people, inside and outside the health service, that CHCs can be a powerful force.

Community Health Councils were set up in 1974 as a gesture towards public participation in the NHS. They are the consumer voice in the health service and are consulted on all changes which the authority wishes to make in the running and planning of the service. CHCs have the right to information about the health service, access to the press, the right to inspect health service premises and they can speak at AHA meetings. They can only represent local opinion however: they have no management powers.

Many CHCs (there is one for every health district in the country) do not restrict their activities to consultation with the AHA. Thus campaigning for a more sensitive health service by involvement with local action groups, researching areas of need, and, importantly, helping people with individual complaints, are all within the scope of the councils.

Although much stronger and more effective than other public consumer organisations, CHCs are imperfect bodies. Imperfect because, apart from the obvious weakness which results in complete separation of representation from management responsibility, health councils are undemocratic, having appointed members who are often socially and geographically unrepresentative. The thirty members are appointed by the local authority (15), voluntary organisations (10) and the Regional Health Authority (5).

The CHC, naturally, had a primary responsibility to inform local people of the crisis. Meetings were organised with residents' associations and action groups, and the press gave the patients' views good publicity. But the outcry was growing and soon the protests of the trade unions and the CHC were accompanied by opposition from medical and nursing staff. Although some satisfaction was gained from the fact that for the first time, consultants, family doctors and nurses were publicly opposing the AHA, the arguments used were potentially divisive.

Some consultants heralded the collapse of the health service by pointing to their long waiting-lists and calling for more resources. Other campaigners illustrated waste and bad administrative and medical management. Some of us, while recognising the scope for economy and the need to evaluate medical practice, also felt that under-financing was pivotal to Liverpool's (and the NHS's) problems. It was clear that a common understanding between all objectors on the nature of the crisis was desirable.

The initial aim of the trade unions, staff associations and the CHC was to secure the AHA's co-operation in demanding more resources from the Department of Health to keep the health service in Liverpool at an acceptable level.

With one week between the publication and the ratification of the cuts, there was very little time to organise. This was one of the main obstacles in the whole cuts campaign; but fifty union representatives from NUPE, COHSE, ASTMS, UCATT, COASA and the TGWU, along with local action groups (Merseyside Right to Work Campaign, Women's Action Group), the CHC and the two nursing organisations — the Royal College of Nursing and the Royal College of Midwives, swelled the public gallery at the next AHA meeting. This was the first time that there had been any public representation at an AHA meeting in Liverpool, in spite of the fact that its monthly meetings are open. The Authority's practice of holding its meeting at 4 p.m. on a Friday afternoon in the University's remote and inaccessible Senate House, no doubt contributed to the poor public attendance.

The AHA was clearly expecting trouble and had taken the precaution of calling on the police force to patrol the doors of the building. The AHA members, embarrassed by the angry crowd, were subjected to heckling and calls to resign, 'in view of the disastrous record of maladministration'. People in the public galleries were incensed when the Chairman, having refused to meet a union deputation to discuss the proposals, decided to take the item in private.

Nobody moved from the public gallery when the Authority's Chairman asked the public and press to leave the room. Eventually the AHA members themselves rose and moved on to an adjoining room to jeers and slow handclaps from the onlookers. People waited around, not knowing when the meeting would be reconvened.

After about an hour most people reluctantly moved off. They did not know until they read in their newspapers next morning that the meeting had been continued in private. This was quite out of order as the AHA should have passed a resolution at the beginning of its meeting if it intended to take items in committee. The Authority issued a lengthy press statement saying that the cuts had been forced upon it by the Department of Health's financial policy. Some of the proposals had not in fact been ratified, and the AHA indicated that cuts might not be necessary if staff would co-operate fully in the 'non-filling of vacancies' policy. These concessions did little to appease the unions or the CHC.

A mass public meeting was called by NUPE for 14 June. It was the first occasion on which NUPE and COHSE, the major health service unions, shared a public platform with ASTMS, the District Labour Party, the TUC, the CHC and, surprisingly, the Royal College of Nursing, not renowned for its militancy. The knowledge of the trade union representatives varied alarmingly. Some spoke simplistically and generally on public expenditure cuts, displaying little knowledge of Liverpool's particular problems.

The Royal College of Nursing representative, who vigorously opposed the cutbacks, was obviously reluctant to face the inevitable consequences of that decision — industrial action. I myself spoke for the CHC, condemning the panic decisions of the AHA, promising the strongest opposition to the cuts. The Authority cannot close hospitals or parts of hospitals without permission from the local CHC. If the Council refuses, the Authority has to go to the Secretary of State for permission. Even if the Secretary of State overrides the CHC opposition, objections to closure can be a valuable delaying tactic. I also spoke about the AHA's monthly meetings, their secrecy, poor debate and lack of contact by the members with either staff or local people. This first public meeting was attended by about 500 local people, mainly staff from Liverpool hospitals. The press had given wide advance coverage and next to reporters in the first row sat the new Area Medical Officer for Liverpool. All the AHA members and officers knew of the meeting, but the Area Medical Officer was the only one to attend.

At the end of our speeches, he stood up and asked to address the meeting. Although some people had a certain admiration for his courage in attending, he was viewed with extreme suspicion by the majority of people present. To the workers in local hospitals who had virtually no idea of the internal politics of Liverpool's health service, this man was the enemy, even though he had taken office only two weeks earlier.

He made a gross error of judgment when, having been given permission to address the meeting, he came to the front, turned to face the people and opened his remarks with one word 'Friends'. The rest of his sentence was lost in hisses and jeers. The main theme of his address was that we may have to sacrifice something today to achieve a better health service tomorrow; that some changes in the pattern of the health service were desirable; hospital services, for instance, could be pruned and the savings put into care for old people. There was no opportunity for this type of discussion. People were not really concerned with the philosophy of health care delivery. They were concerned about jobs and any change meant the possible loss of jobs. The Area Medical Officer was unable to put his case and finally withdrew.

The meeting finally decided to give the AHA one week to consider the proposed cuts and organised a deputation to picket the Authority on the appointed day, calling on the AHA Chairman to give a personal answer to the resolution. One week later thirty people waited in vain outside the AHA offices for the Chairman to meet the deputation. After a brief occupation of the offices of senior managers, the chief administrator and medical officer agreed to an impromptu meeting. Following this stormy exchange a formal meeting was arranged between staff and patients' representatives and senior managers, members of the AHA and the elusive Chairman.

Meanwhile, the man people wanted to see was on the train to London. The Chairman of Liverpool AHA and the Chairman of Mersey Regional Health Authority had arranged to see Roland Moyle, Minister of State for Health, about the crisis in Liverpool. The Minister had expressed his concern that the £1m cuts had been announced by administrators before consideration by the AHA, and, in spite of the public anger a secret meeting generated, it was thought that the two Chairmen might be severely criticised by the Department of Health for the mismanagement in Liverpool and that they were making a case for more resources.

Hopes of this were soon dispelled when the Chairmen returned. A press notice revealed that the Minister supported the need for cuts to help to pay for the new teaching hospital. The two Chairmen made it clear that they had not gone to London to ask for more money for Liverpool's health service.

NUPE and the Community Health Council immediately sent telegrams of protest to Roland Moyle. Having called for joint talks between the Minister, the AHA, the unions and the CHC, they considered they had been completely deceived by the sudden private meeting.

During this time, a public appearance of solidarity between most of the campaigning bodies was maintained. Local consultants, doctors and nurses had broken into separate protest groups, of course, but their solidarity with trade unions had never been expected. More serious was the tension at co-ordinating meetings between the unions themselves, particularly COHSE and NUPE, both battling for membership. There was also too much concentration on solidarity in withdrawal of labour when tactics should have centred on work-ins — and too little discussion of defence committees. Had the time between the cuts proposals and the inquiry been longer, defence committees would have become an important plank of the campaign.

Joint staff/patient defence committees were considered to be vital to equipment. There were already reports from other areas in the country of services closed by AHAs removing equipment without warning. It was clear from small public meetings that residents concerned about the closure of a local hospital needed to be involved with the staff on a programme of action, and it was suggested that staff committees working in every hospital would be supported by a continuing local picket outside.

The CHC too was in a difficult position. The decision to join with trade unions was strongly criticised by other health councils and by the health authority. The argument against joint discussion and representation was that the CHC would lose its 'independence' if seen to speak with the staff. The patients' view, it was suggested, should be 'separate'. Clearly, from the Authority's viewpoint, a united front was a real threat. The reluctance of other health councils to take joint action with staff on cuts stems from the fact that, essentially, CHCs are middle class, conservative bodies with corresponding attitudes towards trade unions.

The separatist view was also expressed on our CHC. But we had always adopted the stand that if CHCs are concerned about services to patients, they must be concerned about staff morale and welfare. In order to get the best possible health service, members decided it was important for the Council to align with all who think similarly on any one issue. In retrospect, it seems that one of the most valuable actions taken by the CHC was its involvement with staff organisations over the health care crisis in the city. Solidarity was, in fact, maintained, and on 28 June representatives of trade unions and the health council met the Chairman of Liverpool AHA and senior officers to discuss the cuts.

Cautious optimism crept over the meeting when NUPE offered to call off lightning strikes if the AHA agreed to suspend its policy of not filling vacancies. It was also suggested that a working party consisting of representatives of trade unions, management and the CHC should prepare an alternative strategy for Liverpool's problems. The administrator of the AHA agreed to put the proposals to the full meeting of the Authority the following Friday. Needless to say, the Authority refused the call to suspend the policy of not filling jobs, and it unanimously objected to the CHC being present on a working party with staff and management. The unions' answer to this was that if the CHC could not be included in the team to examine the health service in Liverpool, the staff organisations would withdraw. Consequently the working party was abandoned.

During the month which had elapsed since the £1m cuts' announcement, evidence had been pouring in to COHSE of waste and mismanagement at one of the city hospitals — Sefton General Hospital. For the first time in the memory of most long-serving administrators, two nursing sisters, both members of COHSE, had spoken militantly against conditions in local hospitals. These two sisters beavered away within the hospital gleaning information from doctors, consultants, other nurses and administrators about the medical and administrative management of the hospital. Within four weeks they had enough evidence to show the serious nature of Liverpool's problems.

The two nursing sisters not only collected evidence of mismanagement and waste at the hospital — reckless spending of equipment not used and material bought at a higher price than necessary, for example — they doggedly tried to inform hospital staff, by calling meetings, and local people, by taking petitions round pubs, of the need for immediate action.

When Roland Moyle agreed to meet a deputation from the trade union which sponsored him as a member of Parliament, NUPE were invited to join the deputation. There is no doubt that their contribution to the struggle was a major factor in the successful demand for an investigation into the management of Liverpool's health service.

On 26 July 1977, exactly two months after the £1m cuts' announcement, Roland Moyle, a NUPE-sponsored MP, agreed to an enquiry into aspects of Liverpool AHA.

The united action of staff and patients' representatives had stopped the worst of the cuts — at least until the Committee of Inquiry reported. For the first time in three years, managers of Liverpool's health services were to watch six months pass without major industrial unrest, although morale of staff was low and absenteeism so serious that the service to patients continued to suffer. The relief which followed Roland Moyle's statement broke into anger and frustration when he announced that the Inquiry would be conducted by the Regional Health Authority. It was quite unacceptable for this Authority to investigate one of its own areas, and senior officers at the Mersey Regional Health Authority were swiftly told by unions and the CHC that they would not give evidence to a committee which consisted of members of the Authority. Such a committee would have no public credibility and having come this far, common justice must not only be done, it must be seen to be done.

The Regional Officers seemed willing to negotiate, and staff organisations and CHCs were invited to nominate committee members. Eventually agreement was reached on an independent committee, half appointed by the Regional Health Authority and half by the staff organisations, under the umbrella of the Regional Health Authority and Chairmanship of Professor Roger Dyson of Keele University.

There was one more battle to be fought, over the committee's terms of reference. Negotiations took forty-seven days and were confined mainly to the trade unions and the Regional Health Authority, although the CHC submitted its views.

The committee of inquiry into Liverpool AHA finally met on 2 October 1977. It had to work fast, as a deadline of three months was set for the publication of its findings. During those three months the committee considered 250 items of evidence, held eleven days of oral hearings and visited local health facilities. Many community groups gave written evidence, and the CHC, trade unions, medical committees, nursing associations and administrative staff were among those who supported written submissions by oral evidence, in discussions which lasted up to four hours.

The local press gave coverage to most of the evidence. Significantly the trade unions, CHC and community groups made their submissions public, while the AHA evidence remained secret. This private treatment of public business was a constant source of criticism levelled at the Liverpool AHA. Until 1974 the NHS came under virtually no public scrutiny and, after reorganisation, managers clearly had problems in embracing the new participative method of management and the greater public accountability demanded by CHCs.

It is fair to say that officers concerned with the regional and AHAs expected the trade unions, NUPE in particular, to be trounced by the Committee of Inquiry. In fact when the Committee published its findings on 18 January 1978, it was the AHA who came in for the severest pounding. Criticism of the trade unions was slight. The committee's report completely justified the public demand for an inquiry and supported many of the points made in evidence. Health authority officers and members, wincing from stinging rebukes, could take a little succour from the committee's acknowledgment of the special difficulties facing health managers in the city, and the recognition that under-financing was central to the problems.

The report made thirty-six recommendations for improving the health service in Liverpool. A greater efficiency in some areas was expected, but the committee said it was baffled by the Authority's decision to close one of the local hospitals. The view of the committee was: 'If the health authority are going to close everything, then the public are going to fight everything.' Two significant recommendations were the retention of this local hospital for the next decade at least, and a no-redundancy guarantee (with conditions) for all staff in hospitals to close when the Royal Liverpool Hospital opened. Officers were criticised for their 'paternalistic' handling of industrial relations and cautious approach to developing much-needed services. Members of the AHA, the local authority and the University of Liverpool also came under fire.

The battle is now on with the Regional Health Authority and the Department of Health for more hard cash for Liverpool — one of the committee's recommendations. But throughout the report runs a warning that 'the problem in Liverpool is one of attitudes as much as resources'. Since the health service locally is still largely run by the same people, it is clear that Liverpool still faces enormous problems.

So what has been achieved? A sceptical view is that an inquiry was a political manoeuvre to take the heat out of the Liverpool crisis and to some extent this is true.

In spite of the obvious opportunities for economy within the NHS — cutting down the large amounts of drugs (which possibly do more harm than good), eliminating wasteful or unnecessary medical routines are two examples — the service is fundamentally under-financed. Unless we see adequate resources pumped into the NHS, both locally and nationally, the service must continue to deteriorate. But at the very least, the level of awareness and understanding which Liverpool people and local health workers have about the health service, has risen greatly since the campaign.

In spite of its limitations, the CHC was a vital cog in the campaign. The trade unions had the muscle-power — they could withdraw their labour. But the CHC had two important contributions to make — it had up-to-date information and therefore provided a crucial service to community groups and trade unions, and it had an understanding of the working of the whole health service in the city. Traditionally, and understandably, staff were concerned about matters which affected them individually. Local people were worried about their nearest hospital and trade unions were primarily preoccupied with jobs. The CHC ensured that 'quality of care' over the whole range of health services became as much an issue in the press as job security.

The council tried to involve a network of community-based groups in the action against the cuts and achieved some success, although its efforts were undoubtedly frustrated by the speed with which events happened — only two months from the announcement of the cuts to the setting up of the inquiry. Nevertheless the meetings held with community councils, tenants' associations, political and women's groups laid a firm foundation for the future. The Committee of Inquiry clearly saw the importance of the CHC's role and its involvement with the trade unions. The cuts proposals 'brought together the trades unions and the Community Health Council in a determined effort to resist the proposals'. This incident, more than anything else, contributed towards bringing Liverpool's problems to the attention of a wider public.

Although we were satisfied that the campaign for the inquiry into Liverpool AHA succeeded, it should be stressed that this was not our main aim. Our prime objective, with the trade unions, was to make joint representation, with the AHA, to the Department of Health for more resources. This request was ignored and our second proposal — a working party of staff, management and health councils to examine the problems in Liverpool, prepare a case for the Secretary of State for Health and an alternative strategy to alleviate the city's crisis, was rejected. There was, finally, little alternative to the demand for an inquiry.

It could be that the joint action of the CHC and the trade unions will ultimately achieve very little in Liverpool. I suspect that this was not the case and, more positively, think it possible that joint action between trade unions, community groups and CHCs in other areas will meet with less obstruction from their

AHAs. It is significant that, one year after our unsuccessful efforts to engage the Liverpool AHA in joint representation for more resources, the Chairman of the National Association of Health Authorities writes to all members of Parliament, urging their support for a better share of the nation's resources for the NHS: 'It [the NHS] cannot give the care, either in hospital or in the community, that would be within its power if it were properly financed, staffed and equipped: patients suffer, morale within the service falls. The community has to ask itself how long it can afford to let this slide go on.'

11   Leeds public transport: linking bus workers and community groups

Kevin Ward

'In England the crucial importance of integrating community and industrial struggles is being increasingly recognised in theory. What remains is to fuse these struggles in practice.'[1] This case study describes how such practical links were created and joint organisation developed between bus workers and the 'community' in the context of public expenditure cuts.

The Labour Government made several announcements of cuts in 1975 and 1976.[2] Although cuts in particular services had obviously been implemented before this, it seems that the Government's intention was drastically to curtail all categories of social services expenditure well into the 1980s. In response to this, 'cuts committees' had been established in various parts of the country which attempted to mobilise opposition to the cuts in order to defend jobs and services. Early in 1976 the Leeds Campaign Against the Cuts was set up by an ad hoc group of activists in the absence of initiatives from either the Leeds Trades Council or any political party. Eventually the campaign secured the support of a number of trade union branches and community groups. Regular propaganda bulletins were distributed focusing on how the national cuts were affecting local services and jobs. This information was distributed widely and was obviously valuable when no other groups were producing such material. But as the year progressed there was an increasing feeling that the campaign lacked any specific action focus, which could draw together trade unionists and community activists. It was decided, then, to concentrate on specific issues in more depth.

Public transport — a single issue

In October 1976 the 9/12 Branch of the Transport and General

Workers' Union (TGWU), covering nearly 2,000 bus workers in Leeds, voted at a mass meeting to accept £50,000 cuts in the bus budget when management gave an assurance that, at least in the short term, neither jobs nor earnings would be affected.

Yet in July 1977 when the West Yorkshire Passenger Transport Executive (PTE) applied to the Yorkshire Traffic Commissioners for fare increases ranging from 24 to 33 per cent, the same branch voted overwhelmingly not to collect the increased fares, if they were approved.

Branch members were present along with members of community groups at a public hearing into the fare increases at which the Traffic Commissioners presided. Normally these applications for fare increases are granted fairly automatically, and very few bus workers and people dependent on public transport are aware that they can attend a hearing and object. The Chairman of the Traffic Commissioners noted at the hearing: 'it is difficult to assess exactly the number of objectors involved but we accept the view that several hundred thousand people either wrote or were represented at the enquiry'.[3] It is no mere coincidence that within nine months, members of the public became concerned and active around public transport, the trade union branch became threateningly militant, and eventually bus workers and bus users were combining around joint action. Before examining the development of the campaign, however, it is first necessary to look at the choice of public transport as 'a single issue'.

Why choose transport?

It is relevant to ask why, once the Leeds Campaign Against the Cuts had decided to focus on single issues in addition to general propaganda, public transport was chosen as a single issue. It was certainly not because transport was seen as more or less important than other services such as health or education; the Leeds Campaign Against the Cuts was very anxious to avoid arguing for one service at the expense of another. Transport was chosen because of a combination of objective, organisational and local factors.

Objectively at that time (late in 1976) public transport nationally was under severe attack. The Government had decided that revenue support to buses in England and Wales was to be reduced by more than half its (then) present level by 1981. Excluding British Rail, public transport subsidies were to be reduced from £134.7m in

1975-6 to £60m in 1978-9. Overall public transport was faced with the largest percentage cut of any proposed public service cut. Also local authorities had been advised by central Government not to introduce new or improved schemes of concessionary fares. It seems then that public transport was not simply facing a difficult future but in fact was in great danger of almost disappearing as a public service.

Organisationally, transport seemed to provide an easier focus than some other issues. Public transport in the form of bus services affects the majority of residents in working class areas directly and immediately. Inadequate services had already led to strong feelings of anger and frustration in some areas. 'The buses' was a clear issue for many members of local community groups who were directly affected when buses failed to turn up or when fares were increased. It was felt that if this frustration could be given a clear 'action' focus, then it could provide the basis for a campaign instead of being directed against the bus workers.

It is worth contrasting public transport in this context with another issue, such as education cuts. In Leeds, recently, several community groups have established contact with teachers and begun to develop common action around such issues as oversized classes because of staffing shortages, and inadequate facilities at their local schools. However, although a number of parents are angry at the effects of the education cuts on their children, it is very difficult to formulate action tactics which will appeal to large numbers of parents. Also, conditions in schools are 'one step removed'. The children are affected but the parents do not often see the results of the cuts *directly* and *immediately*. Another factor is that there are many people who do not have children at school and these then are not affected even indirectly by cuts in educational expenditure.

Locally there seemed to be a great deal of potential in developing links with a group of rank-and-file bus workers who had formed a pressure group within their union in 1976 called 'Platform'. Several members of the Leeds Campaign Against the Cuts had established contact with 'Platform' and held detailed discussions with them about the implications of the bus workers accepting the £50,000 cuts in October 1976. It seemed possible to initiate links between these bus workers and various community groups already in contact with the campaign.

'The buses', then, was chosen as an issue to concentrate upon, not because it was more important than other services but because of a combination of factors outlined above.

Who suffers most?

Nationally, almost half of all households have no access to a car and so are totally dependent on public transport. Broad national percentages such as these, however, can often gloss over the real inequalities. A brief examination of such data as the 1971 census provides some indication of who really suffers most when public transport services are drastically reduced. Obviously, certain groups such as the handicapped will be affected wherever they live; however, an analysis by ward of household car-ownership patterns in Leeds clearly shows how much of an underestimation of the real problem national figures can be. In the Holbeck ward (a working-class area in the south of the city), 84.5 per cent of households and in the East Hunslet ward, 78 per cent, had no access to a car. Thus, the majority of residents there are dependent on public transport for their mobility. These areas provide a stark contrast to wards such as Weetwood, a pleasant residential area in the north of the city, where only 31.3 per cent of households have no access to a car, and 16.6 per cent of households actually have access to two cars.[4]

People on low incomes, then, usually living in 'poorer' areas such as Holbeck and Hunslet which have been described as giving 'an overall impression of neglect and decline',[5] are totally dependent on public transport. Their mobility is restricted and yet mobility is now, as the 1976 Consultative document on transport policy recognised, is much more necessary than ever before, 'for as car ownership spreads, schools become larger, hospitals are regionalised, out-of-town shopping centres multiply and the council offices are situated further away; meanwhile the local shop and post office have often disappeared'.[6] Many people are therefore forced into mobility because of the shifting of facilities such as jobs, schools and shops away from the places where they can reasonably be reached. 'This centralisation of facilities is usually defended by an "economies of scale" argument. For instance, hypermarkets or superstores are said to reduce prices, but in reality, they only save the retailer the bother of distribution, increase his profit margins and externalise his costs of transport (i.e. pass them on to the consumer).'[7] Yet in spite of this forced mobility, fewer people are actually using the buses:[8]

a further reason for the decline in bus travel (in addition to increasing car ownership) is that fares have increased relative to other prices in spite of increasing subsidies. Fares rose by 94 per cent between April 1970 and April 1975, 13 per cent more than the general increase in all prices. Recent experience suggests that a 10 per cent rise in fares relative to other prices leads to a reduction of the order of 3 per cent in passenger numbers.

'Since 1974 in West Yorkshire, bus fares have risen by 151 per cent and will almost definitely rise again by a minimum of 12 per cent in February 1978. This rise in public transport fares directly affects the lower income groups and their ability to travel.'[9]

In this context, it is important to examine the position of women. In 1975 51 per cent of male workers drove to work (whereas only 13 per cent of female workers did).[10] This means that even where there are households with cars, the women (often with children) may be left totally dependent on public transport for mobility. A woman may wish to work herself, but her choice of job may be restricted to a limited number of bus routes.

Overall, there is the anomaly of residents in areas such as Hunslet and Holbeck suffering the effects of the imported mobility of those driving in from the suburbs and beyond — noise, dirt, pollution and busy roads to cross. These same residents have, for a number of years, suffered the severe inconvenience of motorway construction as the M1, the M62 and the M621 have been extended right into the city through 'their' areas. Yet ironically enough they are least likely to own cars themselves, as the car ownership ratios referred to above clearly show. It is obvious then that low income groups, but particularly those living in inner-city areas and also those on peripheral council estates, are the ones who suffer most as public transport has declined, fares escalated, and mobility become even more essential, as various facilities have been located further away.

By concentrating on public transport issues, therefore, it did seem possible to draw out a number of wider issues both with the bus workers themselves and also with members of community groups. The Leeds Campaign Against the Cuts therefore decided to concentrate on public transport for several reasons: (a) nationally, public transport was facing the heaviest public sector cutbacks, (b) local conditions were favourable to the establishment of links between 'workers' and 'consumers' in the form of the campaign's contacts with 'Platform' (the bus workers' pressure group) and community groups, (c) 'the buses' seemed to be a clear issue for the majority of members of community groups — easy to understand and protest about, and from which wider issues could be drawn, (d) tactically (as the campaign developed) there was specific action that could be taken in the form of objecting to the Traffic Commissioners when the County Council decided to increase fares.

The development of the campaign

Reference has already been made to the formation in Leeds in 1976 of a (small) rank-and-file group of bus workers called 'Platform', whose aim was to act as a pressure group within their trade union. The nucleus of 'Platform' consisted of a small group of approximately twelve busmen (including several shop stewards) who worked in different depots throughout the city. This group attracted considerable support from other busmen, particularly in the running of the union and for more militant action against the decline in public transport which would follow from the cuts in public expenditure. The group produced a six-weekly paper, also called *Platform*, which they described as a rank-and-file paper for bus workers. Approximately 750 copies of this paper were sold in the Leeds branch, which consisted of more than 1,500 members.

Nationally the TGWU had mounted an SOS (Save Our Services) campaign, which in Leeds, early in 1977, had involved the distribution of a petition. 'Platform' worked to strengthen this limited campaign against the cuts. They were then a pressure group within the union and were not attempting to establish a separate unofficial group. Their aims were spelled out clearly in their paper:[11] 'The Leeds *Platform* is not just a paper. We are a rank and file pressure group within the 9/12 Passenger Branch of the TGWU. We stand for total opposition to cuts and redundancies. An end to fare increases. An unconditional return to free collective bargaining. Thirty-five-hour week without loss of pay. Regular election of all Union Officers by the members they represent (full-time officers to receive the average wage of their members).'

Members of the Campaign Against the Cuts had made contact with the 'Platform' group and held detailed discussions with them about the implications of the bus workers accepting the £50,000 cuts in November 1976. These bus workers agreed that cuts would obviously affect both bus workers and the community. It was decided to produce propaganda jointly. Thousands of leaflets and bulletins were produced, which were distributed among community groups, to peak-hour bus queues, at union branch meetings, and discussed with sympathetic shop stewards.

As the joint propaganda leaflet pointed out, bus workers would suffer through the cuts: there would be loss of jobs by natural wastage at first. Later, because of the fare increases, the number of passengers would drop and this would result in a cutback in bus services. From this would follow redundancies and wage cuts in the form of reduced opportunities for overtime. Obviously the community would suffer through the cuts as services deteriorated. It was pointed out that as fares were rising much faster than incomes, fewer people were already using the buses.

It became clear that public transport was an issue in which links between workers and consumers could be seen very clearly. A member of the Leeds Cuts Campaign was seconded to the 'Platform' group which felt that if the public began to protest about inadequate bus services, then this would help to put pressure on Union officials to consider more militant action against the cuts. This worker attended the weekly meetings of 'Platform', provided limited research information and created the links between them and various community groups. By early 1977 close contact had been established with a number of bus workers and shop stewards and propaganda had been widely distributed to workers and consumers.

It could be argued that if the Cuts Campaign wanted further action to be taken they should have attempted to involve the local Trades Council. Unfortunately, the local Trades Council had failed to provide any ongoing and broad campaign against the cuts; it could still be argued however, that the TGWU representatives at the Trades Council should have attempted to initiate such a campaign, particularly as it affected transport. Unfortunately, this was not possible, since at that stage the TGWU Branch had not even elected representatives to attend the Trades Council. (In fact this in itself was one issue which 'Platform' were attempting to rectify through taking it up at branch meetings.)

The Labour-controlled West Yorkshire County Council was faced with the county elections in May 1977. This Labour Council had increased bus fares by 131 per cent between 1974 and 1976;

it was the worst county spender on public transport in the country, and it spent more on roads than any other county, spending as much as London did and as much as South Yorkshire and Merseyside put together. The election served to provide a publicity forum which could be used to expose these facts and also to argue for alternative transport policy. At first it was decided that one of the shop stewards would stand as an 'anti-cuts candidate'. However, according to the then Chairman of the Passenger Transport Executive of the County Council, this was not possible because the bus worker as an employee of the County Council was not eligible to stand in county elections. It was then decided to formalise links between bus workers and consumers and at a public meeting held in April 1977 the Public Transport Group (PTG) was formed. The nucleus of this new organisation came from 'Platform' and Leeds Campaign Against the Cuts, but it soon had a great deal of wider support from bus workers and community activists. The PTG received publicity at the time of the election by appealing for a new transport policy based initially on that of South Yorkshire, a neighbouring authority which had pledged itself to no fare increases up to 1986! The PTG argued that whether Tory or Labour won the election, the results would be the same — massive fare increases.

After the Tories won the election, the Group drew up lists of sympathetic contacts and prepared leaflets and press releases in anticipation of an announcement of massive fare increases. It was decided to use objections to the Traffic Commissioners as the main focus of a broad campaign. Thus when the Tories announced fare increases of up to 33 per cent the campaign was prepared. Radio, press, and television coverage was received and the Group appealed to people to take action by objecting to the Traffic Commissioners. Leaflets containing simplified information about the technical aspects of objecting and also broad statements of policy were immediately sent to all active community groups, not just in Leeds but also in other parts of Yorkshire. Trade union branches and political parties were asked for support and assistance. A number of the bus workers spoke at community group meetings and helped to establish a very practical, as distinct from a purely theoretical, link between workers and consumers.

Some organisations such as Transport 2000 were obviously interested in the issue as soon as the PTG received publicity; they were also slightly suspicious: perhaps they felt that this new Group could have threatened their role as a pressure group concerned with public transport; perhaps the predominantly middle-class composition of Transport 2000 did not react too favourably to a group which seemed explicitly 'political'. At all events, they could not ignore the issue or the momentum which the PTG were developing around it and so they urged their members and their contacts to protest to the Traffic Commissioners against the proposed increases. Other groups, such as several predominantly working-class community associations in areas such as Holbeck, reacted very enthusiastically when bus workers spoke at their meetings urging action against the fare increases by both workers and consumers. Objections from organisations representing thousands of people arrived at the Traffic Commissioners' office. Although it was an immediate issue, it was also extremely effective in drawing out wider implications. At the community group meetings, the bus workers appealed for immediate opposition to the fare increases which the county were imposing. But they also pointed out very clearly how central government, as part of its cuts package had severely chopped subsidies to public transport. They were able to point out the effect of these cuts at a local level in terms of inadequate staffing, lack of spare parts for buses, etc., when people asked 'Why no number 86 bus turned up the other night.'

As the publicity had some impact, the group were approached by officials of the TGWU and asked to assist in drawing up a very large petition against the fare increases. The full-time officials of the TGWU had been criticised by 'Platform' for their failure to develop a strong campaign locally against the attack on public transport. To a certain extent this reflected the difficulty of moving a trade union away from its traditional and limited concerns with wages and conditions towards becoming involved in a much broader campaign. Now, however, these officials agreed with us that the only way to oppose the fare increases was by concerted joint action. From this point onwards the TGWU statements made reference to the support they had from community groups. The success of the organising work and publicity within the branch was seen very clearly when, after a recommendation by the shop stewards committee, the branch voted not to collect the increased fares if these were approved by the Traffic Commissioners.

Thus by June it seemed that the campaign had been successful both at the consumer level and also at the trade union level. The

Traffic Commissioners announced 19 July as the date of the hearing. The PTG immediately called a meeting of all objectors to discuss tactics. How did we want the hearing to be run? Which arguments did we think would have the most effect? The meeting agreed to press for the following procedural points:

The hearing should be held in the morning.

Everyone who had objected, and everyone who was a member of an organisation which had objected should be allowed into the hearing.

All objectors should be allowed to put their case and to cross-examine the PTE witnesses.

The PTE would be asked to present copies of their evidence to the objectors before the hearing.

The large number of objectors had already forced the Traffic Commissioners to move the hearing from their offices to a hall in the town centre. A total of 142 objections had come in from all over West Yorkshire and included trade union organisations, community groups, pressure groups, political groups and numerous individuals. The meeting unanimously agreed that if all the objectors were not allowed in or if there wasn't room, the hall would be occupied until suitable accommodation was found.

The hearing

The Chairman of the Traffic Commissioners appointed to adjudge the hearing was an employee of the Department of the Environment, the other two being councillors from outside West Yorkshire. The procedure is much like a public inquiry, although it is referred to as a court. At the hall the objectors found that those who had been notified of the hearing were allowed into the main body of the hall, while others were directed to the gallery. The Chairman opened by outlining the procedure he would follow.

The West Yorkshire Passenger Transport Executive had applied for a 24 per cent increase in fares. They were represented by a solicitor and two witnesses (members of their staff) who would put the case on financial and route management grounds. The statutory objectors (local councils) would then be allowed to cross-examine. Other objectors could ask questions through the Chairman (whatever the supposed difference between statutory and other objectors, it faded out as the hearing went on). Finally each objector would be allowed to make a statement. Before the hearing started, the objectors were on their feet demanding evening sessions as 'the people most affected by the increases couldn't come to hearings during the day' — and that copies of the PTE evidence be made available to them with time to study it. The Chairman refused the evening sessions saying written objections had been received and would be taken into account.

It was difficult to argue strongly for this as there were about 300 people in the hall. The PTE's initial response was that there was no legal requirement to produce copies of their evidence and that it would be expensive and time-consuming to do so. The Chairman turned down the objectors' request. However, when the objectors later interrupted the financial witness saying it was impossible to follow his evidence, the chairman adjourned the hearing early for lunch and instructed the PTE to get copies of their evidence for distribution.

The PTE argued that there were three reasons for the increases: inflation, restrictions on the amount of money available from the council and a decline in passengers. The grant from the county council had been reduced by £3.1m and the PTE had by law to balance its books by the end of the year. If the 24 per cent increase was not allowed they would make a loss of £4m in 1977 and £5m in 1978.

For the most part the objectors, in their cross-examination, left the economic arguments of running a bus service aside, and concentrated on detailing the hardship that would be caused to the elderly, the disabled, women, employed workers, etc. by the increases. The unjust nature of the increases at a time of wage restraint was mentioned by a number of objectors who felt that if the increase didn't break the price code it certainly broke the social contract. There was a strong feeling that the extra money should come from the rates not the passengers. A number of important points were brought out in the cross-examination:

The PTE had by law to provide a service as well as balance its books. But all the calculations they had made were based on economic demand and not social need.

The actual increase required in the revenue from fares was 18 per cent but they had to go to 24 per cent because any increase in fares meant fewer people could afford to use the buses.

The West Yorkshire Transport Policy Programme 1976 had stated that 8 per cent was the highest possible increase without 'endangering the public transport system or causing hardship to passengers' and the PTE witness admitted that nothing had happened since 1976 to change the situation.

Partial victory for the objectors

As the hearing went into its third day, the objectors felt the PTE would get the 24 per cent or perhaps be granted slightly less. Thus the Chairman's decision came as a surprise:[12]

> The Traffic Commissioners were approving fare increases amounting to 50 per cent of the amount asked for . . . the remaining half of the application they were approving to come into effect in February 1978 . . . although they were granting the application in two stages they would be happy to grant dispensation not to proceed with the second stage in the light of further evidence . . . in view of the considerable public reaction it was also proper for us to ask the County Council to give further consideration to public opinion.

Some of the objectors felt that the decision of the Traffic Commissioners was a major victory; others, that it was a significant partial victory. Collective pressure had resulted in the PTE only getting half its planned increase, thus saving bus users about £1.2m in fares. The Traffic Commissioners in their summing up declared: 'we accept that large increases in fares will create considerable difficulties and in many instances hardships for many people'. The Commissioners complained that the County Council who are responsible for transport policy were not present at the sitting:[13]

> most of our time has been taken up with matters which are the responsibility of the County Council. Yet we have not been able to ask direct questions to the Council. It has seemed that the public has been left to find out the background of the hearing . . . elected members of the Council, representing more than two million people have the ultimate responsibility for taking into account the *social* implications of their transport policy.

The Traffic Commissioners in West Yorkshire, then, unlike those in some other areas, agreed with objectors that it is necessary to take account of social as well as purely economic factors in transport policy. Obviously this decision does not establish a legal precedent but it is information which groups in other areas could usefully refer to.

It is interesting to note that, before and throughout the public hearing, there had been extensive press coverage. When the result was announced, however, none of the local papers, radio, or TV reported the fact that the Traffic Commissioners had spent a considerable part of their summing up criticising the Council for submitting fare increases which were 'unreasonable'. The local papers focused on the problems of the financial losses to the PTE rather than the benefits to the public.

One result of the decision was that the shop stewards committee of the bus workers reversed their previous decision not to collect the increased fares. They felt the campaign had been successful in significantly reducing the PTE's application and that consequently the bus workers would not have the continuing militancy to refuse to collect the 'reduced' increased fares. A number of the shop stewards later regretted this decision.

After the decision of the Traffic Commissioners had been announced, the County Council immediately lodged an appeal to the Minister for Transport which was heard at a public enquiry in Leeds in October. The result of that enquiry was announced on 21 December 1977. In his conclusion, the inspector said that the Traffic Commissioners had argued that the 24 per cent increase was 'too drastic and liable to cause unjustifiable hardship. They were not satisfied from the evidence that all alternatives had been properly explored.' The report went on to say that the steep increase in fares 'would hardly have been necessary but for a cut of 44 per cent in the Council's revenue support' (contribution from the rates). This cut of £3m compared with the extra £3.2m of revenue the appellants were seeking. The inspector concluded: 'I recommend that the Traffic Commissioners' decision be upheld and the appeal from the Transport Executive dismissed.'[14]

The implication of the inspector's report is very clear. West Yorkshire County Council cut the support from the rates to public transport and then ordered the PTE to make up the difference by a fare increase which would have caused unnecessary social hardship. However, rather than remedy this it seems that the County Council and the PTE are now trying to make up the difference by cutting services, despite the opposition of bus workers and bus users in Leeds, Bradford and Kirklees.

From fares to re-schedules and wages

The PTE announced in the autumn of 1977 that they were planning to introduce major 're-scheduling of routes'. This is a euphemistic term for cuts in services which could amount to 'savings' of approximately £200,000. Attempts have been made to increase union opposition to these 're-schedules' and also to make community groups aware of the implications. Leaflets explaining that re-scheduling means cuts in services have been distributed to all community groups, and in some areas of Leeds there has been opposition to the new plans by the 'consumers'.

The bus workers have recently negotiated a wage settlement which the PTE have succeeded in keeping within the Government's 10 per cent guideline. It is significant that the local press have constantly distorted the issues of busmen's pay. In 1974 they referred to '£100 a week on the buses'. In fact at present the conductor receives £31.45 for a basic 40-hour week (less than 79p an hour) and the highest rate 'on the buses' is £1 an hour for a one-man-operated bus. The Public Transport Group uses this sort of information from the bus workers to keep community groups reliably informed so that management are not able to 'blame' the bus workers' wages for increased fares and cuts in services.

Attempts are made then to create awareness of issues which have not previously been carefully considered. In the past, bus workers have not taken action over fares because it did not immediately affect their wages or conditions. After lengthy discussions, publicity and meetings, however, many bus workers did feel that this was an issue which affected them. Higher fares equals less passengers equals cuts in services equals loss of overtime, etc., became a formula which was widely discussed among busmen.

Similarly community groups in the past have not had information or discussions about the wage levels of various workers. When they become aware of the low wage levels of bus workers they will not then 'blame' them for wanting higher wages and would hopefully support the workers if they went on strike over the issue. It also becomes possible then to examine broader issues concerning the financing of public transport and to examine the role and policies of the County Council and central Government with both community groups and also the bus workers.

It is generally important then to link a number of issues currently affecting 'the buses', whether these be fares, re-schedules or wages.

The correct strategy?

It may seem from the above account that the enquiry was the major focus of the campaign generally. It is necessary then to examine critically the strategy used and consider other possible alternatives. The PTG did not believe that encouraging people to object to the Traffic Commissioners (which led to the enquiry) would 'solve' the problem of public transport in the area or even, in the short term, necessarily halt the fare increases. It was, however, a mechanism which could be used initially to focus attention on the fare increases: trade unions and community groups could be encouraged to take the simple step of objecting and then they were, however minimally, 'involved' in the campaign. If the campaign was successful (i.e. in blocking or at least holding down the fare increases), it was felt that this could be used as valuable propaganda material — 'a victory against cuts'; 'a victory for the Labour movement' etc. — in a city which over recent years had seen very little radical trade union or community action, far less the creation of links between these. It could then act as the basis for a long term campaign around transport. If the campaign failed at the enquiry stage, then the PTG still felt that its development would have meant an increased awareness of the issues around transport and the creation of links between trade unionists and consumers in such a way that a long-term campaign would still have been possible. (Since at least a nucleus of the active bus workers and community activists had never placed much faith in the use of legal mechanisms to solve basically political questions, they would not have been disappointed or disillusioned if the legal mechanisms had failed.)

Non-collection of fares?

It could be argued that the campaign should simply have concentrated on persuading the bus workers to refuse to collect the proposed fare increases. After all, at one stage in Cleveland in 1976, bus workers refused to charge passengers higher fares, and similar action had been planned in Glasgow in 1977, where it was reported that 'bus crews will refuse to implement bus fare increases in their campaign against cuts in transport services . . . the workers argue that if fares go up again, more people will be driven from public transport which will lead to further cuts and redundancies in future.'[15]

In Leeds, however, there were local factors which militated against this possibility in the early stages of the campaign. The 9/12 Leeds Branch of the TGWU had been strongly influenced by the District Secretary, a full-time official who, to judge by his reaction to previous issues, would certainly not have encouraged such action as refusing to collect increased fares. The shop stewards committee in the branch consists of more than twenty members, but at that time in early 1977 only a very small minority of these would have been in favour of this or any other kind of 'militant' action. The rank-and-file group 'Platform' had created a great deal of interest in the branch. Since they had been in existence only for some months, they did not have a strong base from which to put pressure at branch meetings on to the shop stewards committee or the full-time officials for non-collection of fares.

So where could the initiative within the union have come from early in 1977 for the bus workers to refuse to collect increased fares? It seemed clear that pressure would have to be applied from the outside on to the various levels within the union, in addition to the inside pressure which 'Platform' were attempting to develop. Hence the formation of the PTG consisting of 'Platform', several sympathetic shop stewards and a number of community activists who were able to build up the momentum of the campaign. Once this had successfully developed, the various levels within the union had to respond by taking stronger action than they might previously have anticipated, and this eventually included the shop stewards' recommendation not to collect the increased fares if they were approved by the Traffic Commissioners. Thus the weapon of 'non-collection' in Leeds appeared only in response to the successful build-up of a campaign: it was not something which 'appeared' suddenly — especially given the context of the previous policies and attitudes within the union.

Rate subsidies?

In the course of the campaign throughout the early part of 1977, regular publicity leaflets and bulletins were widely distributed around the garages and also to community groups. These contrasted the situation in West Yorkshire with that of neighbouring South Yorkshire, where it had been decided that there would be no increase in bus fares up to 1986 and where a 2-mile bus journey cost 6p, compared with 13p in Leeds. The PTG urged the Labour

Party to reverse the 'road bias' of West Yorkshire and put more resources from the rates into public transport.

This 'rate subsidy' is a more complex issue than may at first appear. It may seem necessary to press for higher rates in order to have more resources for public transport and other services, but one must be aware that rates are a highly regressive form of taxation. As long ago as 1937 the Fitzgerald Committee commented on the regressive impact of the rating system upon working-class households. Since then the situation has worsened. In 1965 the Allen Committee reported that rates were regressive since low-income households contributed approximately 8 per cent of their income in rates, while those with the highest incomes contributed just under 2 per cent.[16] It has been claimed that these findings are supported by family expenditure survey data which have been analysed to show the incidence of rates and other taxes on different income groups for the years 1959 to 1974. The evidence shows that households with low incomes pay a significantly larger proportion of their income in rates than do households with high incomes, and that the most consistent trend is the decline in the burden of rates as incomes rise.[17]

If one accepts this evidence then the political implications are clear: argue for a re-distribution within the resources currently available from the rates (for example, transfer resources from road spending to public transport), but beware of implying that the problems of public transport, or any other service in an area, can be solved by increasing the rates, since this will obviously create great suffering for low-income households.

Conclusion

It is possible to be critical of the campaign in hindsight, since the 'partial' victory merely delayed the implementation of the fares increase which the PTE had originally requested. Instead of getting their increase immediately, they had been granted half then and the rest six months later. But it is important to examine this limited victory in the context of the local situation. Neither the trade unions nor the community groups in Leeds had a recent history of militant action in spite of the decline of various industries and local communities. So it was a considerable achievement for the PTG to develop and co-ordinate the widespread opposition which came from seventeen trade unions, forty-nine other organisations, and sixty-seven individuals who, in the words of the Traffic Commissioners, represented the views of several hundred thousand people.

It is highly unlikely that there would have been any significant developments in Leeds if the PTG had not taken the initiative. Consisting of bus workers and community activists, the group were able to influence action within both the union and also other bodies outside the union, such as community groups.

On the basis of the Leeds experience, it could possibly be argued that in an area where there are strong pressures within local trade unions to oppose the decline in public transport, as reflected in increased fares, reduced services, and reduced manning levels, it may be diversionary to develop a campaign focused around objections to the Traffic Commissioners. In such cases the bus workers may immediately use their main weapon of some form of industrial action (for example non-collection of fares); the necessity then would be for publicity and links to be created with various community groups so that there could be support and encouragement for the busmen's actions, and the development of an organisational framework including both 'workers' and 'consumers' which could fight against further decline.

If however (as is unfortunately often the case) the attitude of the union at various levels is predominantly 'economistic' i.e. concerned only with their members' wages and conditions, then there will be little wider concern over the decline of public transport. In these situations it may be essential to use objections to the Traffic Commissioners for several reasons:

(a) as an immediate tactic which if successful could provide financial help for the majority of low-income households which are totally dependent on public transport: in West Yorkshire bus users were 'saved' approximately £1.2m in this way.

(b) to create greater awareness of public transport issues among community groups, and from this begin to create an organisational framework (consisting of bus users and sympathetic bus workers) which could then develop a major campaign and also put pressure on to the union to take stronger action against the decline in public transport.

An examination of the Government's intentions and those of County Councils such as West Yorkshire reveal a concern (in spite of the recent White Paper on Transport)[18] with developing an economically viable service rather than a public or social service. Public transport is seen as a residual service for those who cannot afford a car and subsidies should only be provided where it is absolutely necessary. 'The Government considers that the maintenance of adequate bus networks will require support at the present level of about £150m [but] hopes that in the longer term the need for support in urban areas will decline . . . [a subsidy] should be paid only where there is a clear requirement for it to meet social needs in transport that would otherwise not be met.'[19] 'Where social grounds for supporting services are weak, management must design fare policies so as to cover costs and produce an adequate return on planned investment.'[20]

Although the outlook appears gloomy when official policies are examined, there have been recent indications that stronger action will become more widespread as the decline in public transport becomes more and more obvious. Apart from West Yorkshire there have been actions and organisational developments in Glasgow, Cleveland, Newcastle, Edinburgh and Liverpool. The primary need is for strong organisational bases to be established in these and other areas, so that the increasing dissatisfaction over declining services can be built upon and expanded.

Notes

1 J. O'Malley, *The Politics of Community Action*, Spokesman Books, Nottingham, 1977.
2 White Paper, Cmnd 5879, HMSO, 1975; White Paper, Cmnd 6393, HMSO, 1976.
3 Transcript of the Decisions of the Public Hearing, July 1977.
4 Leeds Social Area Analysis, 1971; Leeds City Planning Department, 1971.
5 'Hunslet Appraisal: Current Situation', Leeds City Planning Department, 1976.
6 *Transport Policy: A Consultative Document*, vol. 1, HMSO, 1976.
7 *Transport Politics and the Environment*, Socialist Environment and Resources Association, p. 8.
8 *Transport Policy*, vol. 2.
9 West Yorkshire Structure Plan, Draft Report of Survey, West Yorkshire County Council, 1976.
10 West Yorkshire Structure Plan, 2nd Annual Statement, West Yorkshire County Council.
11 *Platform*, no. 3, January 1977.
12 Transcript of the Decisions of the Public Hearing.
13 Ibid.

14 Inspector's Report, PTE Appeal against decision of the Yorkshire Traffic Commissioners, 16 November 1977.
15 *Morning Star*, 25 March 1977.
16 *Report of the Committee of Enquiry into the Impact of Rates on Households*, Cmnd 2582, HMSO, 1965.
17 Frank Field *et al., To Him Who Hath: a Study of Poverty and Taxation*, Pelican, 1977, pp. 126ff.
18 *Transport Policy*, Cmnd 6836, HMSO, June 1977.
19 Ibid., p. 11.
20 Ibid., p. 14.

Part IV Recent State Initiatives

12 Local authority economic planning: a guide to powers and initiatives

Richard Minns and Jenny Thornley

No longer are local councils up and down the country sitting back and waiting for central government intervention to reduce unemployment levels and to stimulate investment in industry. They are beginning to respond to local employment needs by taking a more positive and entrepreneurial role in the economy in their area. Although community groups, trades councils, law centres and others can be involved in formulating the objectives of local economic planning, there are as yet few examples where initiatives have come from anyone other than local authority councillors and officers. Partly because of this fact more attention has so far been paid to the buildings, infrastructure and financial needs of firms than to the number and quality of jobs made available. This chapter outlines the mechanisms being used by local authorities to intervene in the local economy and discusses the advantages and practical difficulties of using each in the current economic crisis. The intention is to provide community organisations with this background material so that they can be more effective in affecting the course and impact of these local government employment strategies.

There are three ways local authorities can support industry in their areas:

1 They can examine *the effects of existing policies* for which they have a specifically designated responsibility on industry and employment: for instance, the effects of redevelopment on industrial premises.

2 They can *facilitate industrial development* by providing sites and infrastructure for factories; information on support facilities in their area; they can improve existing industrial areas and they can help in representations to central government for more financial support for industry in their areas.

3 They can *create new investment and employment* directly through intervention in the financial structure of individual firms or enterprises in one way or another.

The categories overlap to some extent and they are all relatively new areas of local authority activity. None of the categories is used systematically throughout the UK and there is little statutory guidance as to their use. In fact there is no statutory responsibility for economic or employment planning at the local authority level. Local authorities are expected to encourage development in any way possible in accordance with traditional local powers of development control and within the confines of national policies such as regional policy and new towns policy. However, the current economic situation has highlighted an increasing number of demands and proposals by local authorities for some greater powers in the field of local economic planning. The increase in activity in categories 2 and 3 above, in particular reflects this greater awareness that some additional powers are needed to fulfil new responsibilities. It is our contention that the economic situation demands more involvement by local authorities in these two areas, and that particular attention should be given to the third area — the need for involvement in the capital structure and financial planning of companies.

In order to discuss the second and third areas of local authority support for industry, let us consider how a company's finances and assets are constructed. Figure 12.1 shows the capital structure of a firm, its finance available or capital employed, and its finance expended or the employment of capital. In this chapter we want to contrast finance for specific items in the balance sheet, such as loans for buildings, with financial assistance which takes account of the total capital needs of the firm, for example, a package of equity, loans and grants.

Historically, financial assistance by the state has mainly consisted of assistance in the form of subsidies from central government and has mainly been aimed at specific items of expenditure without taking into account the capital structure of the firm as a whole. This assistance from central government has included assistance with taxation (through deferring certain tax payments), with wages (through Regional Employment Premium in the Assisted Areas), with stocks (through stock-relief) with machinery (through grants and tax-free depreciation) and with interest (deductible before tax). Assistance from local government has, in contrast,

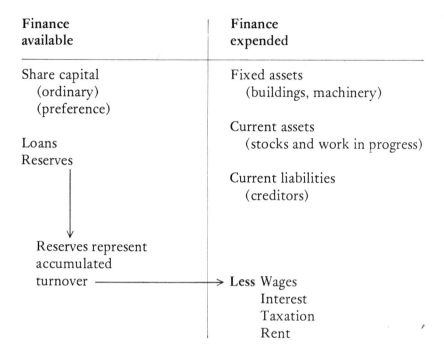

Finance available	Finance expended

Share capital
  (ordinary)
  (preference)
	Fixed assets
	  (buildings, machinery)
	
	Current assets
	  (stocks and work in progress)

Loans Reserves	
	Current liabilities (creditors)
Reserves represent accumulated turnover ——————→	Less Wages Interest Taxation Rent

Figure 12.1. Company financial statement

been very limited. It has taken the form of assistance with rents (rent guarantees and reductions), and with buildings (assistance with erection and improvement and/or loans and grants towards the costs).

Table 12.1 summarises the legal situation for local government at the end of the 1977 Parliamentary session. Although authorities had some general and Local Act powers to assist industry, even these have not been extensively used. In addition, local authority powers to assist industry are concerned primarily with the preparation, provision, maintenance, or improvement of *land and buildings*. All local authorities can, for instance, make loans for the construction of buildings, but only on land sold or let by them, under the provisions of the 1963 Local Authorities (Land) Act. Some authorities have extended their powers by private Act to include buildings on private land too.

However, only a few local authorities have managed to go further than this and obtain powers to lend money for plant, machinery and general equipment. Scunthorpe, Coventry, Shetland, South

Table 12.1. Powers relevant to specific items of expenditure in the company
financial statement

Local authority powers to assist industry contained in general and Local Acts

Power	Act	LAs
Loans for erection of buildings on land sold or let by LA, up to 75% valuation	1963 Local Authorities (Land) Act, S.3	All
Rent free or reduced rent for buildings on land let by LA, on short-term tenancy or with agreement of Secretary of State	1972 Local Government Act, S.123 .	All
Power to carry out work to prepare site of any industrial building or for improvement or provision of services and facilities and/or to make loans and grants toward their cost	Local Acts	29 LAs
Guarantee or contract to secure payment of rent on an industrial building	Local Acts	14 LAs
Loans for land purchase and erection of buildings on any land up to 90% of valuation	Local Acts	17 LAs
Loans and grants towards cost of machinery and equipment	Local Acts	5 LAs
Interest relief grants on LA loans: grants toward rent of building on non-LA land	Local Acts	1 LA

Glamorgan County, and Tyne and Wear County have obtained
specific powers to provide finance not associated with land and
buildings. The GLC attempted to secure these powers in 1974 but
was refused them on the grounds that they would bestow upon 'a
relatively prosperous area' better provisions than could be
obtained in the Assisted Areas. Since then the government's inner
city proposals announced that certain authorities, including some
in London and other non-Assisted Areas, were to receive powers
to lend to industry (Table 12.2), and that additional finance could
be made available for this purpose.

For a company to survive and grow, however, it may need more
than specific assistance with a piece of land, a building or a piece
of machinery. It may require some broader view to be taken of its
financial structure as a whole. There has recently in fact been an

Table 12.2. Local authorities designated as inner city areas to receive powers
to lend to industry

*Partnership areas**	*Other areas†*
Lambeth	N. Tyneside
Liverpool	S. Tyneside
Birmingham	Sunderland
Docklands	Middlesbrough
Newcastle/Gateshead	Bolton
Hackney/Islington	Oldham
Manchester/Salford	Wirral
	Bradford
	Hull
	Leeds ✓
	Sheffield
	Wolverhampton
	Leicester
	Nottingham
	Hammersmith

*These areas will be given powers
(a) to lend up to 90% of valuation for land purchase and erection or improve-
     ment of industrial buildings on any land.
(b) establish Industrial Improvement Areas where the authorities can carry
     out, or assist owners to carry out, conversion of buildings, etc.
(c) provide an initial rent-free period in letting of factories.
(d) help with cost of site preparation.
†These areas will be given powers (a) and (b).

increase in selective financial assistance at the national level through
the Industrial Reorganisation Corporation (IRC) and the National
Enterprise Board (NEB), and through the 1972 Industry Act. This
has enabled central government to look more carefully at the total
financial potential of individual enterprises, providing loans and
equity capital to companies where a commercial return can be
expected but where the balance sheets have become 'strained' or
where the company is going through a temporarily bad period.
Central government, through the NEB, for example, can provide
working capital or new investment capital in a way which enables
it to take into account the total financial structure of the company,
its asset base, its growth potential, its competitive situation and
its ability to become financially independent without continuous

government assistance. The object is to create viable, profitable enterprises. In the first year of the NEB's operations, a group pretax profit of £51m was made by the NEB's companies (a rate of return of 11.8 per cent), and shortly afterwards the NEB sold one of its first investments, in Reed and Smith, for a profit of £755,000. This money can then be used to reinvest in other ventures.

Most financing organisations in the public sector, which have been set up in the last few years, including the NEB, the Scottish and Welsh Development Agencies, the Northern Ireland Development Agency, and the Highlands and Islands Development Board, examine the total capital structure of a company when considering its need for finance. Loans and equity capital are viewed as part of a package of financial assistance. In particular the need for equity capital has been increasingly recognised by public bodies. Public financing bodies can provide equity capital in order to give firms a stronger base from which the firms can then approach joint stock banks for overdrafts and term loans. In addition, when these public bodies examine the financial structure of a company and give appropriate assistance, they frequently continue their involvement with the total financial structure of the company, giving advice of a continuous nature and monitoring the company's performance so that, if necessary, additional assistance can be provided at short notice.

Powers to give loan guarantees have often been suggested as an alternative to the provision of risk capital. They prevent financial disaster to a firm caused by loan obligations, whilst avoiding any of the dangers associated with public authorities owning shares. The experience of the Northern Ireland Development Agency suggests that loan guarantees are clumsy to arrange and operate. They bring all the liabilities of providing high risk capital, but none of the advantages of any return on risk for the authority. If risk capital is to be provided as part of a financial package to a firm, then it must be treated on its financial merits. Loan guarantees may have their place, but only as part of a package which may also include the provision of equity capital.

It might also be thought that interest-free loans or grants could be used instead of equity capital. Government grants are usually attributed to a firm's reserves until used and can form a useful addition to the financial assistance for firms. Interest-free loans are also useful but they remain a liability, unlike grants. As in the case of loan guarantees all these alternatives have their place as part of a total package of financial assistance. But they have only a specific short-term utility because they amount to short-term subsidies which may or may not be sufficient for the long-term growth, viability and asset build-up of a company. There is no substitute for equity capital if equity capital is what is needed.

It has become apparent that small companies are particularly in need of special financial assistance. As a result of inflation and high interest rates, their traditional financial resources contained in their accumulated reserves have been increasingly eroded. They have found it necessary to consider alternative sources of capital, but have found it difficult to attract equity capital from the increasingly influential financial institutions, insurance companies, pension funds, venture capital institutions and merchant banks, who all deal with larger amounts of money than those required by smaller firms.

Any attempt to assist the small firms' sector in obtaining equity would be an enormous task. At the present time there is a growing number of state agencies designed to provide finance for industry and some of these will be able to assist small firms. It is becoming clear, however, that existing agencies, such as the Scottish and Welsh Development Agencies, and existing policies, such as Assistance to the Regions, are not appropriate for providing selective financial assistance to firms below a certain level of market capitalisation.

It is important to consider whether local authorities should perform a role in this structure of state financial assistance and whether they should complement their increasing economic role, especially their role in the inner cities' programme, by having the power and resources to take into account the total financial structure, especially of smaller companies. This would mean being able to provide equity capital as well as loan capital according to the financial situation of the company. Looking at the problem in a different way, should local authorities play a substantial part in the risk of an enterprise for the purpose of creating viable enterprises, services and long-term employment prospects in their areas?

There are three different ways in which local authorities could adopt this approach.

(a) by providing ordinary share capital under special powers or under miscellaneous general powers, and combining this with powers to provide loans and grants;

Table 12.3. Local authority powers to assist industry contained in general and Local Acts

Powers relevant to the total financial structure in the company financial statement

Power	Act	LAs
Power to incur expenditure in the interests of their area or part of it or all or some of its inhabitants, so long as they are not authorised or required to make any payment by or by virtue of any other enactment	1972 Local Government Act S.137	1 LA — for shareholding purposes 1 LA — to assist the formation of a co-operative with loan capital
For PTE purposes, a PTE may form, promote or assist a company	1968 Passenger Transport Act S.10(1) xix	All PTEs
Power to invest in securities or bodies corporate	Zetland County Council Act 1974 S.23	Shetland
Municipal Enterprise	Local Acts	Various LAs
Power to invest up to 10% of superannuation fund in unquoted securities	1974 LA Superannuation Regulations	1 LA

(b) by forming workers' co-operatives;

(c) by the establishment of municipal enterprise.

All of these methods mean that local authorities can take into account the total financial structure of an enterprise. The last two refer more to the formation of new enterprises. The first one refers more to existing privately run companies. These distinctions are guidelines only, as we shall see.

The powers involved in providing ordinary share capital as part of a wider approach are contained in Table 12.3. Shetland Islands Council managed to secure a private Act of Parliament to enable it to assist companies with share capital, or to form new companies. It had in fact by the end of 1977 supported one existing local company and set up two others for local commercial reasons. Shetland was treated as a 'special case' by Parliament, while Tyne and Wear County Council and West Midlands County Council failed to secure similar Local Act provisions in 1976.

As an alternative, local authorities have used Section 137 of the 1972 Local Government Act by which they can spend up to a 2p

product of their rates in the interests of their area. Nottinghamshire County Council used this provision in 1975 to support
Horizon Midlands Limited, a firm on which the nearby East Midlands airport depended quite heavily. This support helped sell
some share capital owned by a failed parent company. The council
bought 10 per cent of the share capital and has subsequently seen
the market value of its shares triple in price. Meanwhile the profits
of the company increased to over £1m for the first time in the
company's history. Greater Manchester Council have used Section
137 to set up a company limited by guarantee with £5m mainly
for developing land and buildings for industry. The company can
also provide loans, guarantees and equity capital for smaller firms,
acting as the relatively independent executive arm of a new Economic Development Association for Greater Manchester.

The eight passenger transport executives (including London
Transport) which are run by the metropolitan counties, have
powers to promote or assist companies. Most of them have taken
part either in the purchase of existing transport concerns such as
coach operators in order to develop the companies' long-term
potential, or they have been involved in the acquisition of a
minority holding in such a company.

Authorities could instead follow the example of South Yorkshire County Council and put aside 5 per cent of their superannuation fund for industrial assistance in their area, either in the form
of loans or equity capital. The Council has taken advantage of the
1974 Superannuation Regulations which extended to local government funds, provisions which had applied to other funds for a long
time. It enabled them to invest up to 10 per cent of their funds in
unquoted securities, i.e. smaller firms, as part of an attempt to
diversify the pension fund into equities with low price earnings
ratios and good growth prospects. The scheme applies to firms
with a pre-tax profit level of £50,000, wanting capital injections
of £100,000–£250,000. This certainly may not apply to some of
the smaller unquoted companies who are said to find difficulty in
securing assistance with particular kinds of capital requirements.
This may be why the scheme had still not been able to advance
any money after eighteen months of operation.

Finally, Merseyside County Council evolved a scheme whereby
the council would identify small, locally based firms which needed
assistance in its area and then refer them to the NEB for the
appropriate finance. The council would also help to monitor the

progress of the companies once the NEB had provided the finance. No legal powers are necessary for this kind of direct economic activity by local authorities.

The financial implications of local authorities providing equity for small firms should not be underestimated. If all the counties provided £2m–£3m per annum for industrial assistance out of their budgets (as a few authorities have done) and if large district councils acted in the same way and provided £1m, there could be something of the order of £200m–£250m available per annum. Over a five-year period this amounts to more than the National Enterprise Board was initially allocated. If all those authorities operating superannuation funds followed South Yorkshire County Council's example and provided 5 per cent of their fund for capital assistance to local industry, they would have more *per annum* than Equity Capital for Industry[1] has got for an indefinite period. Alternatively, local authorities might want to follow the precedents set by Greater Manchester and Nottinghamshire and use Section 137 of the 1972 Local Government Act which allows local authorities to spend a 2p rate product in the interests of their area. In this case they would have another £130m per annum.

There are over thirty-five authorities which have powers to form companies or acquire equity capital, but this is restricted to companies concerned with land development. Central government has announced that Section III of the 1972 Local Government Act can be used instead of these private act powers. Section III provides subsidiary powers for local authorities to the effect that a local authority

> shall have power to do any thing (whether or not involving the expenditure, borrowing or lending of money or the acquisition or disposal of any property or rights) which is calculated to facilitate, or is conducive or incidental to, the discharge of any of their functions.

The argument put forward by central government is that so long as the company facilitates an *existing* function of the local authority, then no new powers are necessary. The acquisition of land for planning purposes and to secure development is already a local authority function, but, it is argued, promoting industry, as such, is not contained in any statute. As a result, Local Act powers to acquire equity for the purpose of industrial assistance, *per se*, are opposed by central government. Apparently, setting up companies to facilitate the implementation of the Community Land Act or some other existing function such as passenger transport responsibilities is not supposed to be open to the same risks. It is argued that an existing responsibility imposes its own discipline on ancillary shareholding activities. Where there is no existing function, it is alleged, a stream of municipal trading activities might be set up, backed by local government rate finance and thus able to compete unfairly and uncommercially with existing enterprise.

But the legal position is not in fact at all clear. It can be argued that, on the contrary, local government does have *some* responsibility for the promotion of industry and economic planning and that therefore specific Local Acts are no longer necessary for providing assistance in the form of equity. The 1963 Local Authorities (Land) Act, the inner city proposals and the various Local Acts have given authorities certain limited powers to assist industry, as we have seen. Central government's argument has become rather circular. On the one hand authorities can *lend* money to industry by using the general Act provisions or by acquiring Local Act powers to do so. They also have been encouraged by the Department of Industry to encourage productive industry wherever possible. However, they cannot have powers specifically to provide *equity* finance because the provision of such finance must be ancillary to an existing function. The importance of looking at the capital structure of companies as a whole has been ignored, even in the most recent proposals. It appears, however, that local government could now argue that the provision of equity finance *is* calculated to facilitate, or is conducive or incidental to the discharge of an existing function — that of providing loan finance.

A second method of giving direct financial assistance to firms is to assist the formation of *co-operative or common ownership enterprises*. These enterprises, collectively called workers' co-operatives in this chapter, have been formed since the last century for different historical reasons and under different legislation. Consequently, there is much variation in their form and method of operation. However, they have the following principles in common:

1 employees are able to become members of the enterprise by nominal holdings of share capital, usually £5 or less.

2 each member has one vote.

3 there is formal provision for direct employee participation in decision-making at all levels within the enterprise.

4 employees share in profits.

Recently workers' co-operatives have been associated more with central government than with local authorities. Between 1974 and 1975 loans and grants were given to Meriden Motorcycles Ltd, Kirkby Manufacturing and Engineering Ltd and Scottish News Enterprises Ltd; these were all workers' co-operatives formed after factory occupations which occurred when the firms had been threatened with closure. In each case central government went against the advice of the Industrial Development Advisory Board (which considers the feasibility of government investment) and which reported that these firms had poor prospects of long-term viability. The workers' co-operatives were supported by Government to avoid large-scale redundancies in areas already suffering from high levels of unemployment.

Central government has continued to support workers' co-operatives by providing finance under the provisions of the Industrial Common Ownership Act of 1976, and by financing a number of enterprise workshops operating as viable co-operatives through the Job Creation Programme. Often the local authority has also assisted with land and buildings. In both these cases assistance has been intended for new, profitable co-operatives with the objective of providing new jobs, and strict commercial criteria are applied when finance is made available for this purpose.

A number of local authorities have expressed an interest in helping to form new workers' co-operatives with the objective of job creation. So far only Wandsworth has succeeded, having given help to the common ownership enterprise in 1977; one collapsed in the early stages, while the other is still operating. In the latter case, loan finance was made available under S.137 of the Local Government Act 1972. Wandsworth is currently considering using the same power to set up a revolving loan fund which would act as a mechanism for assisting the formation of further common ownership enterprises.

Intervention of this kind involves the local authority more than with shareholding. The local authority must be concerned with the total operation of the workers' co-operative from its formation, not just in its capital structure. The intention is to create an enterprise which ultimately becomes self-financing, and which provides jobs for people who are unemployed, within the local authority area. In a start-up situation where the members of the workers' co-operative are mostly unemployed workers with no savings, external capital must be found for land, buildings, machinery, wages and other items such as telephone installation, etc. In addition to helping with finance, the local authority will probably need to assist the co-operative in finding a suitable product, recruiting or acquiring the right skills for the job, and marketing the product.

The type of firm that is formed in this way depends on a number of factors, such as the skills available amongst the unemployed, the availability of markets for the products, the availability of any second-hand machinery and materials that could be re-used, and the limited availability of finance. There are clearly many more constraints on the type of enterprise that can take on a co-operative form than on companies limited by share capital. The new workers' co-operatives set up with local or central government funds are usually labour intensive, e.g. making component parts for larger firms, assembly work, operating a service or manufacturing a commodity of a specialised kind, or making low-cost goods for sale to the public sector.

In supporting workers' co-operatives, local authorities are involving themselves in a high risk in that any loans made in a start-up situation, and particularly in one which has few capital assets, can only be partly secured. As with any investment made by a bank or financial institution, the loans are only given in the expectation that the co-operative will become viable. Large profits are not expected, however, because the primary objective of a workers' co-operative is unlikely to be growth. The return to the local authority on its investment is likely to be small. On the other hand certain objectives can be more readily achieved from investment in co-operatives than from investment in a company limited by shares.

The attractions of a workers' co-op for local authorities are that:

(1) They provide new jobs for unemployed people in the area.

(2) They provide jobs which are more likely to be permanent because workers' co-operatives cannot be taken over, and are unlikely to relocate from the original site.

(3) They provide jobs which are likely to be of a better quality than those which many ordinary firms provide because the objectives of the workers' co-operative are agreed by the worker-members.

In practice the achievement by local authorities in forming workers' co-operatives has been extremely small, but interest in using this as a mechanism for local economic planning is growing rapidly. It is more difficult than shareholding, because the local authority cannot draw on the expertise already developed in a firm as they can when acquiring shares in an existing company, and they may have to find a product and provide some of the skills as well as providing the finance. However, the basic principles of co-operation should mean that the enterprise will operate in the interests of the local authority without the need for any controlling interests in it, once it has been set up. This is in contrast to shareholding where the local authority as shareholder can, in theory, exercise some control over the policies of the firm but, in practice, interferes very little in day-to-day decisions. Nor can the local authority, as shareholder, control who the firm employs, or the working conditions, nor can it ultimately prevent a takeover or relocation.

Municipal enterprise

Unlike shareholding or financial assistance to co-operatives, this is not a new form of local authority activity. It is defined as the operation of an enterprise by a body appointed by a local authority — normally a local authority department. During the nineteenth century municipal enterprise was very widespread, and concerned mainly with the production and distribution of gas, water and electricity, and the running of ports, harbours, transport services and public works departments. It developed in an ad hoc way with Local Acts of Parliament being followed gradually by general enabling powers.

These activities were taken over from private companies by local authorities and continued to be operated as companies. The local authorities were therefore involved in risk-taking. Heavy subsidies were often made. Losses were incurred because the prices of commodities or services were not set at a level which reflected the costs of production. Rather, prices were deliberately reduced so that the supply of commodities and services would be more systematic and regulated. Although this benefited the population as a whole, its major purpose was to increase the competitiveness of manufacturing industry which used the goods and services in question.

Most of these activities were nationalised in the twentieth century; only direct works and some transport services have remained the responsibility of local authorities. Direct works departments are still run as a kind of municipal enterprise, sometimes making a profit, but more often they are loss-making. Most aspects of public transport are now run as a service by Passenger Transport Authorities (PTAs) in the metropolitan counties and by county councils. There are scattered examples of aerodromes, ports and harbours and the Manchester Ship Canal which are still run as municipal enterprises.

Since 1945 new municipal enterprises have been introduced on a small scale mostly for leisure or cultural purposes, such as sports centres, theatres or festivals. Hardly any were ever intended to be viable and they involve the local authority in no risk.

Recently, a number of local authorities have considered expanding municipal enterprise in their areas. The reasons for this have changed; instead of assisting the competitiveness of private manufacturing industry as in the nineteenth century, municipal enterprise has been demanded in order to improve the local economy and employment opportunities. Some local authorities have pressed for increases in direct works departments. The West Midlands County Council, in its Bill of 1975, proposed that the local authority itself should manufacture commodities for sale in the local area, and suggested commodities which were not already produced locally, such as school furniture, school clothing, bricks, timber and joinery materials. In these recent cases, the local authorities involved intended that the municipal enterprises proposed would not be subsidised and would be run as a normal risk-taking venture. The West Midlands failed to get the necessary powers and DLOs have not been expanded. While these new or increased entrepreneurial activities would have resulted in more local jobs and industry, they would have been very costly to set up at a time when public expenditure was being cut back. They would also be difficult to operate as business ventures, being so closely integrated into the local authority's other operations and budgeting. Other mechanisms have been found for intervening in the local economy which involve less expenditure and less continuous control.

Conclusions

We have described the three major ways in which local authorities can intervene directly in the financial structure of individual firms, and have discussed why local authorities should consider these mechanisms in addition to more traditional assistance for land and buildings. We have concluded that the shareholding mechanism offers the most advantages in the present economic recession.

Support for workers' co-operatives can achieve the objective of providing job opportunities tailor-made for groups of unemployed people in the area, and the management of the firm, although constrained by financial considerations, can be controlled by the workers themselves. Assistance takes place almost entirely during the start-up period. Once the workers' co-operative has become viable, little further support may be needed as it will either be self-financing or may attract financial assistance for growth or technological change from elsewhere. However, during the start-up period the local authority must provide all the initial capital and involve itself in all aspects of the enterprise. At this point the risks and costs in manpower and finance to the local authority are very high.

Municipal enterprise, like assistance to workers' co-operatives, requires the local authority to take the whole risk and cost of starting up a new venture. Because it is operated within the local authority itself, all its activities must be monitored continuously. In addition, it is liable to differential application of council policy according to the political party in power, and it does not attract investment capital from outside the local authority. In other words, the risks and costs involved are greater than with a workers' co-operative.

The main advantage of shareholding is its pump-priming nature. With a relatively small input of risk capital, the local authority can help to make a small firm viable and improve its capital structure so that it can attract further investment from private sources, such as banks and ICFC. Compared with workers' co-operatives and municipal enterprise, the local authority's involvement with a firm in which it acquires shares is extremely small. While regular monitoring of the firm's financial position is necessary, assistance will rarely be needed in marketing, accounting, production, training, and the day-to-day operation of the firm. For these reasons, shareholding can take place on a much larger scale than the formation of workers' co-operatives or municipal enterprise. In addition, once a large portfolio of firms has been built up, the local authority may expect to receive a regular return on its investments from dividends and the sale of shares, and this return can be ploughed back for further shareholding.

It is important to remember that there are additional aspects to arguments for shareholding depending on whether shareholding is looked at from the point of view of community groups, local government or central government. Community groups might want to consider whether companies in which the local authority has a financial interest are fulfilling certain legal requirements provided for in measures such as the Employment Protection Act and the Safety and Health at Work Act. Both local authority and community groups may want to consider what happens when small unquoted companies with local authority equity grow and are taken over by larger companies whose main operations are outside the local area. They should also consider what might happen if a small firm moves from their area. It may be possible to operate fairly simple local planning agreements with some faster growing firms. By providing financial support the local authority could obtain a better idea of growth and expansion plans so that it could be ready to point out or provide additional land and services in the locality.

Community groups may also be concerned about the implications of a local authority operating in an entrepreneurial manner. In order to separate local government commercial operations from its other statutory requirements and obligations it may be necessary to create a structure such as a Municipal Enterprise Board based on the models provided by Passenger Transport Executives or Greater Manchester's Development Association. There should be considerable discussion about who should be represented on these Boards from the local authority, the local community and local branches of trade unions and trade councils.

Finally, central government would be very concerned about the operation of its industrial strategy which provides selective assistance to certain key sectors and to certain firms. This assistance is provided through specific financial programmes and through agencies such as the National Enterprise Board. It is important to consider how local authority economic planning and selective financial intervention could assist small firms in the same key sectors as the central government strategy, and how it could assist firms which were suppliers to NEB firms, such as components suppliers to British Leyland, or firms which could achieve the same objectives as NEB firms, such as contributing to exports or import substitution, and long-term viability, or firms which were generally too small for central agencies to assist in meaningful numbers but which contributed to the innovatory role of the small firms sector.

Before local authority shareholding is accepted by the state on any significant scale, a lot of these points will have to be explored further. It is hoped that community groups and local authorities will give this kind of local economic planning serious consideration and help to develop these arguments with the benefit of their local experience.

Note

1   Equity Capital for Industry was set up in 1976 by the larger financial institutions in order to provide equity capital for medium-sized companies. The institutions subscribed £41m to the enterprise.

Further reading

Richard Minns and Jennifer Thornley, *State Shareholding: the Role of Local and Regional Authorities*, Macmillan, 1978.

Richard Minns and Jennifer Thornley, 'The Case for Municipal Enterprise Boards', *New Society*, September 1976.

P. B. Rogers and C. R. Smith, 'The Local Authority's Role in Economic Development: the Tyne & Wear Act 1976', *Regional Studies*, 11(3), 1977.

13 Employment policy in one London borough

Tom Davies

Introduction: the setting

In the last decade successive governments have been concerned at the possibility that the North American experience of inner urban area decline would be repeated in Britain. In the mid 1970s the Inner Area Studies suggested this was the case and that decline had even affected London, the country's most prosperous city. The Studies, like others, clearly identified economic decline as a major factor in explaining the growing poverty and under-privilege of the inner city.

Previously London had enjoyed relatively low rates of unemployment. However the economic crisis, which had been building up since the late 1960s, has resulted in the late 1970s, in unemployment rates close to or even in excess of those in the Assisted Areas.

London, then, like Britain's other older urban areas, has experienced the twin impact of inner urban decline and a deepening economic crisis. Something had to be done. Local authorities were in many cases quicker to react to this economic crisis than central government. In London the inner boroughs were under particular pressure since all their territory lay within the 'inner city'.

Central government's first reaction was that local authorities had no role in the field of economic policy, traditionally the prerogative of the Departments of Trade and Industry and Employment. Gradually it has slowly come to realise that local authority employment policies, if carefully controlled, need not interfere with its wider, national strategies for manpower planning and the distribution of productive investment. Indeed local authorities' employment measures are taking their place in a carefully deployed battery of policies, with which central government is dealing with the problems arising from the restructuring of the British economy as a whole.

Central government then has become more favourable to local authority action, though within strictly defined limits. Thus the new programmes for the unemployed (like those of the Manpower Services Commission) although acknowledging the role of local initiative, include a large and distant bureaucracy designed to ensure central control. The Inner Urban Areas legislation, too, closely limits the powers, the finance and the areas in which the policies can be applied. Moreover it gives the central role to government departments, Ministers and the Secretary of State. The government departments' hostility to the increase of local powers in the GLC General Powers Bill was directed against any likely loss of central influence over local government employment policies and the possibility of conflict with the government's industrial strategy.

The problem

The London Borough of Wandsworth has experienced its fair share of the inner city employment problem. Since 1966 it has lost well over 50,000 jobs at an average rate of 3,500 per year. It has also lost economically active residents — at a rate of around 2,500 per year — as the population has moved to the outer boroughs and to the south-east. There is a widening gap then between the jobs available and the people looking for work. More particularly the number of skilled workers in the borough has decreased faster than the number of unskilled.

However, the local economy of Wandsworth is not yet dead. There are still many thousands of jobs in the borough provided by private companies, both large and small, and by central and local government. Many of these organisations are economically healthy enough to consider expansion. Indeed some of them have no choice if they are to survive.

Moreover the departure of the large plants, particularly those of the Gas Board and British Rail and some private sector firms, have left large acreages of derelict land and buildings which can be redeveloped for industry. This factor at least is a real advantage. Lambeth, adjacent to Wandsworth, does not have such a land reservoir, for example. Wandsworth has therefore a responsibility not just for the workers of its own borough but for those in adjoining areas too.

The history of the council's policy

In 1972 Wandsworth was among the first councils in the country to recognise that there was a growing employment problem in the inner city, that the council was itself contributing towards it, and that something should be done about it.

Initially the main issue which was identified for action was the displacement of small industries by the council's housing programme. Hundreds of jobs were disappearing each year as the council demolished small run-down factories to clear sites for housing. A full-time officer was appointed to find sites for the relocation of such firms. In addition it was suggested that the council should build a block of small unit factories for these firms and also provide land for firms which preferred to build their own premises. A number of other policies, chiefly concerned with development control, were also put forward.

The council's policy developed from these relatively conventional beginnings and recently became widely acknowledged in local government circles to be the most 'advanced' policy of any of the London boroughs. In May 1978 the Labour administration lost power in the local elections. The new Conservative administration, pledged to holding the rate, has looked to employment policy for sweeping savings. Finance may be available, however, from other sources, and many of the non-radical elements of the policy may survive.

The pressure for development of the previous administration's policy appears to have come from two directions: back-bench councillor pressure, in which aldermen played an important role, and specialist officer pressure, particularly from the Planning Department. The political context in which the councillors moved was influenced by their own work backgrounds (key councillors were professionals working in other local authorities) and by their close links with community organisations (such as trades councils and pressure groups, including Friends of the Earth and the Socialist Environment and Resources Association).

In 1975 the local unemployment figures and new evidence about the loss of jobs from the borough made it obvious that the limited actions which the council had taken (and which did not even yet include the building of the proposed factory block) were insufficient. This led to a re-think of the policy as a whole. While this exercise was going on, a back-bench policy review committee of councillors was looking at the same problem.

The report of that committee, entitled 'Prosperity or Slump', received widespread publicity. It put forward a number of proposals for the revival of the local economy. Its underlying assumption was the controversial conclusion that the private sector was largely responsible for job decline and had 'failed Wandsworth'. Its proposals emphasised the case for the creation of a largely 'local grown' economy, founded upon a combination of industrial co-operatives and municipal enterprise. Public enterprise and self-management were to provide the solution to the decline of the private sector in Wandsworth.

The report coincided with, and was encouraged by, a renewed interest in employment policy in the council at large. The Leader and the Mayor were both particularly concerned. The council established a rolling programme of industrial building and land release. Further proposals dealing with training and discrimination in the labour market were added to produce the combined 1976 'Employment Policy Review' published by the Planning Department. This formed the basis for policy as laid out in the then Draft Borough Plan. Resources were allocated to the programme, through a process of bargaining with established budget committees. This involved shifting spending priorities, with the Planning and Transport Committee emerging as the main implementing committee.

This was a major victory for the chairman of that committee. It is traditional in local authorities that employment should be the province of either the Estates or Chief Executive's Department. In Wandsworth, by contrast, an Employment Development Office was set up within the Planning Department with three full-time officers responsible for industrial development, relocation, small firms, co-operative development and training. All these resources are located in the Planning Department because the then Planning Committee chairman and the Director of Planning were anxious to see employment policy, physical and non-physical, vested in one committee. The new administration has removed responsibility for employment policy from the Planning Committee, placing it with the powerful General Purposes Committee.

The objectives of the previous council's policy

The Labour council's policy acknowledged the tremendous importance of the loss of jobs, the difficulties of local people in finding suitable employment and the powerlessness of the local community to influence economic decisions which are vitally important for it.

There were, accordingly, three objectives for the policy:

(a) To conserve and regenerate the local economy.
(b) To increase the access which Wandsworth people have to jobs which are worthwhile.
(c) To increase the control which local people have over the economy in the borough.

This section briefly summarises these policies, highlighting those most open to community involvement.

Economic regeneration

Conservation and regeneration of local industry was to be achieved by giving security to those employers who do not spoil the environment, particularly those providing employment for local workers (for example working mothers); first by helping local firms who wished to expand by assembling expansion sites; second by assisting with the modernisation of premises for them; third by attracting new firms into the borough; fourth by encouraging the creation of entirely new firms.

The council also encouraged the establishment of a co-ordinated information system for local firms, particularly small firms. A chief element of this was a counselling service called the Small Firms Resource Centre, employing voluntary help. New firms were to be encouraged by establishing an Innovations Centre where inventions could be tested out, prototypes built and test marketing made. These policies were to be operated all over the borough, but certain areas were chosen for special treatment where there are concentrations of industry in obsolete, crowded premises (Industrial Improvement Areas), or where there are concentrations of employers in residential areas (Local Employment Areas). Most of these policies may survive, but only if mostly financed from outside the council, or restructured to minimise council expenditure.

Access to jobs

Local people's access to worthwhile jobs was to be increased, first by improving services (public transport, day care places for the children of working parents and so on) and second by expanding training opportunities. The council was also committed to promote policies against sexual and racial discrimination in the labour market.

In general the council's aim was to ensure that both new and existing jobs in the borough were worth while, using its development control powers and its lettings policy on its own buildings.

The Labour council had an ambitious programme for the release of land so that new factories and offices could be built. The council built its own factories, purchasing land for firms to build their own factories and was about to go into partnership with private industrial developers. (In these cases the council's intention was to retain control over the lettings.) The council also intended to help small firms find funds for expansion.

All this costs money, of course, and the council was, at the time of its demise, spending at a rate of £1.5m per annum on the policy. That budget would have had to expand if the objectives were to be achieved. However, if all the elements of the policy were successful, it was estimated that they would eventually create new jobs in the borough at a rate of something like 1,500 per year; sufficient to begin to close the employment gap, albeit slowly.

Increasing local people's control over the economy

'Prosperity or Slump' highlighted the plight of local workers and the community, helpless in the face of those decisions of big business and the state made outside the borough which had led directly to the loss of jobs from Wandsworth. The Labour council wanted to do something about this state of affairs and build into its policies ways in which local control could be increased.

There are three ways in which the council tried to improve the community's control over the local economy:
(a) by increasing the control which it exercised as the then elected representative of the community;
(b) by increasing the control which workers in the borough could have over the economic decisions of the firms in which they work;
(c) by increasing the participation of community organisations in the decisions taken by the council about the local economy.
We now look at these in detail.

Control by the council

The council was seeking to control economic activities in Wandsworth by:

seeking to participate in any planning agreements which are established by central government where the firms involved might have branch plants in the Borough.

seeking to establish 'local planning agreements' with small firms in the borough who might seek or accept help from the council.

by establishing a 'good employer code' which would be used as a guide in dealing with firms and particularly in lettings procedure.

by expanding the numbers of workers employed in municipal enterprises (and by developing workers' participation in these).

Planning agreements: Wandsworth's participation in national planning agreements was hampered by the obvious problem that the government had managed to secure only one agreement, and that with a firm with no branches in the borough. Moreover the council had not established its right to participate in assessing the local impact of any such agreement. This was further complicated by the presence at County Hall of a Conservative council who were not interested in forming a channel of communication with the government on this matter.

Local planning agreements were held up because the council had not yet implemented its policies for providing help for local firms. The Small Firms Resource Centre, the Local Employment Area and Industrial Improvement Area policies and the provision of financial aid to small firms were all at the stage of seeking or awaiting full powers and establishing budgets when the administration changed. Had they been implemented, then a form of local planning agreement would have been worked out which would have incorporated the 'good employer' criteria and a pledge from the firm to ensure security and continuity of jobs in the borough, in return for the council's providing financial and other assistance.

The Good Employer Code: the Good Employer Code had just been approved by the council when the administration changed. Its aim was to produce a set of criteria which could be used for deciding when the council should have dealings with existing local firms or house new ones. The Labour council considered it to be a nonsense to spend public money in creating new jobs for the local population, or in continuing old ones, if those jobs paid badly, had low levels of skill achievement, were inherently insecure or if the workers in them lacked the right to basic trade union organisation.

One of the first areas in which the Code was to be implemented was in the council's lettings policy. Leases of council buildings and land were to contain clauses to ensure that the occupiers complied with the code. It was thought that the demand for Wandsworth's industrial property, which is very high, would be sufficient to allow the Valuers Department to make a preliminary selection of firms who were already complying with those criteria. Opponents of these clauses felt they would restrict the market, exposing the council to accusations of not behaving in a 'businesslike' manner when administering commercial property on behalf of the ratepayers. It is, however, more likely that the application of these clauses would have had the incidental effect of weeding out the marginal firms of the inner city and thus bring a concentration of more stable firms with the ability to pay good rents over a long time. The Code was withdrawn by the new administration immediately after taking office. Wandsworth had earlier put forward the Code to the other Inner London Boroughs for adoption, but they had turned it down.

Municipal enterprise: the council employs hundreds of workers in its direct building organisation, its laundry and its printing activities. Such municipal enterprises can in some cases sell goods and services to other public bodies and, of course, to voluntary bodies and community organisations. Future expansion of the numbers employed in such enterprise would have depended upon the council's ability to exploit such markets. However, the new administration has decided to run down direct labour in Wandsworth, so expansion is unlikely in this field.

Workers' control

The Labour council tried to increase the direct control which workers have over their jobs by:
(a) encouraging the establishment of industrial common ownership in the borough, and
(b) increasing the number of workers who are unionised.
    The Labour council attached great importance to the establish-

ment of a significant number of jobs in common ownership enterprises. The failure of both private and public sectors to take the interests of Wandsworth workers into account when making their investment decisions had brought the council to this conclusion.

Accordingly the council established a budget for the support (mainly through loans) of co-operatives and appointed an officer within the Employment Development Office with significant responsibility for this policy. In the first year of the policy, the groundwork for the policy was in the process of being established.

A vital element in the groundwork was set up when the Inner London Education Authority, with the council's support, secured finance under the government's Job Creation Scheme to set up a market research project to provide the co-operative programme (as well as conventional firms) with 'packaged' products, whose production possibilities, markets, manpower requirements, etc., have been fully researched. These products can then be 'married' to potential co-operators who will receive any necessary pre-training from ILEA.

The council was also proposing to help finance the establishment of a Wandsworth Co-operative Development Agency whose function would be to provide advice, guidance and assistance, including financial assistance, to potential and on-going co-operatives. The Innovations Centre, which has already been mentioned, was to play an essential role in the generation of new co-operatives; innovators were to receive particular encouragement if they were prepared to become co-operators.

Despite the fact that this framework was still being constructed, co-operatives were already being set up in the borough, although only one had at the time of writing been able to get of the ground (with finance from both the Manpower Services Commission (MSC) and from the council, the latter in the form of a loan). The target for the programme, under the old administration, was to be 200 new co-operators per year.

The future of the co-operative programme is not clear. Its budget is at risk in the effort of the new administration to cut expenditure. However, the Conservative council has accepted co-operative development as part of its employment policy. The policy also depends upon the attitude of the MSC, whose labour subsidy is essential, in introducing its enterprise workshop scheme in the new programme for the unemployed. It will also depend upon the identification of appropriate products and services with viable markets, and upon the potential co-operators receiving training both in basic management and production skills.

The Labour council was working towards the unionisation of the labour force in the borough, both through the lettings policy and through the work of the Community Development Team. The Team was concentrating particularly on categories of workers who are traditionally underunionised such as out-workers, women part-time workers, and workers in small firms. The new administration is pledged to removing the function of the Team.

Participation by community organisations

The Labour council generated its employment policy for Wandsworth with the active participation of local organisations, chiefly through the work of the local Trades Council, and through liaison committees and working parties.

The Trades Council was particularly active in the formulation of the 'good employer' policy through its relationship with Councillors and with the Community Development Team. The Employment Liaison Committee and the Youth Employment and Training Working Party are the two main venues for the participation of local organisations. The former has representatives from both sides of industry and from the voluntary sector. The latter has membership which includes most local activists with a particular interest in employment, as well as representatives of government departments and the Education Authority. Both are still in existence. The former has had its importance increased under the new administration. The latter has been recognised by the MSC as a Local Board for the new programme for the unemployed.

The Employment Liaison Committee has three functions: monitoring the progress of the employment policy, suggesting the broad outline of the policy's future development and communicating the policy to the community. The Youth Employment and Training Working party is concerned with job creation policies for young people and the provision of appropriate training in the borough.

Conclusion

Wandsworth's previous administration, then, was attempting, within a framework of tight government control and increasing centralisation, to introduce a coherent approach to the complex problems of inner city employment. In addition, the council was trying to involve the local community in the process.

Local authorities vary in the extent to which they rely on the voluntary sector and other community initiatives. The Labour council had tried to develop a policy which laid equal stress on the roles of central and local government, the private sector and the community's formal organisations. The intention was thus to increase the impact which local authority policies could have upon a highly intractable situation.

It is on this policy of community involvement, as well as on the employment policy itself, that Wandsworth's Labour council's innovatory employment policy should be evaluated.

14 The politics of job creation

Martin Loney

Mass unemployment is now an international phenomenon and work creation programmes part of the post-Keynesian weaponry for counteracting slumpflation. The Keynesian remedies no longer work. In the post-war period deficit budgets and an increase in the money supply have been used to combat a strong down-turn in the economy. Conversely inflation has been restricted by cutting back public spending and tightening the money supply. Now with growing unemployment occurring simultaneously with high inflation, new methods of control are necessary. The most significant of these have been the incomes policy and the cut-backs in public expenditure. The first has sought to raise the profitability of private capital and thereby encourage investment, while the public sector cut-back has been intended to shift resources into the private sector.

State expenditure has been responsible for a growing share of Gross National Product (GNP) in all western economies. In Britain, state expenditure rose as a proportion of GNP from 42.1 in 1961 to 50.3 in 1971 and to 57.9 per cent in 1975.[1] The public sector cutbacks in 1975 reversed this trend. The government's expectation was that this would reduce inflation and stimulate private sector expansion. In fact the private sector has continued to stagnate and one major consequence of the cutbacks has been to increase unemployment.

The government's entry into work creation schemes may at first sight contrast oddly with its commitments to controlling the growth of the public sector. To some extent declining public sector employment is compensated for by work creation programmes. There is however a crucial difference between the unionised state employee with some measure of job security and the client of the work creation schemes. The latter is paid less and is employed for only a short period. Wages are deliberately set at a level which cannot compete with any available employment in the private sector. In some cases what this means is that those who are unemployed as a consequence of the cuts may be temporarily re-employed doing the same kind of work without job security or union rates of pay. In London, St Pancras Station is being cleaned by a Job Creation Project, work which, in more affluent days, might have been undertaken by a regular workforce. Those involved in the new Youth Opportunities Programme will be paid a standard allowance which the Manpower Services Commission (MSC) believes is 'more appropriate than a wage'.[2]

The Job Creation schemes have received mixed support from the trade union movement. The TUC has been involved in the development of the programme, but at a local level reactions have varied. In Scotland the largest local authority, Strathclyde, is running over twenty training workshops funded by MSC. In London, on the other hand, the NALGO branch in the Borough of Wandsworth have vetoed any Council schemes, arguing that any necessary work should be undertaken by expanding the Council's permanent staff.

Work creation and training programmes allow the government to directly reduce the official unemployment figures without reflating the economy. They enable the government to keep the unemployed in contact with the disciplines of work at the lowest possible cost. In the event of a new wave of expansion the unemployed will have been kept in readiness for renewed activity. In that sense the schemes can be seen as a device for 'oiling' the reserve army of labour. This concern is by no means the exclusive focus of the programmes and indeed as successive economic recoveries fail to materialise it must be difficult, even for the most optimistic bureaucrat, to worry about potential labour shortages.

In early 1976, Chancellor Denis Healey set the target for the reduction of unemployment at 700,000 by 1979. This reduction was to be achieved by an export-led expansion in the manufacturing sector. This expansion failed to take place and economic stagnation coupled with a continued increase in the size of the labour force suggest not a reduction of unemployment, from the 1.2 million of early 1976, but further increases.

The latest MSC projections now suggest that to reduce unemployment to one million by mid-1981 would require an unprecedented growth rate of 6 per cent.[3] The Cambridge Economic

Policy Group whose radical recommendations include import controls and comprehensive planning, have argued that present policies will result in unemployment rising towards five million in the next ten years.[4] In these circumstances, work creation and training programmes assume more importance as measures which demonstrate government action and concern for unemployment and which obscure the major effect of the government's industrial strategy, an *increasing* real level of unemployment. The programme also serves as measures of social control over the unemployed and may well prove to be the harbinger of a much larger scheme which will compel the growing army of the unemployed into periodic low-paid service in the work creation industry.[5]

Shifting the blame

Training and work experience programmes emerged as a major component of the American 'War on Poverty'. The belief in the social pathology of deprived areas and in the low motivation and skill level of the poor themselves suggested that programmes designed to increase the occupational skills and improve the social attributes of the poor would automatically reduce the numbers in poverty. What the 'War on Poverty' sought to do was to adjust the supply side of the labour market in the belief that the demand side would expand accordingly. Based on a false premise, the programme attacked the wrong target. Marris and Rein in a seminal critique on the 'War on Poverty' argued that the failure to gear the local programme to a national expansion in job opportunities resulted in further disillusionment of the poor 'as each door they opened led nowhere, they were continually adding anterooms in which an appearance of hopeful activity disguised the ultimate frustration'.[6]

Unless there are fundamental changes in the structure of Britain's economy, this conclusion will provide a fitting epitaph for Britain's Job Creation programme. In an economy with full employment, work experience programmes are unnecessary; the transition from school to work, and the disciplines of the factory are learned in real life. Special training programmes to give sixteen-year-old school-leavers 'industrial experience' such as those recently proposed by the TUC[7] are no more than a cosmetic. With full employment firms will provide their own training, while no amount of training will create new jobs for anybody other than the trainers. The only rational roles for such programmes would be to reach marginal groups who need to be reintegrated into the labour force, as Marris and Rein argue: 'The difficulties of young people from the ghettoes in mastering the demands for employment, or the insensitivity of schools and social agencies, only become crucial as the resources to provide decent jobs and training are assured.'[8]

If the level of unemployment cannot be seen as a function of the skill level of the potential workforce, and in the absence of any evidence that the training programmes reduce the total number of unemployed – except by recategorising a certain proportion as 'trainees' – we must look elsewhere for the rationale behind Britain's Job Creation programme. I would suggest that a prominent feature of the programme is a concern for social order. The Job Creation programme ensures a level of dependence between client and the state, mediated perhaps by a private employer. The habits of obedience and regular attendance are inculcated. On the other hand, since the clients of the programmes remain subsidised and basically non-productive, they cannot easily develop the militancy of productive workers.

The programmes provide a manifest indication of government concern and simultaneously relocate responsibility for unemployment on the workforce, rather than the social system. A recent Youth Opportunities Programme (YOP) advertisement reveals some of the underlying factors. It claims that 'existing schemes have succeeded in helping as many as eight out of ten participants into jobs'. The suggestion is that the YOP will be equally successful. We are told that 'without experience or skill, young people haven't a hope' of work. The suggestion of course is, that with increased skills, unemployment will be reduced, yet in the same period for which the MSC is claiming success, unemployment continued to rise and youth unemployment rose even faster than the adult rate.[9]

Any success the MSC has had could more accurately be seen as a shuffling of faces in the dole queue, as their 'graduates' were able to out-manoeuvre other unemployed young people in the jobs scramble. The limitation of such success is obvious. Once the programme is expanded to encompass a significant proportion of the age group, it cannot hope to succeed, since it makes no impact on the supply of jobs – with the exception of the dramatic growth of the MSC itself. If every unemployed young person is absorbed into the programme, the programme's success rate will be a precise reflection of the level of total employment, though no doubt the MSC will initiate detailed research to find why programmes in areas of high unemployment are not as successful as those in areas of low unemployment.

The Commission's concern for social order is explicit. The alternative to the programme 'is a growing number of young people who feel discarded by "the system"'. What is unstated is that those who are 'discarded' may, feeling they have nothing to lose but their social security benefits, seek to change 'the system' for one which will not leave two million people unemployed.

The concern with social order is not, of course, simply the result of a fear of protests from the left. In fact, the rise of the National Front has probably been a more important factor in increasing funds both for Job Creation and for the inner city. Peter Walker has drawn attention to the more general fear of disorder which may underlie such programmes. This disorder may be reflected in higher crime statistics or, particularly where other grievances are also present, in rioting. In an 'Open Letter to the Prime Minister', the former Conservative Minister for the Environment warned that unless urgent action was taken to improve the conditions of those of West Indian origin living in Britain[10]

> the reality of their bad housing, bad education and high unemployment is of such dimensions, that, unless tackled effectively and quickly, it will bring Britain the crime, the bitterness and the resentfulness that have been such a tragic feature of the American cities that have equally failed to identify the aspirations, hopes and deep disappointments of their coloured population. Birmingham and London possess the main concentration of West Indians. Our first and second biggest cities are therefore threatened unless we succeed in taking effective and imaginative action.

The magnitude of black unemployment was illustrated in a 1977 MSC report which found that 'while total unemployment had increased by 120 per cent since 1974 the numbers of coloured workers unemployed increased by 350 per cent.'[11] James Prior, opposition employment spokesman, told a conference of Conservative trade unionists of the danger of high unemployment amongst the young and particularly amongst young immigrants: 'in the past two weeks in Birmingham and Liverpool, I have listened to disturbing evidence of the growth of crime and vandalism amongst the young unemployed.'[12]

The concern with disenchanted youth has found wider support partly as a consequence of the declining membership of the traditional political parties. The government-funded British Youth Council held a series of discussions with Prime Minister Callaghan's political office and there was talk of a national investigation into the alienation of youth from the political party system.[13] Subsequently it was announced that Edward Heath would chair a new parliamentary committee to examine youth problems.[14]

The Job Creation scheme

One of the first major job creation schemes was established in Canada. This programme, Opportunities for Youth (OFY) and the adult work creation schemes, the Local Initiative Programme (LIP) and the Local Economic Activity Programme (LEAP) provided much of the inspiration for early British efforts. Canada historically has had a higher level of unemployment than most OECD countries and consequently developed its work creation programme earlier. The OFY programme was specifically set up in 1971 to absorb potentially dissident students and marginal youth by providing funds for summer work projects. A confidential evaluation of the programme commissioned by the government observed that[15]

> the decision to focus the summer 1971 effort primarily on students and also to some small extent on the marginal youth sub-culture — as opposed to dealing with youth and other disadvantaged groups generally — must be examined in terms of the perceived relationship between unemployment, inactivity and social unrest. For it was not unemployment *per se* which was seen as creating social unrest, but rather inactivity and non-participation in general.

The British Youth Opportunities Programme is the result of the rationalisation and enlargement of the earlier youth training and work experience schemes. Initially established as a short-term response to youth unemployment, the schemes have grown as the target group has increased. The new YOP must be seen as a major plank in the government's efforts to reduce the participation of sixteen- to twenty-five-year-olds in the regular labour force. The provision of a broad range of training programmes, the establishment of work experience programmes, and the attraction of more school-leavers into post-secondary education, particularly into lower-cost technical colleges and polytechnics, will have a major effect on youth unemployment figures. Looking at the dramatic effect which educational expansion had in reducing labour force participation in North America, one commentator aptly termed the expanded universities 'the new proletarian parking lot'.[16] In Britain cheaper storage space will be found but the metaphor remains apt.

The YOP, like the OFY, is concerned that unemployment will result in 'an ever-increasing number of young people who feel alienated and embittered'.[17] Again, as in the Canadian Programme, concern is with creating activity rather than increasing productivity. Any scheme which began to market its products would be in danger of attack from existing producers for placing them 'at risk'.

The government has so far resisted pressure to put more money into self-sustaining co-operative ventures. Under the JCP scheme 1 per cent of funds were allocated for 'pump-priming workshops including co-operatives', but there is no such provision in the new programmes. Some support might be given to co-operative ventures but demands made for a much larger provision of seed money have not been taken up. Since such ventures, however risky, do provide the possibility of an increase in permanent employment, the government's refusal to sanction a significant programme in this field must be seen in the context of the general conservatism of its economic and social policy.

The major differences between the British and the Canadian schemes lie in the magnitude of the British programme. It is intended that the YOP will cater for 234,000 young people every year, and will provide a place in the programme for every unemployed school-leaver by Easter 1979. The 'trainee' will be paid £19.50 per week usually for up to six months. What will happen to the 'graduates' of this scheme is unclear. In launching the scheme the MSC claimed that a survey showed that 72 per cent of those on the previous Work Experience Programme had found full-time jobs. This is hardly promising. The Commission are unlikely to achieve any comparable success rate on the new programme for the reasons outlined earlier, but even if they did, this would still leave close to 65,000 programme graduates without jobs every year.

The concern with the particular significance of black youth

unemployment which the Commission estimates to be increasing at four times the rate of white youth unemployment, was reflected in the decision to give black youth priority in the programme. Since the programme is supposed to provide a place for every unemployed school-leaver it is hard to make any practical sense of this decision, which like much else bears all the marks of a hasty response to the perceived urgency of the situation. The programme as a whole came under attack as soon as it was launched from the managers of existing training workshops, whose views were co-ordinated by the National Council of Social Service. The managers urged a five months' postponement to resolve what they saw as 'disastrous' guidelines.[18] Whether the scheme will succeed in providing places for 234,000 young people must remain in question. The earlier work experience programme established by the MSC in September 1976 to provide 30,000 young people with six months' experience in factories, offices or shops failed to get adequate support from employers, and the number of places offered in the first year had to be severely reduced. The programme expanded in the following year but still offered only a fraction of the places which it is intended to provide under the new YOP. The scheme may also fail to attract all those eligible, particularly in areas where the cost of living is high and the allowance of £19.50 is regarded as an inadequate incentive to enrol.

To date, local authorities have sponsored most of the schemes and response from the private sector has been minimal. Figures made available in February 1977 showed that local authorities had sponsored 64 per cent of the job creation projects while private companies had sponsored only 2 per cent. The House of Commons sub-committee which reviewed the programmes drew attention to the dominance of local authority projects.[19]

> There has always been something anomalous about their position as creators of extra jobs under the programme. The position seems . . . to be contrary to the national strategy of shaking out employment from local authorities into the manufacturing sector. Worse, as the MSC themselves put it, JCP may be said to be financing relatively low-priority local authority jobs at a time when authorities are having to cancel or defer more important work because of public expenditure constraints.

One consequence of this is that the programmes have had only a marginal effect in increasing the access of unemployed youth to jobs in the private sector.

The fight for full employment

In spite of these criticisms, those in the field cannot reject the programmes out of hand. For the young unemployed even £19.50 per week may be rather more tangible than a sociological critique of the purpose of YOP. Community groups which provide programmes are more likely to offer opportunities which both broaden the trainees' horizons and provide services useful to local people, than are private employers. While the latter may use the programme either to subsidise their usual hiring practices, or to instil factory discipline, community groups can inject a level of 'consciencisation' into their programmes. The use of YOP funds under Work Experience Projects and the Community Service Opportunities Programmes can add to the manpower available to local groups and provide opportunities for local action, however limited.

Voluntary societies had sponsored 10 per cent of the existing projects by February 1977. The projects sponsored on Merseyside give some idea of the range undertaken:

restoration of garage workshop;
setting up of joinery workshops;
provision of adventure playground;
surveys of the needs of elderly and handicapped persons;
conversion of a farm to a youth hostel;
repair work on the houses of elderly and handicapped persons;
construction of area headquarters for St John Ambulance Brigade;
setting up of a charity shop.

Voluntary organisations encounter a number of difficulties in sponsoring projects which are not simply a function of the complexity of funding. Frequently local groups have little experience as employers and lack the skills to develop viable programmes. The suitability of the potential project workers for the programmes is not always considered. In Vauxhall, Liverpool, a Neighbourhood Aid Scheme was set up. Three people with a background in local voluntary work were appointed to supervise three teams of eight young people. The teams were supposed to establish needs among the elderly and attempt to meet them. In fact, the scheme failed:[20]

the supervisors were unable in the time available to learn the necessary skills despite support from trained staff . . . many of the young people, particularly the boys, were unacceptable to elderly and disabled people for the sort of domestic assistance they wanted . . . although social workers and home help organisers welcomed assistance for their needy clients, some of the youngsters were just not suitable.

Other schemes have been more successful and have simultaneously provided useful work for the unemployed and strengthened the credibility and effectiveness of the sponsoring organisations.

Again the Canadian experience is illustrative, for while the OFY programme was clearly intended as a conservatising force it also provided funds for a number of radical ventures. Local projects collected oral histories, supplementing and challenging official histories. Redevelopment schemes were fought, drop-in centres established, tenants' groups created and play-schemes taken to under-privileged areas. Indeed the programme quickly came under attack from business interests and was finally closed down in 1976 and replaced by a more conventional scheme. Nevertheless the first five years showed that the funds could be used in a variety of ways which opened up, rather than closed, political options.

The pressure to secure sufficient places under the YOP scheme, particularly in inner city areas and for ethnic minorities, should serve to mitigate MSC attempts to establish close control over local projects. Projects which are providing places for local residents in areas of high unemployment cannot be easily terminated even when they offend sensibilities in the MSC.

At the same time, those working in the field must be clear of the limits of the job creation programmes. They are not a satisfactory alternative to real employment. Ten years ago the idea that Britain could tolerate a level of unemployment which, in real terms, now exceeds two million, would have been dismissed.[21] Yet the Labour government's industrial strategy with its emphasis on increasing productivity and on shaking out labour is unable to have a significant effect on unemployment levels.

The programmes which the government have put forward remain tied to a scenario in which the state essentially supports private capital and is used to bale out firms in economic difficulties. Government attempts to reduce the labour supply are equally conservative. The proposals for early retirement which are now seen as the cheapest way to cut the dole queues ignore the poverty, isolation, and physical and mental decay which frequently accompany retirement. The attractiveness of the idea is simply that a group of workers can be phased out of the labour force thus aiding the government's programme of restructuring private industry and losing labour. At the same time it can be done without any potential threat to social order — such as is posed by the young unemployed — and without the risk of higher benefit levels undermining the work ethic. In addition the refusal to engage in redistributive welfare programmes — except between different sectors of the working class — means that the benefits offered for early retirement will remain low. The earlier job release scheme which offered selected workers early retirement on £25 a week tax-free was so unattractive that by February 1976 it was found that three out of four people who had applied were already on the dole. Consequently few jobs were released for young workers.

The potential of other proposals which might improve the quality of working-class life, such as the introduction of sabbaticals from industry, has not been seriously considered. This scheme, if introduced on a large enough scale, would have a significant impact on unemployment figures, but an adequate level of funding would necessitate a considerable increase in public expenditure. This is the central dilemma for any job release scheme, for if it is to be attractive to employed workers in productive sectors of the economy, it must provide worth-while benefits. In turn this necessitates the very increase in public expenditure which the government has rejected as a solution to the current crisis. No doubt much could be achieved by redistribution from the small percentage of the population who continue to monopolise the country's wealth, but again such a policy has been rejected by successive Labour governments. In the present situation, however, sabbaticals could merely be used as a means of spreading the burden of unemployment more widely.

The tendency to reduce employment opportunities may well be structural. Future industrial recovery could accelerate moves to capital-intensive production, while British industry already suffers from considerable overmanning. What this suggests is that future demands should concentrate not simply on more employment but also on programmes which provide worth-while alternatives to work, while not inducing the dependency which characterises existing welfare and job creation programmes. Sabbaticals linked with a range of other demands (e.g. full pay, adequate leisure facilities etc.) are a clear alternative allowing the worker to return to the job afterwards in a revolving programme of release. The sabbatical experience in turn may well have significant effects on shop-floor consciousness. Other demands may focus on work-sharing and reductions in the working week, but these must be rooted in the recognition that for most, overtime is not a desired alternative to a few hours in the allotment, or the key to two weeks in Benidorm. Overtime is, rather, a necessary factor in maintaining the weekly budget. This would suggest that reductions in working hours will only be possible through rapid economic expansion, which is unlikely, or by successful struggles for redistribution, not within the working class but between social classes.

Peter Townsend succinctly summarised the alternative for the future. 'The labour movement has a choice either of continuing to drift meekly with international capitalism and weakly attempting to moderate or minimise the human consequence of predatory economic imperialism, by a mixture of tax adjustments and largely cosmetic job creation schemes, or of establishing an alternative structure of full, equitable employment for all the population.'[22] This, as Townsend makes clear, will require substantial government intervention in the economy and a challenge to the traditional prerogatives of private capital. How far the government will resist such a radical departure is suggested by the lengths to which the social democratic German government has gone. Faced with significant unemployment for the first time in a generation, the government has established some 160 mock firms. These firms trade with each other, keep detailed accounts, have nominal capital and are responsible to imaginary shareholders. All their operations are purely theoretical. The firms' sole function is to absorb and train the unemployed against the day when they might find a real job.

In a world where hundreds of thousands starve every year and many more live in poverty, there may well be reasons why people discarded by the system should be encouraged to think of alternatives. The Job Creation Programme, however, is not an area on which community workers or trade unionists should turn their backs. Rather, the fight for permanent, socially useful employment must be extended through the programme. The absurdity of a social system which creates mock factories because it cannot maintain real ones, and which runs work experience programmes because young people cannot get experience of work, must be made manifest.

Notes

1 I. Gough, 'State Expenditure in Advanced Capitalism', in M. Fitzgerald *et al.*, eds, *Welfare in Action*, Routledge & Kegan Paul, 1977, p. 22. See also I. Gough, Unit 31A, 'Social Work, Community Work and Society', DE 206, Open University, 1978.

2 First Special Report from the Expenditure Committee, Session 1977-8, The Job Creation Programme; Observations by the Secretary of State for Employment, 24 November 1977, p. 7.

3 'Heath's Three Day Blueprint', *Guardian*, 23 March 1978.

4 *Economic Policy Review*, no. 4, Cambridge Department of Applied Economics, 1978.

5 For a discussion of the background to the current economic crisis, see A. Gamble and P. Walton, *Capitalism in Crisis, Inflation and the State*, Macmillan, 1976.

6 P. Marris and M. Rein, *Dilemmas of Social Reform*, Penguin, 1974, p. 125.

7 *New Society*, 9 March 1978, p. 546.

8 Marris and Rein, op. cit., p. 127.

✗ 9 'The Young on the Dole', *Economist*, 7 January 1978, p. 80.

10 *New Statesman*, 18 June 1976.

11 Quoted in 'Black Joy', *New Society*, 5 January 1978, p. 20.

12 *Guardian*, 5 September 1977.

13 *Guardian*, 26 September 1977.

14 *Guardian*, 8 March 1978.

15 Quoted in M. Loney, 'A Political Economy of Citizen Participation', in L. Panitch, ed., *The Canadian State*, University of Toronto Press, 1977, p. 4.

16 Loney, op. cit., p. 460.

✗ 17 'Their Future is Britain's Future: Dare We Jeopardise It?', MSC, 1978, p. 3.

18 *Guardian*, 28 February 1978.

19 Seventh Report from the Expenditure Committee, Session 1976-7, Job Creation Programme, vol. 1, p. xxiii.

20 Unit 17, part 1, 'Social Work, Community Work and Society', DE 206, Open University, 1978.

21 For a discussion of the way official figures underestimate unemployment, see P. Townsend, 'The Neglect of Mass Unemployment', *New Statesman*, 7 October 1977.

22 Ibid.

Part V **Production for Community Needs**

15 Community action over local planning issues

Bob Colenutt

Introduction

The ideas that the residents of working-class areas are engaged primarily in struggles about the environment and are not much involved in workplace and employment struggles; and that conversely, the local workforce is not much concerned with environmental issues may now be a myth. This is the conclusion that is emerging from community actions up and down the country where local residents and workers have participated together in local planning issues.

Plans for local areas, whether 'informal plans' or those required by law (District or Local Plans as they are often called) have provoked more interest and stimulated broader alliances than local authorities may have bargained for. In this paper, we shall look at the growth of opposition to planning policies in Southwark; first, policies towards office development, and then policies towards public services, discussing the reasons for the alliances that have emerged and the scope for further collaboration between residents and the local workforce. We shall also refer to the role of community work in this process.

Conflict over office development policies

Back in 1971, when Southwark council prepared a plan for the Thames-side area in the north of the borough, there was little conception among the planners or politicians in the Town Hall that the plan was controversial or that it would create a movement of grass-roots opposition that would have wide political repercussions. The Strategy Plan for Thames-side affected an area of a square mile bounded on the north by three miles of wharves and warehouses and tapering south towards the Elephant and Castle. It was an area where industry and housing were mixed, small shopping parades and corner shops were prolific, and open space was confined to patches of grass and courtyards in housing estates. The area also carried (and still carries) the main roads heading for the bridges across the Thames, in particular Blackfriars Bridge and London Bridge leading to the City of London, and Tower Bridge linking access to the East End. The thirty thousand people then living in this area did not constitute a single community but a number of smaller communities distinguished by the type of housing (council or trust property), location (old metropolitan boroughs of South-wark or Bermondsey), their length of residence in the area and their connections with the major local industries.

Local politics had been dying in Southwark and Bermondsey since the war. Membership of local ward parties was at a low ebb, and the Labour group on the Southwark borough council exer-cised control with little opposition either from within the Labour Party or from outside, in the community. Local councillors were likely to be nominated by a tiny handful of Labour Party mem-bers. Some tenants' associations did exist on the estates but they were almost exclusively concerned with rehousing from slum tene-ments. There was little awareness in Southwark or elsewhere of the meaning or possibilities of planning and participation in planning.

The Strategy Plan changed all that. The plan itself was an 'infor-mal' plan which altered the land use zoning of the riverside and the adjacent area from industrial, commercial, shops and housing, to 'City and West End Uses' — i.e. offices, hotels and other com-mercial developments. Its purpose was to give the council authority to grant planning permission for the increasing applications for offices. These applications were building up as the property boom triggered an overspill of office demand from the City of London across the river to North Southwark. The social and economic implications of this spreading office development were of crucial importance to the local residents and workforce. Basically the area would cease to serve the needs of the old working-class com-munities, providing houses, jobs and shops etc., and would become part of the financial, commercial and tourist centre of the capital, instead.

However, the council reckoned without the upsurge of commu-nity action that accompanied the property boom in London and other cities. Word was spreading about other protests against speculative development and community workers were beginning to encourage such movements in some areas. An action committee was formed in North Southwark in response to the Strategy Plan consisting of tenants' associations, trades councils, and individual residents. The committee was assisted by community workers based at a project run by the National Institute for Social Work Training. Later this committee, called the North Southwark Community Development Group (NSCDG), was able to obtain a five-year grant under the Urban Aid Programme to set up a Community Planning Centre staffed by two full-time workers. The presence of this Centre and its workers in the community played an important part in the protest movement because they were a resource of facilities, energy and skills for NSCDG.

But what tied the local groups together was the glaring conflict between local needs for reasonably-priced housing, shops, open space, and industrial jobs on the one hand and the pressures for speculative development on the other. These pressures were (and still are) helping to drive out some of the industrial firms and local shops. By bidding up the price of land they were also inhibiting local authority intervention.

The battle between the local groups and the council was focused on the future of major development sites such as Hays Wharf and also over the effects of 'hope values'[1] created by the council's planning policies for North Southwark. Opposition to the council centred, initially, on the lack of public consultation over the Strategy Plan. The controversy about the inadequacy of consultation was an important factor in drawing local residents, the trades council and other local groups together. In fact, it was this aspect of the council's policies which, at the beginning, caused the most hostility towards the council – a distrust that only increased when planners and council members tried to justify themselves at public meetings.

Later on, the opposition concentrated on individual office developments and the policies of West End and City zoning. For example, the North Southwark Community Development Group attacked the council's own plans for a site called Bankside, where it was proposed that the council go into partnership with developers to build a large office block and a theatre. On this prime riverside site, the Group wanted to see council houses with gardens. The council's initiatives obliged them to submit their own planning application for housing. The purpose of this move was to force a public inquiry over the use of the site and to challenge the council's overall strategy at the same time.

The Community Planning Centre undertook surveys of industry, shops and housing in order to reveal what was happening to the area. Help was also given to tenants' associations undertaking their own household surveys to find out what people thought of the area and what they would like to see on particular sites. Planning applications were investigated and information passed around to the tenants' associations most affected. When there were public inquiries over development proposals, vigorous and well-researched contributions were made by local groups.

Without support inside the council, all of this activity and ammunition was to no avail in changing council decisions. Between 1970 and 1976 585 planning applications for offices were submitted for sites in North Southwark, of which 466, affecting 349 different sites, were allowed. Only on a few notable occasions were office applications turned down as a result of local protest. But each of these successes and each delay effected merely strengthened the determination of local groups. The very consistency of the council itself in supporting offices, hotels, tourism and prestige schemes sustained and stimulated the opposition forces.

This experience convinced local activists that a change of tactics might add a further dimension to the struggle. They felt that a voice in the council and better representation for local people was needed. So the membership of local ward Labour Parties was slowly built up until the community groups were in a position to replace five of the councillors representing the area. The biggest build-up of membership was in the wards closest to the riverside where most of the development pressures were evident. The differences between the new councillors and the old ones was principally that the new members had their base in the tenants' associations, trades councils, and the NSCDG while the old guard were suspicious and separate from this movement having become part of the Town Hall establishment. It is important to add that trade union delegates to the Labour Party played an important part in this political changeover.

The closeness between trade union activists and tenant activists in the Labour Party was not always matched when pressure was being mounted by community groups against the Strategy Plan and individual development proposals. Even though this part of

Southwark provided jobs for nearly seventy thousand people and was experiencing a rapid run-down of industry (a survey of fifty industrial firms in 1974 was repeated in 1978 and showed that 30 per cent of the jobs had disappeared in four years), many workers did not regard Southwark's office strategy as a threat. In well-organised workplaces, the trade unions were able to negotiate substantial redundancy payments for longer-serving workers. Alternatively they accepted the closure as long as some of the workforce were transferred to other plants or moved with the company. The real losers were the least organised members of the workforce — women generally, unskilled workers, short-term and part-time workers, especially if they were employed in non-union firms.

For these reasons only a few workplaces responded to overtures from community groups to take a stand on redevelopment issues. At Courage's bottling and brewery plants, for example, both simultaneously affected by plans for run-down and closure allied with office development plans, the union made no response to offers of help and co-operation from the NSCDG and the trades council. The main concern of the branch appeared to be obtaining promises from the management about the size of redundancy payments and transfer to other Courage plants. On the other hand, the postal workers at the large sorting office in North Southwark joined with community groups in opposing a large office block scheme in Borough High Street.

Much of the trade union response was located in the Bermondsey and Southwark Trades Councils. They affiliated to the NSCDG, made use of the facilities at the Community Planning Centre and joined fully in the protest about the Strategy Plan and various office developments. Not all members of the Trades Councils felt strongly about these issues; but dockers who had worked on Hays Wharf and the Surrey Docks were particularly incensed by Southwark's collaboration with companies who had seemingly 'sold their workers down the riverside'. On the other hand, representatives of some of the blue-collar unions hardly seemed to care. Local residents who were also active in their trade unions, however, took the issue to the Trades Councils, and those trade unionists living elsewhere in the borough who were concerned about the employment base of the borough became involved in the protest movement. In particular, members of the civil service and local government unions took an interest in council policies. Politically, then the issue became a focus for a wide range of trade unionists active in Southwark politics.

The Trades Councils were able to complement the environmental arguments made by residents by concentrating on the employment implications of more and more office development. The Southwark Trades Council formed an Employment and Planning Committee to monitor and analyse employment changes in the borough. A major report called *Employment in Southwark* was produced with the help of the Community Development Project. This document examined the reasons for the decline of industrial jobs in each sector and the growth of the office sector. It pointed to the wastage of skilled workers, the reduction in earnings for industrial workers who had moved to office occupations, and the decline in apprenticeships. Southwark Trades Council proposed an alternative employment strategy which combined a halt to further office development with a major effort by the borough council to protect remaining firms, where possible, and to construct and modernise factory buildings. These ideas were publicised as widely as possible and used when lobbying the council.

The impact of this on employment in the borough was limited, not just because the council was hell-bent on its own policies but because the forces responsible for the loss of industrial jobs and the invasion of offices were so powerful. The borough had by this time accepted the need to develop factories, albeit by going into partnership with private developers. The major remaining areas of disagreement were over the amount of offices and the extent of municipal intervention but the Trades Councils could do little more than try to create some sort of public debate about the issues. Perhaps the most important outcome was the strengthening of the political network stretching from tenants' associations and trades councils into the Labour Party by the formation of a general set of common policies, or at least common attitudes, towards employment.

The trade unions have not yet called for industrial action. Only one resolution, that I am aware of, has threatened such action. This came from the Greater London Council (GLC) direct labour branch of UCATT (the construction workers' union), which has resolved to black a site in Lambeth near the river where the Tory GLC has decided to scrap the previous Labour plans for council housing and seek a massive office and hotel development. Whether this union branch or the Trades Council will be able to stop other building workers going onto the site of the office remains to be seen. But it is an important new step and gives encouragement to those in the community who have been battling against such schemes for several years without much political or industrial muscle behind them.

Yet there is scope for other kinds of industrial action from the public sector unions who are close to the Trades Councils. These unions recognise that planning policies which place office buildings before open space, council housing and community facilities have implications too for jobs in local government. Further steps towards active trade union criticism of council policies are taking place only slowly. Perhaps the explicit link-up between land use planning and public expenditure in Southwark's 'Community Plan' and the Local Plans for North and Mid/South Southwark will draw in these unions more completely. This is what we shall look at in the next section.

Public services and local plans

Traditionally, planning has been concerned with questions of land use, transportation, and the physical environment. Public participation exercises have normally asked people to comment on options for the allocation of land uses; i.e. what should go where. Meanwhile, other aspects of living such as the social issues, community structure, finance, unemployment and political conflicts have not been regarded as 'planning matters', as the planning lawyers call them. Planning matters for them are problems such as the distribution of employment and population, the appearance of buildings, traffic flow patterns, and matters of density and layout. There is much discussion of what constitutes a 'development' requiring planning permission, and constant debate about whether individual development proposals conform with existing plans. Planning is thus seen as a specific local authority responsibility primarily concerned with the distribution of 'developments'; it is not regarded as a focus for examining every council policy affecting an area.

This restrictive view of planning is changing. After the debacle of the Strategy Plan for Thames-side, which was a non-statutory plan, Southwark Council began to prepare a statutory Local Plan for North Southwark. This Plan requires, by law, several rounds of public consultation, beginning with a debate about the problems of the area. At the public meetings so far, local people have shown no inclination to confine themselves to the traditional planning categories, even though the planners have tried to steer the discussion in that direction. Local residents have insisted that the planners listen to complaints and suggestions about every aspect of life in Southwark: maintenance of council estates, parks and streets; closure of the local facilities such as libraries, public baths and toilets, and problems caused by lodging houses. The Trades Councils have demanded a debate on unemployment, skill training and cut-backs in public expenditure.

This has coincided with the controversy nationally about public expenditure and its effects on services and jobs. Southwark introduced a 'nil growth' policy in 1976-7, a 1 per cent cut in revenue spending in 1977-8, and is proposing nil growth again in 1978-9. The consequences of this for the community, while not immediately dramatic, have nevertheless caused resentment. The redecoration cycle in council flats was extended, several types of repair became the responsibility of tenants, street maintenance was sharply reduced, public toilets were closed, library hours were reduced, home help services were cut and positions in social and community services were left unfilled.

The council's financial strategy affected the Local Plans in other ways too. Local demands from tenants' associations and trades councils for land acquisition, more council house building, more intervention in the property market, more advance factory building, and the rehabilitation and expansion of the direct labour were often countered with the warning that the money was not there or if it was it would have to be transferred from other areas of council spending. Thus, the advance factory building programme is to be financed from council reserves which could have been used to improve social services or housing. So, for the first time, Local Plans have become explicitly tied up with the council's overall spending strategy and thus in turn with the government's economic policies.

Southwark council's own management policies have made these links even clearer. A Community Plan was introduced (written almost entirely by council officers) which was a statement of the council's policies for all its departments. This plan included financial appraisals and estimates of the employment implications. Land use planning was integrated into the overall Plan so that it could be seen as part of the borough's corporate management approach.

There was, therefore, no reason for community activists whether in tenants' associations, the Labour Party, or trade unions to see planning as something separate from other areas of political activity. This has particular implications for the public sector unions representing local government workers because it is quite obvious that cuts or redeployment policies have effects both on the quality of life of the residents and on the jobs of other workers in the borough. The two major local government workers' unions in Southwark, NUPE and NALGO, have now begun to take a much closer interest in the council's overall financial strategy and are working with community activists to put flesh onto the statistics of budgeting and cuts. This may have important implications for the relationship between community groups and local trade unions. Similar work has been undertaken by the Joint Docklands Action Group for community groups in the Docklands Boroughs. They see the involvement of the public sector as the key to the revitalisation of Dockland. Indeed, without it, they see no hope of an end to the area's dereliction and decline.

Southwark Trades Council and the NSCDG also regard public spending as central to the debate about planning and employment policies. They are calling for public ownership of land, the construction and rehabilitation of factories by direct labour, the expansion of the council house building programme in the north of the borough, and more local authority assistance to community projects. Tenants' associations in the council sector are almost completely dependent on the council for the maintenance and management of their estates. In fact the whole question of the maintenance of the environment is as central to residents' views on their area as it is to council expenditure. Local Plans and the cuts in public spending have now made this clear and have created new bonds between trade unionists and residents' associations.

Conclusion

The experience we have gained in Southwark over the past six years suggests that, at least in our area, the much-discussed dichotomy between local residents and the local workforce may no longer be such a great divide. Although there are circumstances, as we have noted, in which the workforce did not join in community actions, there are important links. Plans such as the Thames-side Strategy, which have serious employment implications, and Local Plans, which raise a very wide range of issues, have brought community and trade union activists together. The demand for more adequate consultation over plans has been another meeting point for different groups. The co-operation has not so far led to industrial action over planning issues but it has led to the development of close links, with the sharing of information and mutual support.

Joint action over planning issues whether employment, jobs, public expenditure, or housing has taken place in the arena of local party politics. With a strong representation of local tenant activists in the Labour Party and trade union delegates attending the General Management Committees of the constituency Party, political alliances between trade union delegates and ward delegates have developed.

Similarly, the Trades Councils are forums where trade unionists and community activists are working together over employment and other planning issues. The Trades Councils have not always been able to involve many of the branches affiliated to them, but the network is there for future developments.

The debate about public expenditure has also created new alliances between tenants' groups and trade unionists. When the effect of cuts or controls over spending is evident in both the community and in the local authority workforce, the two groups have something in common. Moreover, in inner city areas like Southwark, where the key to regeneration lies with the public sector, public spending is the critical factor both for residents and workforce. Local authorities may well be forced to develop their own local economies by building factories, setting up industries, and expanding public sector employment. Equally, the shops, community services and environmental maintenance that residents need must be provided by the public sector. As local councils take more control over the management of their own areas, the alliances between trade unionists and residents are likely to be strengthened.

Note

1   The 'hope value' of a piece of land refers to the practice of speculators buying land at inflated prices in the expectation that values generally will rise rapidly in the near future. It can also be used to denote the 'hope' that a change of use, for more profitable purposes, will be allowed by the council's Planning Department. For a more detailed exposition see P. Ambrose and B. Colenutt, *The Property Machine*, Penguin, 1975, ch. 1, 'Office Development: Rents, Values and Profits'.

16 Sunderlandia (Builders) Ltd

Pete Smith

Preamble

The promoters of Sunderlandia Ltd came together through a small but rapidly growing organisation called the Industrial Common Ownership Movement (ICOM). ICOM has developed since the late 1950s from the Quaker convictions of Ernest Bader,[1] who founded the organisation under the name of Demintry[2] in 1958 as a broadly-based forum of ideas and activities directed at democratising the control of work situations and neutralising the power of capital. It is a non-party-political organisation that campaigns for legislation that would reinforce its objectives in law, and will co-operate with any government that is prepared to enact such legislation. ICOM embraces people from disparate backgrounds who actively support its principal objectives which are basically two-fold. First, the enterprise should be owned and controlled by the people working in it. Labour should hire capital rather than capital hiring labour. Second, the enterprise should progressively aim to dealienate the relationships between people at work on the one hand, and between people and work on the other.

To this end ICOM fields a small full-time staff[3] who not only give advice and support to groups setting up such enterprises as Sunderlandia but correlate information and developments from all over the United Kingdom. In addition, in 1971 ICOM established a revolving loan fund called the Industrial Common Ownership Finance Ltd (ICOF)[4] to help in providing 'seed' capital for those groups that satisfied the ICOM principles mentioned above or the terms laid down under the Industrial Common Ownership Act 1975. ICOF has its own officer to vet and investigate loan applications and to advise on the presentation of feasibility studies, and the revolving loan fund is supervised by its own trustees, which include ICOM representatives. In 1975 ICOM was successful in promoting a Private Members Bill that was presented to Parliament by David Watkins MP, with the support of an all-party committee through which ICOM conducts its political operations.

The Industrial Common Ownership Act 1975 places on the statute book for the first time legislative recognition for an enterprise exclusively owned and controlled by its working members. In addition, it makes a modest provision of finance in two forms. First, it provides grants of up to £30,000 p.a. (for five years, in the first instance) for agencies recognised under the Act to give advice and support for the promotion of common ownership enterprises. Second, it provides up to £50,000 p.a. (for five years, in the first instance) to be used as seed capital for those groups who both satisfy the definition of a common ownership and are an industrial enterprise as defined in the Act.

The notion of workers' control is not a new one. In one sense, it goes back to the Diggers, a seventeenth-century peasant movement which believed in the common ownership of land. This theme has been taken up by the Syndicalist Movement in industrial Europe and again by the Industrial Workers of the World (the Wobblies) in the USA. The notion preceded Marxism, but in turn Marxism reaffirmed the belief in the ownership and control of the means of production. Not only is this objective embodied in Clause 4 of the Labour Party Manifesto but most trade union rule books make some explicit reference to the question of workers' control. The Institute of Workers' Control[5] in Britain today acts as a forum for trade unionists, academics, students and politicians. It has little direct involvement in the creation of worker-controlled enterprises, its main thrust being the development of a political strategy directed at the state.

The current debate on workers' control covers a wide spectrum of party political and philosophical expression. Perhaps the main divide in all this is between those who see it as a means of obtaining basic changes in society and those who see it as part of the movement for change itself. ICOM believes that ownership is synonymous with control. Within the movement, however, there are those who see it as either collective or 'granulated' capitalism and even Christian socialists who regard it as a basis for religious and spiritual revival. Others see it as an opportunity to develop a working strategy for fundamental change in an advanced industrial society. Whatever their position, most of those involved in the debate accept that before people reject capitalism, they have to both understand it and experience its contradictions. Large sections of our population have had neither experience.

This debate is part of the internal dynamics of ICOM, and members of Sunderlandia, in particular, don't see themselves as either a panacea for unemployment or the sole agent for social change. It is clear though that ICOM and the individual enterprises like Sunderlandia have an important role to play with much scope for co-operation with the wider labour movement.

The formation of Sunderlandia

The three promoters of Sunderlandia came from widely disparate backgrounds, and although they shared a belief in the establishment of common ownership enterprises, their motivation and perspectives differed somewhat. Michael Pearce has an architectural background and had been in joint practice in Zambia for the whole of his working life. Apart from the socio-political conditioning of his African experience, he was concerned about the illogicality and contradictions in the building industry as a whole and particularly anxious to redefine the role of the architect in relation to the builder and client. The second promoter was Robert Oakeshott, an academic journalist who had spent a number of years working for the Zambian government prior to returning to the UK. He had been the prime mover in Zambia of an experimental education and production community at Shayashe River School between 1968 and 1971. This unfortunately failed in its objectives, apparently through personality conflicts and bad management.[6] The third promoter was Pete Smith, who, until becoming involved with the project, had worked in the chemical industry and been actively involved in trade union activities as a Transport and General Workers' Union shop steward and convener. His primary interest in the project was that of workers' control in industry and it was hoped that his experience of working-class struggle over fifteen years would be some contribution to the successful establishment of common ownership enterprise.

The three promoters came together in 1972, and with the support of a grant from the Rowntree Social Services Trust, Robert Oakeshott was able to conduct the bulk of the research for the feasibility study. In addition to pursuing the principle of common ownership, the promoters decided that the objectives should include good, cheap housing for people and the alleviation of youth unemployment, as well as the maximum of skill training. (It was later found difficult to resolve the contradictions between these objectives.) Sunderland was shown to be a highly suitable location for this experiment. It had, and still has, one of the highest rates of youth unemployment in the country. Second, it has a very high proportion of older owner-occupied housing, most of which was eligible for government house improvement grants. Apart from a strong market in a socially attractive sector of the building market, home improvement presented an opportunity for a high degree of skill training in a situation of labour-intensive production, thus affording the opportunity to take on a fairly high ratio of apprentices to tradesmen. (The ratio of tradesmen to apprentices proved to be one of the main miscalculations of the promoters that subsequently contributed to heavy losses in the first year and a considerable amount of internal conflict.)

Common ownership can take various legal forms. The ICOM (1977) model rules register an enterprise under the Industrial and Provident Societies Act (1965-1975) as an Industrial Co-operative and are the easiest and cheapest way to form an ICOM enterprise. These, however, were not available at the time, and Sunderlandia was registered under the Companies Acts (1948-1967) as a company limited by guarantee and not having a share capital. The project was to be financed by loanstock from three initial sources: the promoters, individual well-wishers, and sympathetic institutions.[7] In addition it was expected that individual working members would contribute to loanstock out of savings, but it was recognised that it would be in no way realistic to expect members to cover the cost of creating their own jobs. A rather complicated formula was devised to give capital a real rent of 3 per cent and protect the principal against inflation. The high rates of inflation between 1973 and 1975 meant that Sunderlandia would be paying real rates of interest in excess of 20 per cent, and hence the device was abandoned in favour of pegging 'money rent' to the local building society rates.

The Memorandum and Articles of Association make it clear that the ownership and control of the company rested within the sovereign democracy of the General Meeting. Normally any employee would become a member of the company after three months, but this could be extended by either party or conversely changed by the General Meeting.[8] The core tradesmen were recruited by circularising the trade union branches of UCATT with the co-operation and support of the local full-time official and the North East regional office. All members of Sunderlandia were expected to join their appropriate trade union, and UCATT proved to be consistently supportive throughout the whole of the first two difficult years. Often craftsmen were recruited by word of mouth, which seemed to be a common method of labour recruitment in the construction industry. The apprentices were all recruited from the Sunderland labour exchange, though some had worked for the Community Industry project. (This project offered young people temporary employment for one year in jobs supervised by craftsmen after which they returned to the dole queue unless they were fortunate enough to find a permanent employer.)

The intention in Sunderlandia was for every member to acquire at least one skill and to share the laborious and onerous labouring tasks. In practice it was found necessary to make exceptions, as there are in the building industry some skilled labouring tasks. Drainer/flaggers, for example, although classified as labourers, are in fact highly skilled. Similarly, roofing and plasterers' and brick-layers' labourers are all roles that require considerable building knowledge and skill. Notwithstanding this, the idea of sharing dirty and arduous tasks was largely accepted and on the whole worked well.

The day-to-day management of Sunderlandia was implied to be through a fairly conventional line management structure in the first instance. Clause 10 of the Preamble in the Memorandum and Articles of Association states: 'An enterprise should work for the eventual disappearance of the distinction between management and non-management. But given present realities, it would be a deception to pretend that the distinction does not exist and the organisation of an enterprise must take it into account.' Against that, the Articles contained a more explicit statement of how the members were to move to a self-management position. Article 84 states: 'The Company must spend a sum equivalent to not less than 5 per cent of the annual wage bill on the education of members and other employees and at least half of that expenditure must be on non-technical education. Agreement of the trade unions must be sought to the education programme.' Through this mechanism it was envisaged that as members acquired the wider technical skills and developed the socio-political awareness required for self-motivation and mutual co-operation, the conventional management structure would wither away.

The overall management of the company was vested in the Board of Directors of six members elected from the body of the General Meeting, and two outside Directors. One-third of the elected members resigned each year and the outside Directors came up for election annually. It had been envisaged that a dual structure of line management on the one hand and trade union representation on the other would operate during the transition from a conventional management structure to a self-management structure. A system of self-managing autonomous groups would develop to replace the dual structure as the educational programme mentioned above took effect. Communications were developed through monthly General Meetings, and representatives of the Loanstock holders, consumers (clients) and the community could voice their opinions on various topics at these meetings, but were not entitled to vote.

Sunderlandia in operation

Production began in July 1973, after most of the apprentices had experienced a nine-week pre-production training at Wearside Technical College. During the same period, while still with their former employers, the tradesmen held regular meetings with the promoters, which now included a second architect, Charles Cockburn. He had learnt about the project through the press and was enthusiastic enough to move from London (and more lucrative employment) to work with the project. These early meetings were extremely successful. The promoters knew nothing about the mechanics of building work and the weekly meetings were vitally informative for them. At the same time, the tradesmen gained confidence in working together and demonstrated their ability to think clearly about many basic management problems. These meetings achieved a great deal in fostering the philosophy of control by the workers. It seemed reasonable at the time, therefore, to abandon the idea of any 'line management' structure and go straight for autonomous group working. This proved to be a costly mistake.

Work began on revitalising Sunderland cottages, and within twelve months Sunderlandia had up to twenty separate contracts in progress. Notwithstanding the fact that contracts were reasonably priced, the company was making heavy production losses, and it became evident that some basic problems existed in the organisation and day-to-day operation. Disillusionment set in as the tradesmen began to sense an acute absence of management initiative. This was evident in the inefficient utilisation of labour and the poor material supplies on site. It was also becoming evident that the high ratio of apprentices to tradesmen (on average 3½:1, but in some trades as high as 5:1) was proving to be inoperable and a source of anxiety to the tradesmen.

It was on this second issue that the tradesmen focused their attention, and despite the resistance of the promoters they demanded that the apprentice ratios be reduced in order to create more efficient and manageable workgroups. It was the one single change that would result in immediate improvements in production performance. The choice was to dilute the ratio either by taking on more craftsmen or by dismissing a number of apprentices. The latter course was chosen, and although some were against that decision, it had a decisively positive effect. In asserting their self-confidence by making that decision, the tradesmen felt they had some effective control, and what was beginning to look like a sham of workers' control became a reality once again.

The third-quarter production figures showed a surplus of £999 as against losses of £7,071 and £2,575 in the first and second quarters respectively. The extent to which this turnaround in production is directly attributable to the reduction in apprentices is not clear, and the fact that the fourth quarter saw a loss of £5,120 would indicate that other factors were at play.[9] The steady improvement in productivity, measured in value of work done per head, is more likely to be the result of the general learning curve: a slight improvement in management effectiveness coupled with a more assertive self-management on a large number of small sites.

It is also important to note that during the third quarter the company began its first large contract, the modernisation of twenty houses for the Durham County Housing Association, worth in excess of £95,000. The first phase of revitalisation work (demolition, followed by new brickwork) is always the most profitable part of the contract and requires the least support in the form of materials and administration from management. Such a breathing space enabled an overstretched and inexperienced management to service the Sunderland cottage contracts more efficiently while at the same time enabling everyone on site to be gainfully employed.

On the other hand the successful management of a large site requires a much higher calibre of management and co-ordination
than that of £2,500 contracts on Sunderland cottages; when about
50 per cent of Sunderlandia's capacity found itself engaged in the
more complex building operations on this large contract, organisational weaknesses began to show. The lack of onsite leadership
and strong back-up facilities on a large site meant that the potential advantage of a concentrated workforce on a repetitive contract
became the source of fairly heavy losses. The underlying problems
of co-ordinating materials and labour and utilising both effectively
on site were persisting. The failure to define a 'line management'
in the first place had led to a leadership vacuum. Individuals who
showed leadership or management initiative were repressed by the
anarchism of style shown in the pre-production meetings. Many of
the tradesmen saw this to be the case, and others not only saw it
to be the case but used the situation in a disruptive and exploitative way. Confusion and mistrust abounded and, in an attempt to
put the various problems into perspective, a report was produced
in March 1974.[10] This was intended to be a discussion document
for resolving the developing crisis. Such was the ill-feeling that the
report itself was not considered seriously and some of its recommendations were not discussed or acted upon until much later.

Apart from the conflict between tradesmen and apprentices on
the one hand and tradesmen and management on the other, there
were certain basic points that the promoters had failed to communicate to the members of Sunderlandia. The problems of social
relationships that the members were now facing were the price of
bad communications. It was clear that, in the main, people did not
understand the motivations of the promoters or the motivation of
the loanstock holders. The questions people were asking were: 'Is
Sunderlandia a communist organisation?'; 'Are the promoters
communists?'; 'What is the motivation of the people who have put
money into the company?'; 'What ultimate control do the loanstock holders and promoters have — if any?'.

In a culturally conservative area like Wearside, such issues are
highly emotive. It is hardly surprising, therefore, that a number of
the members, particularly such tradesmen who were sincerely
committed Catholics, should be sensitive about any implied association with Marxist politics. They recoiled and were discontented
at criticisms made by outsiders in the town, or by people who
visited the enterprise who suggested that the promoters were

communists. Such criticisms were easily fired by myopic local politicians, competitors and the local Federation of Building Trade Employers, who had every reason to want to see Sunderlandia fail. It seemed of some urgency that such questions should have been discussed openly and with complete honesty. There was a need for Sunderlandia to dissociate itself completely from any party political dogma and illustrate that above anything else the enterprise was a democracy.

It was equally important to put in a clear perspective the role and status of the loanstock holders. To people who have never held a share certificate or a capital interest in business, the idea of having money sunk into a business is a complete mystification. People did not question the loanstock holders' right to a return on capital; that is traditionally an unquestionable right of the capitalist. However, it is also considered an unquestionable right of investors to have some control over the operation of the enterprise. The fact that the company's Articles stated the contrary did not change these feelings in the minds of the membership. It seemed reasonable to assume that, until the members became loanstock holders themselves in accordance with Article 7, they would always regard the loanstock holders and the promoters with awe.

To a large extent, however, most of these emotive issues were simply an outward manifestation of the frustration resulting from five distinct areas of administrative weakness which led to recurring losses. They were:

1 Lack of forward planning.
2 No internal account of stock and distribution.
3 No costing and purchasing systems that people could relate to.
4 No improvement in production through the light of recorded experience.
5 No clear existence of welfare, education, and social objectives, as distinct from production objectives.

Added to these internal problems was the fact that the building industry was entering into its worst recession since the 1930s. This, coupled with unprecedented inflation, was making the market competitive and tight, and finding work tended to take precedence over the immediate internal problems. Apart from the setting up of two working parties, one to study how to implement loanstock contributions, and the other to look at organisation and management, little was done to resolve the problems that existed at that time. The fight for economic survival became the total preoccupation, and a survey conducted by two Dutch business students some twelve months later, made similar findings as the March 1974 report.[11]

Sunderlandia was experiencing here a principal conflict in trying to create an oasis of socialism in a capitalist desert. It faced the contradiction of working within a market economy while attempting to develop socially useful production. In addition to this, it was also attempting to provide secure employment and in a self-actualising work environment, at a time of very high unemployment, particularly in the construction industry. In fact, workers' co-operatives are frequently criticised on the grounds that dealing with these conflicts leads to the dissipation of energies that would otherwise be directed at the capitalist state. This is the most valid criticism of workers' co-ops under industrial capitalism and one that becomes more valid as one co-operative comes in direct competition with another. For this reason producer co-ops should see themselves as a semi-didactic development within the context of a wider political struggle. If market contradictions are dealt with objectively within the democratic framework of its enterprise they form the basis of re-education and the focal point of co-ordinated political action.

All this does not say, however, that there were no positive developments. The demands from the tradesmen were for a competent conventional management structure, which would include good site managers on the larger sites, a contracts manager in the office, and a rational and smoothly organised purchasing and supply service. Those of the members — particularly the promoters — who were in quasi-management roles, were in no position to provide such leadership, partly because they were overstretched and partly because they did not have the relevant background. It was encouraging to find, therefore, that some of the larger building sites 'threw up' their own leadership. The more mature and responsible tradesmen, particularly joiners and bricklayers, began to take co-ordinating functions on site and generally this worked extremely well. At the same time various individual initiatives were taken to gain management techniques and skills. Charles Cockburn, recognising the need for production planning and control, not only took special responsibility for some of the smaller sites, but attempted to introduce some critical path analysis for the larger work programmes. However, since a number of these initiatives were in conflict with the idiosyncratic styles of others in quasi-management, they were never institutionalised and given the force of authority required to be really useful.

The problem of finding sufficient work was becoming a continual problem. Paradoxically there was a high need for housing improvement in the Sunderland area. The problem was not one of housing quantity: vigorous council building and continuing emigration have ensured an adequate number of housing units. The problem was, and still is, that of improving a decaying old housing stock. In 1973 it was estimated that some 8,000–10,000 housing units were eligible for housing improvement grants.[12] About two-thirds of these were owner-occupied, the remaining third were tenanted and it was estimated that about 1,500 of these units belonged to the National Coal Board. Council officials were worried about the slow rate of take-up of grants and discovered that deterioration may have been outpacing improvement.

Sunderlandia believed that the slow rate of take-up of grants was due to two main factors. First, the people most in need, particularly elderly owner-occupiers, could least afford even the 25 per cent portion of the grant they had to pay. Second, the bureaucratic red tape associated with a relatively simple undertaking like home improvement is quite overwhelming for all but the most robust and determined individuals, or the institutional landlord. One original intention of Sunderlandia had been to offer house improvement clients a complete building service. This would include the design and submission of plans for local authority planning and grant approval, and then to try and reorganise the whole administration connected with the building inspectorate and the payment of grants. This proved to be an expensive and time-consuming operation that did not generate work quickly enough or in sufficient quantities. Although such a comprehensive service was desirable it was considered that the best vehicle for such a community service would be the establishment of a voluntary and democratically controlled housing association registered under the Industrial and Provident Societies Act of 1965. An investigation was conducted, again with a grant from the Rowntree Social Services Trust, into the establishment of a Sunderland Housing Association. A steering committee was elected, a number of whose members were Sunderlandia members, to implement the findings of the investigation in October 1975. It took from then until December 1977 to register the housing associate as the Banks of the Wear Housing Association, and obtain the first three properties that are now being prepared for improvement.

The Housing Association and Sunderlandia will be of mutual support in the near future, but this has in no way alleviated the hard lean years of 1975-6. As unemployment in the construction industry nationally rose to over 300,000 building operatives during 1975, the 'lump' and other 'sharp' operators began to move in on the small contracts market, and the major contractors increasingly tendered for medium-sized conversion projects simply to keep the core of their organisation together, through a deep recession. In an attempt to survive this squeeze, Sunderlandia decided to move into the speculative building market by developing eleven units on a small site at Ryhope, County Durham.

Other things being equal, Sunderlandia may not have embarked on such an ambitious project without having had much more experience. On the other hand it did give the members an opportunity to demonstrate perhaps their greatest social and professional asset. That was Mike Pearce's ability to design an environmentally sensitive housing estate of interesting 'starter houses'. The estate is extremely attractive in design, and gives better value than most. The objective was to design and build a house that would be within the reach of the first-time buyer, and which could be easily extended to accommodate changing family needs.

It was this contract, coupled with a large revitalisation project for the Newcastle City Council, that saw the company's survival through 1975-6. During the same period, Sunderlandia became agents for Tremco, a roof maintenance system, and although it did not generate much work initially, it became of major importance to the company's survival through a large contract with the Peterlee Development Corporation. There was a period during the summer months of 1977 when the roofing contracts were the company's 'bread and butter'. In order to complete this work, however, additional unskilled labour had to be taken on because some of the skilled tradesmen refused to work on roofing. It seemed that the notion of the elite of the labour aristocracy still persisted, and this issue again reflected the fact that Sunderlandia had so far failed to enable people to regard the enterprise as their own and to evoke the commitment that one would expect from people who owned and controlled their own enterprise.

Conclusion

A complete assessment of the first five years of a common owner-ship enterprise cannot be dealt with in a short essay such as this. Sunderlandia is as much about how people relate to each other at work in a situation of social justice, as it is in being a successful commercial venture in a capitalist society. This is the principal contradiction in all producer co-operatives. However, some lessons can be learnt from the experience so far and, although this is always a risky business, some speculation about the company's future can be made.

Although they are interdependent, it is important to distinguish between the external and the internal factors affecting the company's progress. There is a clear need also to distinguish between the efficient commercial and productive organisation of a common ownership enterprise and the sovereign democracy of the worker-owners who are its members. This needs to be clearly reflected in the structure of its 'line management', though the style of such management should be such that it provides the maximum partici-pation in collective decision-making and self-actualisation through work. This is more easily achieved in production than in other areas such as financial management and marketing, and the latter areas are a longer-term development. For this purpose it is essential both to have the appropriate conventional management skills and in addition for these managers to identify with the social, econ-omic and political objectives of common ownership enterprises. For this reason it may be necessary to limit the size of the oper-ation to the availability of such skills.

The sovereign democracy of the members should interact with this enlightened management structure through the guides and checks afforded by the constitution of the enterprise, using the structure of the General Meeting and such bodies it elects to repre-sent it. The trade unions have, in the main, considerably developed the skill of shop-floor organisation and this is one of the many im-portant roles that they should play in the development of worker-controlled enterprises.

Although the promoters recognised the need for such a struc-ture, they failed to implement it, despite the fact that Clause 84 of the company's Articles made provision for resources to be avail-able for its implementation. The provision of such resources are as important as materials, tools and a market, if a common ownership enterprise is to be successful. This is particularly the case in the construction industry with its tradition of a nomadic labour force and hard-line management. Building workers are hard men, the work is rough and insecure, and as a result they express a high degree of independence and little trust or identity with their employers. To overcome that kind of hard socialisation requires a high degree of re-education. In hindsight this is what Sunderlandia should have concentrated on. Admirable as the training of young people in a secure job environment might be, it can be embarked upon only from either a secure commercial base or by government agencies underwriting the costs of such training.

Sunderlandia has now a fully trained labour force and needs a period of time to consolidate its profit-making operations. If a more favourable market develops, it will have the opportunity to correct some of these early mistakes in its organisation. The building industry is particularly sensitive to cyclic economic forces, and it must be noted that the company has survived five years in a downward market; a period when over 3,000 registered building enterprises and countless jobbing teams have folded. With injections of government money from the 1977 budget just working their way through in the form of construction projects for inner city areas,[13] and building society interest rates falling to 8 per cent in early 1978, the industry may be poised for recovery.

Commercially, Sunderlandia would be able to take good advantage of an upward market. There is an area of mutual support between the Banks of the Wear Housing Association and the company as a common ownership enterprise. Both are an integral part of the community and should be sensitive to each other's needs. Furthermore the Ryhope housing development has attracted considerable interest from local planners and those individuals who are concerned with the environmental quality of housing. It is likely that the future will bring increasing opportunities to build more housing of this type. A number of mid-Durham pit villages have infill plots (space for one or two houses). The scattered nature of these plots and the environmental planning constraints in these often attractive villages dissuade the profit-maximising speculative builders from this section of the market. If Sunderlandia can combine its outstanding design skill with a high degree of efficient self-management then it could capture a specialised and socially useful section of the housing market.

In conclusion, one should look at some of the wider social and political implications of the revived interest in worker co-ops. Persistently high unemployment levels coupled with unprecedented rates of redundancy and an increasingly tight labour market for young people during the 1970s, have contributed to the growing interest in ICOM. Sunderlandia, along with over 200 groups who have registered under the ICO Act, are evidence of that.

But to whom are common ownership enterprises useful? It can be argued that they are most useful to capitalism by ameliorating conditions in what might otherwise be politically unstable areas such as the depressed regions of Northern England and the industrial conurbations of Southern Wales and Scotland. There is little room for doubt that this is the motivation of the 'granulated' capitalist school and the Christian socialists. The development of co-operatives of this kind has been made easy by the availability of the Manpower Services Commission Job Creation Programmes (JCP). Despite the high failure rates of JCP-linked co-ops, it is clear that the Commission will support them because of their ameliorative effects on unemployment rates. However, it could be argued that social engineering of this kind will take place in any event and the constraints that it imposes are no more, or less, insurmountable than those facing radicals in the trade union movement or the community (witness the problems of the Community Development Projects).

The important safeguards to build into a common ownership project are full expression and control by its members and adequate resources for re-education. Sunderlandia's Articles of Association had these features and in addition insisted on trade union membership by its members. The purpose of this is twofold. First, to safeguard against what might be termed 'revisionism' (assuming, of course, that the trade unions are progressive) and second, to provide a channel of outward communication with the wider labour movement.

It has also been argued that worker co-ops are complementary to capitalism in so far as they can operate successfully in marginal areas of the economy where entrepreneurial capital cannot extract sufficient return on investment. This may well explain, to some extent at least, the greater success of the whole-food co-ops and those groups that couple their enterprise with alternative life-styles. On the other hand, those people who do operate in collectives are not only demonstrating against the capitalist system but making a valuable contribution to a society that needs to reassess its economic, social and political values. It certainly is true to suggest that, in the main, common ownership lends itself to the more labour-intensive activities. Scott Bader Chemicals is the notable exception, but some of the 'spin-off' enterprises from Scott Bader are both labour-intensive and potentially high-growth industries within the glass-reinforced plastic market. The question then arises — where an enterprise is successful, can it resist being taken over by capitalists which would result in a loss of control by the working members as a sovereign democracy?

These dangers and questions are, in the main, unresolved. Some protection is afforded by building safeguards into the constitution. Sunderlandia's loanstock agreement does not allow capital either to vote on decision-making or to participate in profit. It simply attracts a rent agreed between the company and the loanstock holder. Capital can of course withdraw, but again, the company can reserve the right to twelve months' notice before redemption. Also any change in Sunderlandia requires a two-thirds majority of all those eligible to vote, and in the event of a 'wind up' any residual assets have to go to another common ownership or a charitable trust.

In the last analysis the only true safeguard is to ensure that the vast majority of members actively participate in the control of the company. The crucial thing to remember is that social and political change needs to come from the grass roots up. To this end one had to begin from where people are rather than where one would like them to be. It may well be that the ideology of workers' control is out of its true historical perspective in capitalist society. It certainly was for the Syndicalists and the IWM. None the less they made a significant contribution to the labour movement in developing a revolutionary vision. It seems also worth noting that the producer-co-operatives in Mozambique which are well-organised and producing socially useful goods and services have been able to transcend the revolution to make a strong contribution to socialist reconstruction.

Notes

1 Ernest Bader was the former owner of Scott Bader Chemicals, Woolaston, which became the founding member of ICOM.
2 Demintry: Democratic Integration of Industry.
3 Industrial Common Ownership Movement, 31 Hare Street, Woolwich, London.

4   ICOF Ltd, 1 Gold Street, Northampton.
5   Institute of Workers' Control, Bertrand Russell House, Gamble Street, Forest Road, Nottingham 7.
6   Timothy Frank Taylor, 'A personal and independent report on Shayashe River School', unpublished report, mimeo., 1971.
7   Memorandum and Articles of Association of Sunderlandia, Appendix 1, Loanstock Holders, 1973.
8   Ibid., Clause 7, Membership.
9   Robert Oakeshott, First Annual Report to the Rowntree Social Services Trust, 1974.
10   P. W. Smith, 'Social account of Sunderlandia Ltd', unpublished report, mimeo., 1974.
11   Sander Dorren and Herman Snelder, 'Run Your Own Business', unpublished report, mimeo., 1975.
12   Tom Holzinger, 'Investigation into the proposed New Sunderland Housing Association', unpublished report, mimeo., 1976.
13   Councils in the Tyne-Wear area were expected to receive about £50m for construction projects under this programme.

17 The Green Ban movement

Roland Watkins

'What the hell use is a thirty-hour week if you have to spend
the rest of your time, along with your wife and kids in a dirty
inner city slum, with lousy schools and no proper hospitals,
while ten million square feet of office space stands around
empty and useless in Sydney alone?' Jack Mundey – NSW
Branch of Australian Builders Labourers' Federation.

Origins of the Green Ban movement

The Green Ban movement was born in Sydney, Australia, in 1971
and established itself here, in Birmingham, in 1976.[1] It is one of a
growing number of examples of workers trying to come to terms with
the difficult question of the social value of their labour. A 'Green
Ban' is a withdrawal of labour by building workers from projects
which are regarded as being against the best interests of community.

The idea of imposing Green Bans is a challenge to conventional
production and investment decision making, in which the profit
motive outweighs basic considerations of social usefulness. It also
challenges the paraphernalia of Town and Country Planning Acts,
supposedly devised by government to regulate the activities of
property owners. This regulating process has proved profoundly
unsatisfactory. Most people looking round today's cities, full of
ugly – and often empty – concrete office blocks, pedestrian
underpasses, multi-national stores with standardised shop fronts
and products, are quite unable to see the benefits of planning
activity carried out in their name. By contrast, Green Ban, through
the power of the building workers, bring the community into a
direct relationship with the property developer; the bias towards
developers, inherent in our so-called democratic planning processes,
is thereby cancelled out.

The Green Ban movement in Birmingham: the campaign to save
the Post Office

In January 1976 the Green Ban Action Committee was set up in
Birmingham with the specific initial aim of saving the Victorian
Post Office. This was threatened with redevelopment by a speculative office scheme. The Building, once the nerve centre of the
city's postal services but now 90 per cent empty, had been listed
in 1972 as being of architectural interest. Outline planning permission had already been given in 1972, and public knowledge of the
scheme had been alerted only by minor irregularities surrounding
the approval of the detailed drawings in December 1975. The
scheme seemed unnecessary (given the large amount of existing
office space unused in Birmingham), as well as destructive of a
building which was attractive and still usable.

A group of people opposed to the scheme therefore called a
public meeting and invited the Australian building workers' leader
Jack Mundey (who was in London at the time) to speak. At the
end of the meeting the Green Ban Action Committee (GBAC) was
formed, composed principally of environmentalists and building
workers. The broad aims of the Committee were to spread the idea
that workers should have more say in the kind of work they do
and that all work should be socially useful, without damaging the
environment. The Committee undertook to 'bring together groups
interested in the environment, with trade unions, to promote
active campaigns including Green Bans; second to spread knowledge of the way Green Bans work, and of conservation and environmental issues'.

Reaction from the Postal Board's developers – CDA Ltd – to
the Committee's formation and its intention of saving the Post
Office, was immediate and hysterical. This perhaps reflected their
understanding of how developers had been squeezed by the Green
Ban movement in Sydney. Sir Frank Price, the brains behind CDA
Ltd and once a leading Labour councillor, explained: 'we are on a
dangerous course, and anyone who supports this type of Fascism or
extreme Communism will want his head examining'.

Nevertheless, support for the campaign to save the Post Office
poured in. It came from the district or regional level of all the
major unions (except, unfortunately, the Union of Postal Workers).
Many individual branches sent donations and the Trades Council
and West Midlands Trade Union Council added their support in

response to motions forwarded to them. Seven local MPs and fifty councillors of all parties, but predominantly those in the Labour Party, added their support to the campaign.

The Committee's strategy was to campaign initially for the planning permission to be reviewed and possibly cancelled. The market demand for offices had changed since 1972 and there was also more public concern about the environment. It was felt that the Postal Board, being a public body, should be able to respond to the new environmental and social issues being raised. But if the Board and the planning authority were not convinced by rational argument that the redevelopment of the Post Office was a wasteful use of resources, then trade unionists would be asked to place a Green Ban on both the demolition of the Post Office and the construction of the new office blocks.

From the outset, therefore, the Committee was involved in traditional pressure-group tactics, as well as the direct action implied by Green Bans. But the support obtained during 1976 to save the Post Office was not just a means of reopening the 1972 decision to build office blocks on the site. It was also a necessary precondition for requesting any militant action from the building workers in the future. The regional executive of the Union of Construction, Allied Trades and Technicians (UCATT) were by this time in strong sympathy not only with the preservation of the Post Office but also with the general aims of the GBAC. The four-point motion passed in response to a letter from GBAC included a resolution that the Executive 'will seek ways of using the industry's resources and skills in a manner which meets social needs and benefits the community'.

With the official support of UCATT behind them, the Committee launched a petition which was to circulate at all levels within the community. It called on government to stop the destruction of the Post Office and prevent its replacement by high-rise office blocks. An explanatory leaflet was produced and sent, with copies of the petition, to local organisations and trade union officials for circulation to their membership. A well-supported demonstration on a Saturday morning in March achieved further publicity. An illustrated broadsheet setting out the aims behind Green Bans, as well as the purpose of the Save the Post Office Campaign, was produced with the donations sent from supporters.

Throughout the spring and summer, members of GBAC stood outside the Post Office on Saturdays, collecting signatures for the petition. It was the support from members of the general public that convinced them, beyond any doubt, that the Campaign was worth while. People complained bitterly about the planning system which had allowed Birmingham's city centre to be transformed into a concrete wilderness designed for cars, commuters and the international chain stores. There was, they said, no variety or quality left and ordinary shoppers had to descend into subways, where they wandered between the concrete roots of the roads and office blocks above. The transformation of the centre of Birmingham, from a unique market complex with a strong Victorian flavour into a bad imitation of Oxford Street, had been achieved during the 1960s and early 1970s with a minimum of public concern. The City, led by councillors who were often themselves property developers, took an entrepreneurial role. Any criticism was fobbed off by pointing to the financial advantages of property development to the rate payers — even if these advantages were a figment of politicians' imagination. The City council, in practice, were quite surprised therefore at the breadth and depth of the opposition stirred up by the GBAC. Eventually about twenty thousand signatures were collected.

In August the council called a meeting in response to a request put to them by the West Midlands TUC. The outcome of this was an investigation of the cost of revoking the planning permission. A further meeting in November 1976 was attended by representatives of the Postal Board, their developers — CDA Ltd, the Victorian Society (who had been campaigning for a revised office scheme which retained the Victorian facade), GBAC and their architects from the New Architecture Movement (NAM), who were drawing up plans for alternative use of the Post Office. It was chaired by the leader of the council, himself a director of several property companies, who made it clear that, because the estimated cost of revoking the permission was between £250,000 and £750,000, this course of action was out of the question. The Postal Board were intransigent and even refused to consider the Victorian Society's compromise. At every point under discussion there was deadlock.

The way is now open for the first British attempt to impose a Green Ban. If or when this occurs, the Committee's tactics will be to picket any attempt at demolition, occupy the building and then call for UCATT and other trade unions to support the Green Ban. Although lists of pickets have been drawn up, it seems however that direct action is still a long way in the future. Ironically the collapse of the property market and the glut of offices in Birmingham means there is no immediate threat to the Post Office. It is even possible that nothing will happen before the planning permission needs renewal — in December 1979.

Alternative uses of the Post Office

It is perhaps fortunate that it has not yet been necessary to approach the Regional Executive of UCATT to request a Green Ban on the site. Given the high unemployment rate in the building industry, the union may not feel in a position to declare a ban on any potential work for its members. The breathing space provided by the irrationality of commercial property development has therefore been used to switch away from a mere 'save-it' campaign, towards the development of a campaign to convert the building to a Leisure Centre. Although cheap in terms of materials and machinery, such a scheme would be labour intensive, creating almost as many jobs for building workers as the office block scheme. If, in the future, UCATT imposes a Green Ban on the Post Office, it will not be 'losing' work for its members — only choosing one kind of work instead of another.

Even during the early days of the campaign many people, though sympathetic to the preservation, said: 'But what can you use such a large old building for?' In March 1976 GBAC therefore asked the Postal Board for permission to inspect the closed parts of the building to see for themselves what potential, if any, the Post Office had. After six months of negotiations this permission was granted. It was quickly apparent that the two large sorting halls would be ideal for indoor sports requiring a great deal of space, e.g. football, cricket, golf, basketball, badminton, archery or bowls. This left a range of smaller rooms suitable for everything from judo to music rehearsals. GBAC, with the help of NAM, decided to draw up a detailed scheme for conversion to a Leisure Centre.

Besides being practical in terms of the existing spaces inside the building, and more acceptable to UCATT, the Leisure Centre proposal also has the advantage of meeting social needs. Birmingham is extremely short of leisure facilities. There is only one publicly owned indoor leisure complex — on the northern side of Sutton Coldfield — and more specialised facilities are just as inadequate. Plans for various major sports schemes were all hit by the cuts in public expenditure during 1975–6 — the most dramatic being the city's decision not to stage the next Commonwealth Games.

But the appeal of the Leisure Centre did not seem to reach other organised sports and community groups. GBAC found the majority of the sports associations focused on their own particular activity. They needed more facilities but preferred to work towards getting them in their own way at their own pace. There was also a reluctance to work with people who were making strong demands on the political system and raising issues about the value of work and the importance of leisure. The same attitude had come from many members of the Victorian Society who thought that GBAC was 'too political'.

Most community groups and residents' organisations also saw themselves as having narrow terms of reference. They recognised that people in their area might use a Leisure Centre but did not feel it their job to get too involved with issues located outside their own particular sphere. Some even saw a city centre leisure complex competing with local leisure demands; few people were prepared to push for both local and central facilities simultaneously.

The lack of support from sports and community groups reflects the difficulty of involving organisations which are set up for one purpose, in campaigning for something else. There are constitutional problems, though often these are used as excuses for giving a polite No! People recognise too that broad and ambitious campaigns make great demands on their time — usually their own leisure time. They prefer to restrict themselves to relatively easy objectives. In these circumstances the crucial importance of linking particular struggles or campaigns is not appreciated sufficiently.

Nevertheless, GBAC decided to proceed with the Leisure Centre idea, using general public and trade union support as its mandate. During 1977 the detailed plans of the conversion scheme were completed by the NAM and submitted formally for planning permission at the beginning of 1978. Obtaining local authority support in this way would in no way commit the planners to revoking the permission for offices. But it would be further evidence of the viability of the scheme, which would help to bring in further public and trade union support.

Broadening the issues

The trade unions have also been approached more directly about the fundamental issues raised by the Green Ban Movement.

In January 1977 a conference was held, entitled 'Industry and the Environment in the West Midlands'. The aim was to encourage interest among trade unionists for working alongside conservationists on specific campaigns against the pollution and waste generated by the quest for profits. There were also wider discussions about public and private transport, nuclear energy and the building industry.

The conference provided GBAC with a number of useful contacts, including local representatives from Lucas Aerospace who had recently launched their own proposals for gearing their work to social needs. It was mainly through these contacts that it was possible to organise quickly against a proposed increase in bus fares in the summer of 1977.

GBAC sees transportation and especially the motor industry as an important area for future work. It is an industry which employs a large number of people in the Midlands and there are many problems about both its organisation and its products. Some of these are being tackled through the National Enterprise Board and state involvement. But there is little evidence that anyone is looking at these issues with energy saving, pollution, or the important role of public transport in mind. When the West Midlands County Council announced intended fare increases of up to 30 per cent in July 1977 there were even some trade unionists who said, 'Good, now people will buy more cars!'

The campaign to prevent the bus fare increases was not successful, as the Traffic Commissioners – who make the final decisions – are precluded from examining the all-important issue of subsidies. But it did allow trade unionists (members of TGWU, NALGO, AUEW, NUPE, UCATT) and conservationists to experience at first hand the nonsense of the system whereby 'independent' Traffic Commissioners mediate the 'public interest' without any reference to the political decisions which caused the bus fares to be increased.

The campaign, which is continuing, will in future be looking at tactics beyond the sham democracy of the Traffic Commissioners' enquiry, to prevent any further erosion of public transport services. In September 1977 several bus garages were in favour of refusing to collect the extra money; but failure to plan this adequately in advance convinced TGWU officials that this course of action would not work. The next round of increases may see a change in this situation.

GBAC also took a decision to work closely with UCATT on matters of common interest, outside the context of Green Bans. This it was hoped would strengthen mutual respect and understanding. There was, for example, an urgent need to bring home to building workers the dangers of working with asbestos. The big companies that control the industry are desperately trying to diversify into alternative materials in order to be prepared for the day when public pressure eventually forces the government to ban its use altogether. This pressure rarely comes from building workers because, like most people, they are under the impression that the occasional use of asbestos is not likely to be harmful. This view is quite wrong. Machining asbestos (which inevitably creates a lot of fine dust) – even just once in a confined space – can cause asbestosis and lung cancer.

The aim of the Asbestos Conference in April 1977 was, therefore, to provide UCATT officials and shop stewards with the necessary technical information about asbestos and its dangers. It also provided a forum for discussing the best tactics for banning the use of asbestos on sites and pressuring employers for safety equipment or alternative materials. Following the conference a leaflet was produced and circulated to UCATT branches throughout the country.

Members of GBAC have also been involved in the regional campaign to save Direct Labour Departments. GBAC recognises that all direct labour contracts are socially useful and that the quality of workmanship and the quality of working conditions are usually superior on direct labour sites. Direct labour represents, therefore, an alternative to the existing disorganised privately-owned building industry, riddled with lump labour, working for short-term commercial gains and mindless of the future use or quality of the building under construction.

The work of GBAC during 1977 took place against a background of the Grunwick dispute, the breaking of the firemen's strike by the use of troops, and the Criminal Trespass Act which will restrict occupations of factories and building sites by workers in dispute. The ability of workers to challenge decisions made by the state or by employers in traditional ways was one of the major political issues of the year, and it is clear that the workers lost ground.

But during the same period an increasing number of people came to see that the arrangements for democratic control of both public and private investment were very tenuous indeed. This was clear from the Windscale Inquiry into the nuclear waste processing proposal, as well as at several motorway enquiries where frustrated objectors eventually took militant action to stop the enquiry proceeding. Direct action, of the kind favoured by GBAC to challenge some of the economic assumptions of our system and some of the hurdles set up to muffle and divert the voices of ordinary people, was very much in evidence. But there is also a danger that taking action of this kind on a large scale will produce a reaction in the form of more aggressive attempts by the state to curb it. To some extent this has happened already in Australia where, in the wake of Green Bans and the anti-nuclear campaigns, legislation is being considered to bring trade unions 'under control'. In Queensland, for example, all anti-nuclear demonstrations have been banned.

GBAC has therefore begun to look for other areas where workers have potential power which they might use in the future to influence decision making. This aspect of the work of GBAC does not centre on a concern to develop traditional forms of direct action, but is an attempt to ensure that existing trade union access to power is exercised fully and in the interests of the community and the environment. Clearly, worker participation in management offers scope in this direction. But with the shelving of the Bullock Report it looks as though no scheme introduced in the near future will vest much authority in workers' representatives.

A more promising possibility lies in the growth of pension funds and the dependence of property development on their form of finance. The money held by pension funds actually belongs to workers; it is deferred income. There is no question that it should be their right to have a say in how it is invested. In practice, control of investment decisions is in the hands of a small group of professional investment managers who have nothing in common with the workers whose money they handle. Trade unions are sometimes allowed to nominate representatives to the boards of their pension funds, but never in sufficient numbers to take control. In any case, these bodies are often rubber stamps rather than decision-makers. As a result they are not taken seriously. Discussion about pension fund investment rarely occupies a place on the agendas of national trade union conferences, let alone local branch meetings.

Yet pension funds occupy an increasingly important place in the economy and will become more important as emphasis is placed on better pension schemes. These schemes — some of which are administered by insurance companies — now rival company profits as the major source of 'new' wealth available for investment. The amount runs into millions of pounds each week.

In the past decade pension funds have been the main regulator of speculative building of offices, warehouses and factories. They contributed to the property boom of 1972–4 by their investment policies and also to the collapse in 1974–6 by their refusal to invest any more. Since the collapse, however, the pension funds have continued to buy property — but more cheaply. Whole property companies have been bought out and some experts consider that in a few years property companies will be replaced by financial institutions, i.e. pension funds and insurance companies, which will own both property and land and will employ their own property dealers. If Birmingham's Victorian Post Office is redeveloped for offices it will almost certainly be paid for out of a workers' pension fund.

Although no action has yet been taken on pension funds, the implications for the Green Ban movement are obvious, especially where the built environment is concerned. If the property market is almost totally dependent on pension funds, then, in theory, the output of building workers in this part of the industry can be controlled by miners, postmen, nurses, etc., but only after these workers win some control through their trade unions over these financiers from the City of London who, at the moment, invest their money for them.

In this way, workers would themselves choose how to invest the deferred income from their own labour. In some trade unions this demand has already been made in the context of investment in South Africa. Over a period of time, they may become convinced to invest not in speculative office blocks but in buildings of social value. This would help not only the community of which they form a part but also those building workers who want to work on worth-while projects. The same relationship between worker-controlled pension funds and other areas of production, e.g. the ideas contained in the Lucas Aerospace Stewards Corporate Plan, can also be envisaged.

There is, therefore, more than one way of imposing community control of production with dependence on existing methods and without recourse to the increasingly discredited system of public enquiries, courts of appeal — tribunals of various kinds — nearly all of which are run by an increasingly discredited group of judges, retired civil servants, councillors and MPs. But all these methods depend on the unused power of the trade union movement. This strength needs tapping by those community groups seeking solutions to the problems caused by existing forms of government. It needs tapping by people who are concerned about the quality of life tomorrow as well as today. It needs tapping urgently if only to prevent its becoming manipulated (as with pension funds) by people with the same lack of concern for social need that has characterised nineteenth- and twentieth-century industrial capitalism.

At present GBAC sees the main potential as direct action of the kind which has already happened in Australia. But this is using power in a purely negative way. In the present situation stopping anti-social investment is important. Moreover it challenges basic assumptions about the nature of work and about authority. But it does not guarantee a switch to an acceptable alternative. The Green Ban movement therefore has to look to the long term as well. This means creating not just an awareness of the social value of work but also an awareness of the urgent need for social and environmental responsibility. As Jack Mundey puts it, 'we must start working towards the kind of life we can afford on a finite planet'.

Note

1   For a more detailed discussion of the Australian origins of the Green Ban movement see Gary Craig's interview with Jack Mundey in Paul Curno, ed., *Political Issues and Community Work*, Routledge & Kegan Paul, 1978, ch. 11.

18 Technology for community needs

Mike Cooley

The significance of the Lucas Aerospace workers' initiative

There is now widespread interest in what is vaguely called 'community activity'. A motley collection of politicians of the Right and the Left, church leaders, local councillors, social workers and the inevitable professional planners are all pronouncing in a grandiose pluralism, the need to 'revitalize our communities'.

A much more serious aspect of this 'community rejuvenation' is the drift towards what I shall call industrial feudalism. Our economy is now dominated by the passive multinational corporations and financial institutions. These vast corporations spearhead the so-called 'technological revolution' and distort its development to meet their drive for profit maximization. The underlying assumption is that of a rapacious economic system fired by ever-increasing consumption and production. Apart from the waste of energy and materials their throwaway products bring in their wake (not to mention widespread pollution), they are becoming increasingly capital intensive rather than labour intensive (see below). Throughout the so-called 'technologically advanced nations' they are displacing millions of workers and are permanently destroying jobs and skills — creating structural unemployment while extending their control over the cultural as well as the economic and social lives of the mass of the people.

Because work in the past has been a dire economic necessity and because in the past fifty years it has been performed in fragmented, alienated tasks, this has come to obscure the vital importance of work to human beings. If you ask somebody what they are, they never say, 'I am a Beethoven-lover — a Bob Dylan fan — a James Joyce reader.' They will always say, 'I am a teacher — a fitter — a carpenter', or whatever. In other words we relate to the rest of society through our work and, in addition, we develop as human beings through the performance of meaningful work.

The vast multinationals are increasingly conscious that there is going to be a backlash from society at large in reaction to the way they are distorting its development. Some of my colleagues who are well-placed technocrats in these vast companies tell me that they are about to engage in what they call programmes of 'enlightened self-interest', and are planning to move into the community and job creation field. The idea is that they will provide some funds, and second executives (with all the elitism that that implies) to set up small-scale enterprises. In this way they hope to be able to placate the public on the one hand but, on the other, thereby to be left free to get on with the serious business of maximizing their profits at the commanding heights of the economy. Computerisation and automation will mean that small numbers will be required to run these large corporations in which they will try to separate an elite from the rest of the community and transform them into true 'corporation men'; they will satisfy them, economically, with company cars, company houses, company health services and other facilities denied to the rest of the community.

A large sector of those who remain — the unemployed — will be left to fiddle around with 'community work'. These activities will be deliberately chosen because they yield no economic power. Indeed it will be a sort of therapeutic, do-it-yourself social service! The industrial feudal lords will sit in the multinational headquarters while the 'peasants' will scratch out a living in the deprived communities in which they reside. They will, of course, be assured that this kind of work will be non-alienating and will enhance their self-reliance; and both of these are highly desirable goals in themselves.

In practice they will spend their time repairing, cleaning up, modifying and recycling the rubbish which the multinational corporations are imposing on them. While it is conceivable that some of these jobs will be craft-based and provide an outlet for some initiative and self-activism, the reality will be that they will have no real economic power or industrial muscle. Thus a significant proportion of the population will never have a 'real job' with all the frustration, alienation and other social multiplier effects which this situation will give rise to. The labour movement will be split between the employed elite — no doubt highly organized on the 'business union' basis as in the United States — and the unorganized, relatively powerless mass.

Against this dismal background, the challenge of the Lucas Aerospace workers can be seen in its considerable significance. Here are thirteen thousand workers, highly skilled by hand and by brain, with a long experience of industrial struggle. Their demand is not just for the right to work, but for the right to work on socially-useful products which would be relevant to the communities in which their seventeen Lucas Aerospace sites in the United Kingdom are located. A detailed account of how they arrived at this position and the products they have in mind is given in light of the potential it reveals for similar activities in large companies elsewhere.

The contradiction between what technology could, and actually does, provide

We have a level of technological sophistication such that we can design and produce Concorde, yet in the same society we cannot provide enough simple heating systems to protect old age pensioners from hypothermia. In the winter of 1975–6, 980 died of the cold in the London area alone. We have senior automotive engineers who sit in front of computerized visual display units 'working interactively to optimize the configuration' of car bodies such that they are aerodynamically stable at 120 miles an hour when the average speed of traffic through New York is 6.2 miles an hour. It was in fact 11 miles per hour at the turn of the century, when the vehicles were horse-drawn. In London at certain times of the day it is about 8.5 miles an hour. We have sophisticated communication systems such that we can send messages round the world in nano-seconds, yet it now takes longer to send a letter from Washington to New York than it did in the days of the stagecoach. Hence we find the linear drive forward of complex esoteric technology in the interests of the multinational corporations and on the other hand the growing deprivation of communities and the mass of people as a whole.

The second contradiction is the tragic wastage our society makes of its most precious asset — that is the skill, ingenuity, energy, creativity and enthusiasm of its ordinary people. We now have in Britain 1.6 million people out of work. There are thousands of engineers suffering the degradation of the dole queue when we urgently need cheap, effective and safe transport systems for our cities. There are thousands of electricians robbed by society of the right to work when we urgently need economic urban heating systems. We have I believe, 180,000 building workers out of a job when by the government's own statistics it is admitted that about 7 million people live in semi-slums in this country. In the London area we have about 20 per cent of the schools without an indoor toilet, when the people who could be making these things are rotting away in the dole queue.

The third contradiction is the myth that computerization, automation and the use of robotic equipment will automatically free human beings from soul-destroying, back-breaking tasks and leave them free to engage in more creative work. The perception of my members and that of millions of workers in the industrial nations is that in most instances the reverse is actually the case.

Fourth, there is the growing hostility of society at large to science and technology as at present practised. If you go to gatherings where there are artists, journalists and writers and you admit to being a technologist, they treat you as some latter-day Yahoo, to misquote Swift. They really seem to believe that you specified that rust should be sprayed on car bodies before the paint is applied, that all commodities should be enclosed in non-recycleable containers and that every large-scale plant you design is produced specifically to pollute the air and the rivers. There seems to be no understanding of the manner in which scientists and technologists are used as mere messenger-boys of the multinational corporations whose sole concern is the maximization of profits. It is therefore not surprising that some of our most able and sensitive sixth-formers will now not study science and technology because they correctly perceive it to be such a dehumanized activity in our society.

All these four contradictions – and indeed many others – have impacted themselves upon us in Lucas Aerospace over the past five years. We do work on equipment for Concorde, we have experienced structural unemployment and we know day by day of the growing hostility of the public to science and technology.

Lucas Aerospace was formed in the late 1960s when parts of the Lucas Industries took over sections of GEC, AEI and a number of other small companies. It was clear that the company would engage in a rationalization programme along the lines already established by Arnold Weinstock in GEC. This, it will be recalled, was the time of Harold Wilson's 'white heat of technological change'. The taxpayers' money was being used through the Industrial

Reorganization Corporation to facilitate this rationalization programme. Whatever consideration was given to the social cost, Arnold Weinstock subsequently made redundant 60,000 highly skilled workers. This may have made GEC look efficient, but the taxpayer had to pick up the tab first for the payment of social services, and second, the nation state as a whole suffered the loss of the productive capacity of these talented workers.

We in Lucas Aerospace were fortunate in the sense that this happened about one year before our company embarked on its rationalization programme. We were therefore able to build up a combined committee which would prevent the company setting one site against the other in the manner Weinstock had done. This body — the combined committee — is unique in the British trade union movement in that it links together the highest level technologists and the semi-skilled workers on the shop floor. There is, therefore, a creative cross-fertilization between the analytical power of the scientist and the technologist on the one hand and, perhaps what is much more important, the direct class sense and understanding of those on the shop floor. As structural unemployment began to affect us, we looked around at the manner in which other groups of workers were attempting to resist it. We had in Lucas already been engaged in partial sit-ins, in preventing the transfer of work from one site to another and a host of other industrial tactics which had been developed over the past five years. But we realized that the morale of a workforce very quickly declines if they can see that society, for whatever reason, does not want the products that they make. *We therefore evolved the idea of a campaign for the right to work on socially useful products.*

The Lucas proposals

It seemed absurd to us that we had all this skill and knowledge and facilities and that society urgently needed equipment and services which we could provide, and yet the market economy seemed incapable of linking these two. What happened next provides an important object lesson for those who wish to analyse how society can be changed.

We prepared 180 letters which described in great detail the nature of the workforce, its skills, its age, its training, the machine tools, equipment and laboratories that were available to us, and the types of scientific staff, together with the design capabilities which they had. We wrote to 180 leading authorities, institutions, universities, organizations and trade unions, all of which in the past had one way or another suggested that there was a need for the humanization of technology and the use of technology in a socially responsible fashion. What happened really was a revelation to us: all of these people who had made great speeches up and down the country, in some instances written voluminous books about these matters, were smitten into silence by the specificity of our request. We had asked them very directly what could a work-force with these facilities be making that would be in the interest of the community at large – and they were silent, with the exception of four individuals, Dr Elliott at the Open University, Professor Thring at Queen Mary College, and Richard Fletcher and Clive Latimer at the North East London Polytechnic.

We then did what we should have done in the first instance: we asked our own members what they thought they should be making. I have never doubted the ability of ordinary people to cope with these problems, but not doubting it is one thing, having concrete evidence is something different. That concrete evidence began to pour into us within three or four weeks. In a short time we had 150 ideas of products which we could make and build with the existing machine tools and skills we had in Lucas Aerospace. We elicited this information through our shop stewards committees via a questionnaire. I should explain that this questionnaire was very different from those which the soap powder companies produce where the respondent is treated as some kind of passive cretin. In our case, the questionnaire was dialectically designed. By that I mean that in filling it in the respondent was caused to think about his or her skill and ability, the environment in which he or she worked and the facilities available. We also deliberately composed it so that our members would think of themselves in their dual role in society: that is both as producers and as consumers. We were therefore quite deliberately transcending the absurd division which our society imposes on us which seems to suggest that there are two nations, one that works in factories and offices and an entirely different nation that lives in houses and communities. We pointed out that what we do during the day at work should be meaningful in relation to the communities in which we live. We also deliberately designed the questionnaire to cause the respondents to think of products not merely for their exchange value but for their use value.

When we collected all these proposals we refined them into six major product ranges which are now embodied in six volumes, each of approximately 200 pages. They contain specific technical details, economic calculations and even engineering drawings. We quite deliberately sought a mix of products which on the one hand included those which could be designed and built in the very short term and those which would require long-term development; those which could be used in metropolitan Britain mixed with those which would be suitable for use in the third world, products incidentally which could be sold in a mutually non-exploitative fashion. Finally we sought a mix of products which would be profitable by the present criteria of the market economy and those which would not necessarily be profitable but would be highly socially useful.

Products for the community

I shall explain briefly some of the products we are proposing.

In the medical field Lucas already makes pacemakers and kidney machines. About three years ago the company attempted to sell off its kidney machine division to an international company operating from Switzerland. We were able to prevent them doing so at that time both by threats of action and the involvement of some MPs. When we checked on the requirements for kidney machines in Britain we were horrified to learn that 3,000 people die each year because they cannot get a kidney machine. If you are under twenty-five or over fifty-five it is almost impossible in many areas to get one. The doctors involved sit like judge and juries with the governors of hospitals deciding who will be allowed, as they so nicely put it, 'to go into decline'. One doctor said to us how distressed he was by this situation and admitted that sometimes he did not tell the families of the patients that this was happening because they would otherwise be distressed. We regard it as outrageous that the skilled workers who design and make this equipment face the prospect of the dole queue where they will be paid about £40 a week (which when administered by the bureaucrats is approximately £70 a week), when with a little commonsense if they were paid £70 a week to stay in industry they could at least be producing artefacts which will be required by society. Indeed, if the social contract meant anything and if there were such a thing as social wage, surely this is precisely the sort of thing which it should imply, namely having forgone wage increases in order that we could expand the services to the community at large, we should have the opportunity of producing medical equipment which they require.

Before we even started the corporate plan, our members at the Wolverhampton plant visited a centre for children with spina bifida and were horrified to see that the only way they could propel themselves about was literally by crawling on the floor. So they designed a vehicle which subsequently became known as Hobcart — it was highly successful and the Spina Bifida Association of Australia wanted to order 2,000. Lucas would not agree to manufacture these because they said it was incompatible with their product range and at that time the corporate plan was not developed and we were not able to press for this. But the design and development of this product were significant in another sense: Mike Parry Evans, its designer, said that it was one of the most enriching experiences of his life when he actually took the Hobcart down and saw the pleasure on the child's face. — It meant more to him, he said, than all the design activity he had been involved in up to then. For the first time in his career *he actually saw the person who was going to use the product that he had designed.* It was enriching also in another sense, because he was intimately in contact with a social human problem. He literally had to make a clay mould of the child's back so that the seat would support it properly. It was also fulfilling in that for the first time he was working in the multi-disciplinary team together with a medical type doctor, a physiotherapist and a health visitor. I mention this because it illustrates very graphically that it is untrue to suggest that aerospace technologists are only interested in complex esoteric technical problems. It can be far more enriching for them if they are allowed to relate their technology to really human and social problems.

Some of our members at another plant realized that a significant number of the people who die of heart attacks die between the point at which the attack occurs and the stage at which they are located in the intensive care unit in the hospital. So they designed a light, simple, portable life-support system which can be taken in an ambulance or at the side of a stretcher to keep patients 'ticking over' until they are linked to the main life-support system in the hospital. They also learned that many patients die under critical operations because of the problem of maintaining the blood at a constant optimum temperature and flow. This, it seemed to them, was a simple technical problem if one were able to get behind the feudal mysticism of the medical profession. So they designed a fairly simple heat exchange and pumping system and built this in prototype. I understand that when the assistant chief designer at one of our plants had to have a critical operation they were able to convince the local hospital to use it and it was highly successful.

In the field of alternative energy sources we have come up with a very imaginative range of proposals. It seemed to us absurd that it takes more energy to keep New York cool during the summer than it does to heat it during the winter. If therefore there were systems which could conserve this energy at a time when it is not required and use it at a time when it is, this would make a lot of sense. One of the proposals for storing energy in this way was to produce gaseous hydrogen fuel cells. These would require considerable funding from the government but would produce means of conserving energy which would be ecologically desirable and socially responsible. We also designed a range of solar collecting equipment which could be used in low energy houses and we worked in conjunction with Clive Latimer and his colleagues at the North East London Polytechnic in producing components for a low energy house. I should add that this house was specifically designed so that it could be constructed on a self-build basis. In fact some of the students working on the Communications Design Degree course at that polytechnic are now writing an instruction manual which would enable people without any particular skills to go and learn the processes and at the same time to produce very ecologically desirable forms of housing. One can now see that if this concept were linked to imaginative government community funding it would be possible in areas of high unemployment where there are acute housing problems to provide funds to employ those in that area to build their own housing.

We have made a number of contacts with county councils as we are very keen to see that these products are used in communities at large. We are unhappy about the present tendency of alternative technology for products to be provided which are little more than playthings for the middle class in their architect-built houses. Hence we have already made links via the Open University with the Milton Keynes Corporation and have designed and are currently building in conjunction with the OU prototype heat pumps which will use natural gas and will increase the actual coefficient of performance (COP) by 2.8 times.

We have had long discussions with our colleagues at Chryslers and British Leyland. In fact many workers now see that the choice facing them two or three years ago was not to continue producing rubbishy cars or to face the dole queue. There were a whole series of other options open to them if the political and social infrastructure were there to allow them to do so. We have been working with Richard Fletcher and his colleagues at the North East London Polytechnic on a unique road-rail vehicle which is capable of driving through a city as a coach and then running on the national railway network. It could provide the basis for a truly integrated, cheap, effective public transport system in this country. It uses pneumatic tyres and is therefore capable of going up an incline of 1:6; normal railway rolling stock can only go up an incline of 1:80. This meant in the past that when a new railway line was laid down it was necessary literally to flatten the mountains and fill up the valleys or put tunnels through them. This costs about £1m per track mile − this was the approximate cost of the railway in Tanzania which the Chinese put down. With our system a track can be put down at about £20,000 per track mile, since it follows the natural contours of the countryside. This vehicle would therefore not only be of enormous use in metropolitan Britain but would also be of great interest in developing countries and even in areas such as Scotland and some of the less densely populated areas in Europe.

The last range of equipment I would like to mention is what we call telearchic devices. This literally means hands or control at a distance. If we examine the present development of technology, we will see that machines and systems are designed in such a fashion as to objectivize human skill and thereby diminish or totally replace the human being. This means in practice that industries are becoming capital intensive rather than labour intensive. They are also invariably energy intensive. This is now giving rise to massive structural unemployment in all of the technologically advanced nations. There have been about 5 million people permanently unemployed in the United States over the past ten years; in Britain we have now 1.6 million. Even in West Germany, that most optimistic of the technologically advanced nations, they now have 1 million people out of work and 700,000 on short-time working. In 1974 they increased the number of process computers by 50.3 per cent and in 1975 by 33.8. They will have sixty times as many microprocessors by 1984 and they reckon that in 1982 60 per cent of all measuring and control equipment will include these microprocessors. It is clear that this is going to give rise to a massive dislocation of the workforce, and these concerns are now being expressed by the West German trade union movement, in particular by Ulrich Briefs of the DGB (German TUC). Gradually they too are learning that the more we invest in industry in its present form, the more people we put out of work. When we were considering the design of robotic equipment to maintain North Sea oil pipelines, the more we thought about this the more it became clear the terrible waste we are making of the great human intelligence which is available to us. If you try to design a robot to recognize which way a hexagon nut is about, much less to select the correct spanner to use on it and then to apply the correct torque, it is an incredible programming job and you realize how intelligent people are in the sense that they can do this without really 'even thinking about it'.

So we are proposing these telearchic devices which reverse the historical tendency to diminish or objectivize human skill. Basically they are a range of equipment which will mimic in real time the motions of a human being. This would mean that in the case of mining, the skill of the miner would still be used but the miner could go through the mining process remotely in a safe environment whilst the telearchic device actually did the mining for him. Thus we human beings would continue to be involved in that precious learning process which comes about through actually working on the physical world about us and it would also mean that we would be countering structural unemployment. We would, in a word, be very creatively linking a relatively labour-intensive form of work with a reasonably advanced and responsible technology. We would not therefore be proposing a return to the so-called 'good old days' in which some romantics seem to believe that the populace spent its time dancing round maypoles in unspoiled meadows. We are deeply conscious of the squalor, the disease, the filth which existed in the past and the contribution science and technology has made in overcoming these. What we believe is necessary is to draw on that which is best from our past and link it with that which is best in our science and technology.

Harnessing technology to human needs

The Lucas workers' corporate plan has the distinct advantage that it is a very concrete proposal put forward by a group of well-organized industrial workers who have demonstrated in the past, by the products they have designed and built, that they are no daydreamers. It is proving to be a unique vehicle with which to test the boundaries of the system in a technological, political and economic sense.

We have of course approached the government and we have had every sympathy short of actual help. We have been enormously impressed at the ability of the various ministries to pass the buck; indeed we have experienced at first hand the white heat of bureaucracy. However, support from the trade union movement is growing — large shop stewards committees at Chryslers, Vickers, Rolls Royce and elsewhere are now discussing corporate plans of this kind. One of our colleagues from Burnley, Terry Moran, has made a tour of trades councils in Scotland discussing these matters. The combined committee has organized a series of meetings in the towns in which Lucas Aerospace has sites. We think it is arrogant for aerospace technologists to believe that they should be defining what communities should have. We are seeking through the local trade unions, political parties and other organizations in each area to help us to define what they need and to begin to create a climate of public opinion where we can force the government and the company to act. At the national level the TUC has produced a half-hour television programme dealing with our corporate plan: this is part of its training programme for shop stewards. The TGWU has come out with a statement indicating that its shop stewards throughout the country should press for corporate plans of this kind. At an international level the interest has been truly enormous. In Sweden, for example, they have produced six half-hour radio programmes dealing exclusively with the corporate plan and have made cassettes which are now being discussed in factories throughout the country. They have also made a half-hour television programme, and a paperback book has been produced dealing with the corporate plan. Similar developments are taking place in Australia and elsewhere, and the interest centres not merely on the fact that a group of workers for the first time are demanding the right to work on socially useful products, but that they are proposing a whole series of new methods of production where workers by hand and brain can really contribute to the design and development of products and where they can work in a non-alienated fashion in a labour process which enhances human beings instead of diminishing them.

The corporate plan and the community — the way forward

Whether the Lucas plan succeeds or not will depend to a great extent on the support it is given by community activists. Campaigns for the 'right to work' in the past have suffered the great weakness that the factory was isolated from the community. The Lucas workers seek the involvement of the community and wish to serve it and learn from it. They are deeply conscious that it would be arrogant for Aerospace workers to say what kind of products communities should have, and they have therefore organized a series of meetings in the towns where Lucas factories are located. A highly successful one took place in a local town hall in Burnley and was attended by some three hundred people. Similar meetings have since taken place in Birmingham, Luton and Bradford, and others are scheduled in Liverpool and Wolverhampton. It has certainly horrified sections of the Lucas management that people in the community should be discussing how *their* requirements could be met in '*their factory*'.

A significant extension of the Lucas workers' campaign has been the establishment at the North East London Polytechnic of the 'Centre for Alternative Industrial and Technological Systems'. This is unique in a number of senses; not least in that it is the first time, anywhere in the world, that a research centre is being run jointly by shop stewards and academics. It is hoped to develop a range of products which could be the basis of campaigns at other firms. The centre will also help to establish community workshops to manufacture products which the community itself requires. This relationship will be purely of a 'pump-priming' nature, otherwise there is a danger that it would undermine the self-reliance of the community and continue to perpetuate an elitist relationship. Schemes of this kind could use Job Creation money to produce a long-term shift in the relationships of power. It is quite obvious that the present job creation schemes are deliberately chosen so as to preserve and strengthen existing power relationships.

In some of the projects envisaged, it would be possible to create permanent jobs at a cost of only £4,000 each, as compared with £480,000 per job in nuclear power. The Lucas workers' range of medical products could be manufactured locally and used in integrated community health care teams — and already attempts are being made to set up such a medical/design group.

The Lucas proposals, now linked with the centre at the North East London Polytechnic, will provide a unique opportunity to test out in practice what form of technology communities actually require, and how they themselves can meet their own requirements in communally-based enterprises. The Lucas workers hope to be able to gain widespread support from the communities in which their factories are located, because, as one Lucas worker put it: 'It will not be possible to create an island of responsibility in Lucas Aerospace in what is otherwise a sea of depravity.'